Murray Noonan is an associate member of the Contemporary Histories Research Group, Deakin University. He holds a PhD from Victoria University, Melbourne.

'Since no human practice can be eternal, natural and universal, we must refresh our understanding of capitalist imperialism to keep pace with its actualities. That exercise, in turn, requires revisiting previous explications. All this, and more, is clarified in Murray Noonan's analytical survey. *Marxist Theories of Imperialism* will engage students, be a source book for teachers, a treasure trove for researchers and a spur to action against its subject's current manifestations in the US corporate warfare state.'

Humphrey McQueen, author of *The Essence of Capitalism*

'Imperialism intrigued prominent followers of Marx – Rosa Luxemburg, V.I. Lenin, N.I. Bukharin and Rudolf Hilferding. A few decades later, Paul Fox, Michael Barratt Brown and Tom Kemp severally developed the theme of "theories of imperialism". Kemp's exemplary 1970 study has come to need updating. This has now been done in fine style by Murray Noonan. With a massive research effort, he has advanced both of these Marxian traditions.'

Bruce McFarlane, editor of the *Journal of Contemporary Asia* (1975–2005)

MARXIST THEORIES OF IMPERIALISM

A History

Murray Noonan

BLOOMSBURY
NEW DELHI • LONDON • OXFORD • NEW YORK • SYDNEY

BLOOMSBURY INDIA
Bloomsbury Publishing India Pvt. Ltd
Second Floor, LSC Building No. 4, DDA Complex, Pocket C–6&7,
Vasant Kunj, New Delhi 110070

BLOOMSBURY, Bloomsbury Academic India and the Diana
logo are trademarks of Bloomsbury Publishing Plc

First published in India 2022
Published in 2017 by I. B. Tauris

A catalog record for this book is available from the Library of Congress.
A catalogue record for this book is available from the British Library.

ISBN: 978-93-56400-85-6
For sale in the Indian subcontinent only

Exclusively distributed in the Indian subcontinent by
Manohar Publishers & Distributors
4753/23, Ansari Road
Darya Ganj, New Delhi 110002
Tel.: 23284848, 23289100
Email: sales@manoharbooks.com, manoharbooks@gmail.com

Typeset in Garamond Three by OKS Prepress Services, Chennai, India
Printed and bound in the India by Replika Press Pvt. Ltd.

To find out more about our authors and books visit
www.bloomsbury.com and sign up for our newsletters.

CONTENTS

ACKNOWLEDGEMENTS

Writing this book would not have been possible without the help of many people. Amongst those, there are a few I would particularly like to thank. I have benefitted from editorial advice and enthusiastic support provided by Lester Crook of I.B.Tauris. I really appreciate your efforts, Lester, in getting behind my book proposal and pushing to have it published. Thanks also to those at I.B.Tauris involved in the preparation of this book for publication.

I have also received support from Professor David Lowe and the Contemporary Histories Research Group at Deakin University, which enabled Lisa Couacaud to weave her magic in the creation of an index. Thanks David, thanks colleagues at CHRG and thank you very much Lisa.

I also want to thank Paul Adams and Jamie Doughney of Victoria University, who provided me with insights, guidance and advice on Marxism in general and imperialism theory in particular. Any flaws in this work are my responsibility.

Many thanks too to Tony Joel who has pushed me throughout the process of writing, book proposal and final typescript. I couldn't (wouldn't) have done it without you, Tone.

Last but not least, I want to express my heartfelt gratitude to my partner Susan Digby and our daughter Meave, both of whom have supported me throughout this long and trying process.

INTRODUCTION

THE THREE PHASES OF MARXIST IMPERIALISM THEORY

Introduction

The late Chinese Premier Zhou Enlai suggested that the twentieth century was the era of imperialism and proletarian revolution (Zhou 1973). Looking back from the vantage point of the first decades of the new millennium, imperialism and the theorising associated with it was one of the key concerns of Marxist thinkers of the past one hundred years. Furthermore, there has been a resurgence of interest in imperialism theory with a number of Marxist writers rising to the challenges posed by the hegemony of the United States (US) in the post-Cold War years and the seemingly unavoidable force of globalisation. Imperialism continues to be an important element of critical Marxist analyses of contemporary global capitalism and geopolitics.

What, then, is imperialism? For Lenin and others such as John A. Hobson, Rudolf Hilferding and Nikolai Bukharin, imperialism grew out of developments in late nineteenth- and early twentieth-century capitalism. The shift from the highly competitive capitalism that had underpinned British dominance of manufacturing during much of the 1800s, to the more organised, centralised and concentrated forms found in Germany and the US evident at the turn of the century had far-reaching ramifications. Hobson, in his groundbreaking 1902 work *Imperialism: A Study*, was one of the first writers to make the connections between imperialism and developments in the economies of the advanced capitalist countries (Hobson 1988). Although Hilferding, in *Finance Capital* published in 1910, did not define imperialism, he made it clear that it was an offshoot of the latest changes to capitalism culminating in the rise of what he called 'finance capital' (Hilferding 1981). Bukharin, in a study written in 1915 but not published until some years later, elaborated on and systematised Hilferding's analysis making the link between capitalism and imperialism explicit (Bukharin 1973). So, too, did Lenin, claiming in his book of 1917 that imperialism was a necessary product of a particular stage of capitalism (Lenin 1973). For these writers imperialism was a specific set of phenomena intimately connected with capitalism at a particular developmental stage. Imperialism, though, was not solely constituted by changes to capitalism. There were other factors involved, political, social and for Hobson especially, ideological and psychological (Townshend 1988: [25–6]). Nevertheless, for these writers and their contemporaries who collectively make up the cohort of writers classified in this book as the 'pioneers of imperialism theory', by definition imperialism ultimately was determined by changes to capitalist political economy. Imperialism, for the 'pioneers' as well as those Marxists subsequently engaging with the subject, was and is a historically specific phenomenon; it was and is capitalist imperialism.

It is apposite to define the phenomenon in question. David Harvey has provided a concise summary of the dialectical relationship that underpins capitalist imperialism. For Harvey, imperialism is a product of the territorial and capitalist logics of power, where 'inter-state relations and flows of power . . . [are manifested] within a global system of capital accumulation' (Harvey 2005: 33). Inter-state relations, or geopolitics, during the era of capitalist imperialism (from the late 1800s to the present), have been and continue to be notable for the subordination of the less powerful countries or regions to the powerful capitalist states. Subordination has been maintained through formal political ties (for instance, in direct colonial rule) or informally with political independence masking economic dependence. Tensions in the geopolitical realm culminating in wars of unprecedented ferocity were a feature of the twentieth century. The drive to access resources and markets or to control access to resources and markets helped create inter-imperialist rivalries leading to the outbreak of the two world wars. Whilst inter-imperialist rivalry has not been as decisive a factor in post-World War II international politics, the shoring up of access to and control of markets and resources continues to influence the actions of powerful capitalist nation-states. A case in point is the 2003 US invasion of Iraq, the official justifications for which could not obscure the importance of controlling the resources of the oil-rich Middle East by the sole superpower. The concept of the 'territorial logic of power' is sufficiently flexible to cover the geopolitical changes that have occurred over the past century. The capitalist accumulation process remains what it is despite the vicissitudes of time. Harvey's important clarification of the constitutive elements of imperialism, and how they exist in symbiosis, captures the essence and dynamics of capitalist imperialism. Consequently, this book is heavily influenced by his insightful work.

By emphasising how the capitalist and territorial logics interact to shape the political and economic features of the modern world, Marxist theories of imperialism provide better insights into the nature of the capitalist world system than the two main theoretical approaches in 'International Relations: Realism and Liberal Internationalism'. As Justin Rosenberg points out in his critique of Realism:

> the character of a geopolitical system is no more to be understood as given simply by the plurality of competing units (however sophisticated our account of the mix of the internal and external goals and determination of behaviour) than the character of a society in the conventional sense is understood as the outcome of a plurality of pre-constituted individuals (Rosenberg 1994: 56).

The question of how capitalist social structures influence geopolitics and vice-versa is generally avoided in Realist analyses. Realists, like Kenneth Waltz, view the state-system as an anarchical autonomous realm populated by states pursuing their interests. The state-system is cut off from the influence of domestic issues such as 'ideology, religion, mode of production and social organization' (Burchill 1996c: 85). Liberal Internationalism, on the other hand, posits liberal democracy as the zenith of societal development. Liberal democracy is based on capitalism, which, according to Liberal Internationalists, creates bonds of interdependency, over time leading to the replacing of national competition and the diffusion of 'unilateral acts of aggression and reciprocal retaliation' (Burchill 1996b: 36). Such a view of the beneficial nature of global capitalism and its attendant political forms is optimistic, skimming over structural problems in the global capitalist economy, ignoring inequalities, uneven development, oppression and unilateral acts of aggression by powerful nation-states. The invasions of Iraq and Afghanistan by the US are relatively recent examples of such acts of aggression.

The new third phase of imperialism theory: 'globalisation-era' Marxists

This book makes an important contribution to the existing literature on Marxist imperialism theory by identifying and critically analysing a distinct new phase that started in 2000. One of the principal concerns of Marxist writers in this phase has been the critical assessment of globalisation. Accordingly, in this book their work on contemporary imperialism is given the novel appellation 'globalisation-era' Marxist imperialism theory.

In literature that surveys imperialism theory, there is a general consensus that there have been either two or three phases of Marxist writing on the subject. Whereas Anthony Brewer and Chronis Polychroniou have posited two phases of imperialism theory, Jan Otto Andersson claims that there have been three 'waves'. Bob Sutcliffe agreed with Andersson about the number of phases (three) differing over the periodisation (Brewer 1990; Polychroniou 1991; Andersson 2001 second version; Sutcliffe 2002). Alex Callinicos has claimed that there have been three phases in the history of *imperialism*: first, what he defines as the 'classical imperialism' phase commenced in 1870 and lasted until 1945; the second 'superpower imperialism' phase spanned the Cold War era of 1945–91; and, finally, starting in 1991 and continuing to the present is the third phase that Callinicos categorises as 'imperialism after the Cold War' (Callinicos 2009: 138). Andersson, too, considers the post-Cold War era as a watershed for imperialism and imperialism theory. He postulates that a new third 'wave' or rethinking of imperialism theory had its beginnings in the 1990s propelled by the first Gulf War, the East Asian financial crisis of 1998 and global ecological issues. By the new millennium this third 'wave' of imperialism theory was under way (Andersson 2001 second version). He did not name this phase or wave of theorising as his overview of imperialism and its theorising was published at the start of the phase in 2001.

One of the problems with identifying phases in imperialism theory is that it can be difficult to decide where one phase ends and another begins. There is an element of arbitrariness that attends such compartmentalisation. Nonetheless, it is possible to discern two phases that largely encompass the pre- and post-World War II periods. Having established a basic periodisation, a key contention of this work is that there are not two but actually three phases of imperialism theory. The first phase, that of the 'pioneers of imperialism theory', started with Hobson in 1902 and ended in 1916 with Lenin's *Imperialism, the Highest Stage of Capitalism* (Lenin 1973). The second phase – encompassing the neo-Marxists – is slightly more difficult to define. One the one hand, its beginning straddles the pre- and post-World War II divide with the 1942 publication of Paul Sweezy's *The Theory of Capitalist Development* (Sweezy 1970). On the other hand, it shades into the third phase with Samir Amin's interventions in the discourses associated with globalisation and US hegemony from the 1990s and into the new millennium (Amin 1997a; 1998; 2001; 2005; 2006a). Nonetheless, the neo-Marxists' engagement with imperialism primarily occurred from the late 1960s to the mid-1980s, with decreasing engagement through the 1990s and into the present century. The best known neo-Marxist contributions to imperialism theory – dependency theory and World Systems theory – were responses to the anti-imperialist struggles taking place in Vietnam, Latin America and the US during the 1960s and 1970s. It is this burst of theorising that gave neo-Marxist writing its distinctiveness.

This leads to the distinct new third phase of Marxist writing on imperialism, labelled here as the 'globalisation-era' Marxists. As Callinicos and Andersson have pointed out, the post-Cold War era has been significant for imperialism and imperialism theory. More significant has been the advent of the new millennium. Michael Hardt's and Antonio Negri's book *Empire* (2000) challenged Marxists by suggesting, *inter alia*, that imperialism was now an historical curiosity as there had been fundamental transformations to global social, political and economic conditions. The ensuing critical response to their claims helped spark something of a renaissance of Marxist imperialism theory.

Hardt and Negri were not single-handedly responsible for the upsurge in interest in imperialism. Other factors also have acted as catalysts. One of these was the open pursuit of empire the Bush administration conducted after the September 11 attacks of 2001. One prominent historian, the US-based British academic Niall Ferguson, has encouraged the US government and polity to take up the burdens of formal empire. Ferguson campaigns strongly for the overall positive effects that empire can have not only for the elites but for the majority of the subjects of imperial rule by way of providing infrastructure and institutions, economic development and the rule of law (Callinicos 2009: 2). What is remarkable about this active cheerleading for imperialism is the romanticising of the actual empire experience. That is, the problems and conflicts, famines and immiseration that accompanied British rule in India, for instance, have been downplayed by Ferguson (Mooers 2006: 122–5).

Claims made about the 'strong' version of globalisation by its proponents such as Kenichi Ohmae who see it as ushering in a borderless world (Ohmae 1996), found their echo in Hardt and Negri. *Empire* (2000) partially is predicated on a 'strong' or 'hyper-globalist' account of globalisation. Many of the claims made about globalisation were direct challenges to Marxist imperialism theory. For Marxists writing about imperialism after Hardt and Negri, analysis of globalisation was unavoidable. The ambitious claims made by Hardt and Negri concerning globalisation and the imperial hubris of the US stimulated the enthusiastic return to imperialism theory by the 'globalisation-era' Marxists.

Key objectives

This book provides an update to critical surveys of Marxist theories of imperialism, which is an important task because there have not been any extensive surveys undertaken for over two decades. The last significant works were Brewer's *Marxist Theories of Imperialism: A Critical Survey* (the second edition of which was published in 1990) and Polychroniou's more polemical *Marxist Perspectives on Imperialism: A Theoretical Analysis*, which appeared the following year (Polychroniou 1991). The magisterial two-volume *A History of Marxian Economics* by Michael Howard and John King deals with the theorising of imperialism by quite a number of the writers whose work is examined in this book. Its primary objective, however, is to present a detailed analysis of Marxian economics, not Marxist imperialism theory. The second volume of this influential work was published in 1992 (Howard and King 1989: 1992).

Callinicos, in a book published in 2009, identifies not only a renewed interest in imperialism theory; he argues that there is currently a 'great renaissance' in Marxist imperialism theory (Callinicos 2009: ix). He presents a critical analysis of classical Marxist theories of imperialism, too, utilising a hybrid of Bukharin's and Lenin's theories of imperialism in his analysis of contemporary imperialism and global political economy in the last chapter of his book (Callinicos 2009: 188–227). Callinicos' survey, though, is limited to a selection of the classical Marxists. He was not attempting to update critical surveys of Marxist theories of imperialism.

This book, then, makes a timely and important contribution not only by addressing a considerable gap in the existing literature but also through the identification of and critical engagement with a new third 'globalisation-era' phase of Marxist imperialism theory.

Another chief aim is to track how imperialism has been theorised across the twentieth century up to the present. Both Brewer and Polychroniou have tended to summarise the work of a writer and not trace the development, the changes in a writer's output over time. Neo-Marxists in particular continued their intellectual pursuits over extensive periods and their understanding of and interest in imperialism over time invariably changed. Consequently, this book traces continuities and discontinuities of imperialism theory across three phases and where necessary, over the course of a particular writer's career.

A final aim of this work is to help establish the grounds for richer, more sophisticated Marxist theorising of imperialism. Leo Panitch and Sam Gindin, two of the 'globalisation-era' Marxists, correctly identified the lack of adequate theorising of the state in the work of the classical Marxists (Panitch and Gindin 2004: 6). Classical Marxists tended to emphasise the economic aspects of imperialism, which meant that the political elements often were poorly covered. In addition, what is called in this book the 'theoretical underlabouring' undertaken by Ellen Meiksins Wood and David Harvey has helped clear up issues about the historical specificity of capitalist imperialism (Wood) and the constitutive relationships that define imperialism (Harvey).

The work of 'globalisation-era' Marxists has been invaluable in not only 'tidying up' and clarifying, but also through pointing out shortcomings in the work of some of the 'pioneers'. Therefore, the groundwork has been laid for a better theory of contemporary imperialism. The book concludes by offering some suggestions about what needs to be addressed in the pursuit of more sophisticated Marxist theories of imperialism.

Conceptual framework

The 'pioneers of imperialism theory' are the first cohort of writers analysed. They are divided into two groups, namely the 'reformists' and the 'revolutionaries'. Hobson, as a liberal, is the one exception among the theorists covered who does not count as a Marxist. Along with Hilferding and Karl Kautsky, he was a 'reformist' who did not see imperialism as some inevitable outgrowth of capital development. The 'revolutionaries' are Rosa Luxemburg, Bukharin and Lenin who considered imperialism an unavoidable product of a particular stage of capitalism and immune to reform. The first phase of writing from the 'pioneers' set the foundations for later theorising and became consolidated as the benchmark by which later theorists judged their own and other's writings.

The key representatives of neo-Marxist thinking on imperialism whose work is examined here include Sweezy, Paul Baran, Andre Gunder Frank, Immanuel Wallerstein and Amin. Generally they focussed on problems like the lack of development of the periphery, 'Eurocentrism', monopoly capitalism and the long history of the capitalist world system.

The 'globalisation-era' Marxist cohort of thinkers consists of Hardt and Negri, Humphrey McQueen, James Petras and Henry Veltmeyer, Wood, Harvey, and Panitch and Gindin. The work of these writers not only has been part of a renewal of interest in imperialism theory, some of their contributions have added qualitatively to Marxist imperialism theory. To help to contextualise the theories produced by each cohort of writers, important political, economic, social, historical and biographical elements are also included.

Structure of the book

The first part of the book, which analyses the writing of the 'pioneers', comprises two chapters. Whereas Chapter One examines the work of the 'reformists', namely Hobson, Hilferding and Kautsky, Chapter Two concentrates on the output of the 'revolutionaries' Luxemburg, Bukharin and Lenin. Chapters Three to Six make up the second part, which is devoted to the neo-Marxist thinkers. Sweezy's and Baran's works are the subject of Chapter Three. Chapter Four presents an examination of Gunder Frank's contributions to imperialism theory. Wallerstein's *oeuvre* is the focus of Chapter Five. Chapter Six critically engages with Amin's engagement with imperialism. The third part consists of two chapters, the first of which examines the importance of Hardt's and Negri's intervention. Chapter Eight critically surveys the literature produced by the 'globalisation-era' Marxists. Highlighted at the end of the chapter are some very recent 'globalisation-era' Marxist additions to the literature. In the conclusion, a summary is given of what the book has achieved in examining the theorising of imperialism by the selected writers. Some suggestions are made that will help to enrich future Marxist imperialism theory.

Synopsis and key arguments

By examining how they critically analysed the capitalist development and geopolitics of their times, part one argues that collectively the 'pioneers' made substantive, complex and lasting contributions to the theorising of imperialism. Their work set the parameters for much of what has followed. Indeed, so empirically rich, suggestive and influential were some of the theories that they have become the foundation and benchmark for much of the subsequent theorising on imperialism. This point is borne out by some of the 'globalisation-era' writers who in the current revival of imperialism theory have gone back to the classical Marxist theories in particular, rather than to the body of work produced by the neo-Marxists.

Part one also addresses a valid criticism about classical Marxists' problematic handling of the political aspects of imperialism, which is that the writing on the subject by these 'pioneers' generally tended to focus on the changes that they had discerned in the capitalism of the early twentieth century. In other words, their analyses of imperialism honed in on the economic developments, leaving the geopolitical and political theory side of imperialism rather less developed. The connections between the dynamics of the capitalist accumulation process and the political systems in the capitalist heartlands were rather crudely drawn by classical Marxists. The conceptualising of the state in Lenin's pamphlet and Bukharin's *Imperialism and World Economy* (Bukharin 1973) can only be characterised as instrumentalist. The most trenchant criticisms of the poverty of the theorisation of the state in the offerings of classical Marxists have been made by the 'globalisation-era' Marxists Panitch and Gindin. How their important essay grapples with state theory is covered in part three (Panitch and Gindin 2004).

Although theories always contain blind spots or omissions, placing them in their social, political and economic contexts helps to explain if not mitigate such shortcomings. For Luxemburg, Bukharin and Lenin the political and ideological struggle against the reformism of the Second International was of paramount importance. The drive to war evident in the years leading up to the outbreak of hostilities in 1914 and the capitulation by member parties of the Second International to nationalist sentiment (German Social Democrat deputies voting for war credits, for example) in the latter year, also needed to be explained. These priorities militated against the elaboration of a fully fleshed out theory of the state. The theorising of imperialism undertaken by these three writers had strong polemical elements and, fuelled by militarism, war and the collapse of the Second International, a sense of urgency. So, whilst criticisms levelled at classical Marxists regarding the impoverished nature of state theory in their analyses of imperialism have veracity, it also should be recognised that, in comparison to academics, revolutionaries like Luxemburg, Bukharin and Lenin had differing audiences, priorities and pressures to which to respond.

Part two argues that, originating with Sweezy's *The Theory of Capitalist Development* (1970), neo-Marxist understanding of imperialism began with an acceptance of the foundational writing of the 'pioneers' and particularly Lenin's insights on imperialism. Over time, however, a number of neo-Marxist writers moved away from explicit endorsement of Lenin's theorisation of imperialism and the word itself almost disappears from the lexicon of two of the writers. In place of imperialism, Baran and Sweezy adopted the term 'Monopoly Capital' (Baran and Sweezy 1968). For others, such as Gunder Frank and Wallerstein, imperialism and imperialism theory became noticeably less prominent in their later works. Amin has been more consistent in his use of the term and even in his more recent books he continues to acknowledge his debt to Lenin's insights on imperialism. Nonetheless, there was a demonstrable decline in interest in defining and engaging with the concept of imperialism by the neo-Marxists, with imperialism seen to be either a stage of capitalist development, as monopoly capitalism itself or shorthand for Third World dependency and/or underdevelopment.

Also noteworthy is that neo-Marxists Gunder Frank, Wallerstein and, to a lesser extent Amin, made exchange relations between countries the determining feature of capitalism. From an orthodox Marxist viewpoint, the determining feature of capitalism is found in the realm of production. It follows that, in the writings of Gunder Frank and Wallerstein especially, there has been a problem with their characterisation of the political economy of capitalism, and thus how they have depicted the history and spread of the capitalist world economy. The combination of the declining interest in imperialism and its theorising and the problematic handling of political economy by Gunder Frank and Wallerstein, serve to highlight the less than concise formulations of imperialism by the neo-Marxists as a whole. Here it is argued that, in the hands of neo-Marxists, the conceptualising of imperialism atrophied.

The second argument to be made about the neo-Marxist contribution to imperialism theory concerns the more recent scholarship of Amin. Amin has been critical of the uneven development that necessarily results from the capitalist accumulation process. For him, globalisation had done nothing to redress uneven development and furthermore, the supposed unstoppable force of globalisation was merely the current incarnation of imperialism. The latter proposition about the globalisation/imperialism nexus pre-figured a claim made by two of the 'globalisation-era' Marxists. Amin in his examination of globalisation concluded that it was the form that imperialism took in the current period of US hegemony. It will be contended that by anticipating the claims made by the 'globalisation-era' Marxists James Petras and Henry Veltmeyer (Petras and Veltmeyer 2001b) Amin especially in some of his latest books acted as a bridge between neo-Marxist and 'globalisation-era' Marxist theorising on imperialism. Amin was one of the few academic figures to continue using the concept of imperialism in his writing through the 1990s.

Critiquing of neo-Marxist treatment of imperialism, capitalism and political theory should not be read as a wholesale dismissal of the voluminous and insightful output of the writers in this cohort. Much important research was conducted by Sweezy and Baran, Gunder Frank, Wallerstein and Amin. The last three writers took pains to counter what they saw as 'Eurocentric' biases in Marxist and mainstream social science, shifting attention to the impact that absorption into the capitalist world economy had on the countries of the periphery. In addition, Sweezy set up and contributed editorial expertise to a prominent independent Marxist journal *Monthly Review*, which continues to publish Marxist analysis. Wallerstein's creation of World Systems theory (with able contributions from Gunder Frank and Amin) was highly influential and remains a valuable theoretical approach in the fields of the humanities and social sciences.

Part three argues that Hardt's and Negri's *Empire* (2000) had a cathartic effect on contemporary Marxist scholarship in general and imperialism theory in particular. The book had more than a hint of the millennial about it, with the authors making grand claims about fundamental changes to capitalism and especially the system of states and state sovereignty. Hardt and Negri believed that so much had changed, due in large part to globalisation and the demise of 'actually existing socialism', that it was possible to speak of a de-centred, de-territorialised power called 'Empire'. The 'Empire' that Hardt and Negri claim has come into existence is not specific to one nation-state. Whilst predicated on US military might and superpower status, 'Empire' transcends the system of states and previous forms of empire. Also transcended are previous forms of capitalism and its attendant appurtenances such as imperialism. Hardt and Negri acknowledge the seminal influence of Lenin's work on imperialism, but claim there is no scope for any such analysis in the transformed world of 'Empire'. Notwithstanding the cathartic effect their book had on Marxist scholarship (and other scholars, too, for that matter) the second argument concerning Hardt's and Negri's intervention is that they overstate the transformative influence of globalisation, make bald assertions about the state system and sovereignty, culminating in the flawed proposal about the dawning of a new era, the era of 'Empire'.

Hardt's and Negri's ambitious book confronts some cherished Marxist concepts and positions, compelling the other 'globalisation-era' Marxists to re-visit and critically reflect on the classical Marxist theories. Three themes link the work of Hardt and Negri and other 'globalisation-era' Marxists: globalisation; the state; and the system of states and empire/imperialism.

Engagement with these themes by contemporary Marxist intellectuals McQueen (2003), Petras and Veltmeyer (2001b), Wood (2003), Harvey (2005), Panitch and Gindin (2004) as well as Hardt and Negri has ushered in a new phase of writing on the subject. Rising to the challenges of globalisation, a resurgent US once again projecting military force in various parts of the globe, neo-liberalism and financial vicissitudes, these writers have responded by taking a fresh and often critical look at what the classical Marxist theorists had to say about capitalist imperialism. It is noteworthy that it was the classical Marxist works that have been subjected to scrutiny. For the most part (with the slight exception of Petras and Veltmeyer, who took as one of the fundamentals of imperialism the neo-Marxist trope of the impoverishment of the Third World/periphery), globalisation-era Marxists have bypassed the neo-Marxist musings on the subject. The result has been the identification of serious oversights in the theorising of the 'pioneers' and the calling into question of some of the claims made by Lenin especially.

Identifying deficiencies – such as the rudimentary nature of the analysis of the state in classical Marxist works or calling into question Lenin's notion of the certitude of inter-imperialist rivalry and the problematic 'stagist' approach to capitalist development – has brought the constituent elements of imperialism theory into sharper focus. It is argued that, together with what is called in this book the 'theoretical underlabouring' of Wood and Harvey, 'globalisation-era' Marxists have taken imperialism theory to a higher level of abstraction, and in the process they have provided insightful analyses of the connections between the capitalist accumulation process, geopolitics, imperialism and globalisation. This continues with the work of contemporary writers such as Tobias ten Brink and John Smith whose challenging and interesting offerings warrant careful study. On the basis of these 'globalisation-era' Marxist contributions and by addressing certain problems and oversights that are raised in the conclusion, there is the potential for richer and more sophisticated Marxist theorising of imperialism in the twenty-first century.

CHAPTER 1

IMPERIALISM AS ABERRATION

THE REFORMISTS: HOBSON, HILFERDING AND KAUTSKY

Introduction

For many contemporaries, the first two decades of the twentieth century heralded the end of civilisation. Eric Hobsbawm notes that, for people like the British foreign secretary, Edward Grey, who had spoken of the 'lamps going out all over Europe' upon the commencement of hostilities in 1914, 'the world war [was] the end of a world' (Hobsbawm 1998: 22). The war was remarkable not only for killing and maiming on a scale never before witnessed, but also for the disappearance of empires and the re-drawing of the political map of the world (Hobsbawm 1998b). For such catastrophes to happen, clearly there had been some significant developments in Europe and in the wider world. The effort to understand what had been the causes of the conflagration and how to stop such a calamity occurring again gave rise both to the discipline of International Relations (Burchill 1996a) and the League of Nations. The latter was the first multinational body whose aim was to prevent the outbreak of another catastrophe like the Great War (Hobsbawm 1998b).

The effort to understand did not end there. The social, political and economic changes that had occurred prior to the outbreak of hostilities were critically analysed by the British economist and liberal John A. Hobson. On the Continent, the Austrian-born Marxist Rudolf Hilferding sought to extend and update Marx's critique of capitalism.

Hilferding identified a number of developments in capitalism that had occurred after Marx's death, especially the appearance of an amalgam that he called 'finance capital'. One of the consequences of the publication of Hobson's book *Imperialism: A Study* (1988) and Hilferding's *Finance Capital* (1981) first published in 1902 and 1910 respectively, was that imperialism gained acceptance as the descriptor for not only capitalism's changes since Marx but also the disquieting developments in the geopolitics of that time. Hobson and Hilferding were of the opinion that capitalism, the nature of politics, the political relationships within and between the industrialised nation-states and the multifaceted relationships between colonies and colonial powers all had been transformed by imperialism.

Hobson's understanding of imperialism, informed as it was by his liberalism, led him to offer up some prescriptions to return the British body politic to rude good health. The details of those prescriptions need not delay us here; it is enough to note that Hobson thought that reform of the British economy and its politics would be sufficient to rid the country of the evils of imperialism. Classical Marxists, namely Hilferding, Kautsky, Luxemburg, Bukharin and Lenin, had fundamental differences of opinion about the role of reform or revolution in the strategic vision of working class parties. These differences had a direct bearing on how the classical Marxists configured imperialism and its connections to contemporaneous developments in capitalism and domestic and international politics. Despite the differences in ideological outlook and strategic vision, taken as a whole, the work of the 'pioneers of imperialism theory' was complex, theoretically sophisticated and established the parameters for the analysis of capitalist imperialism.

The 'pioneers' did more than produce rich and complex theories. One of the arguments in part one is that the theorising of the 'pioneers' is not only of historical interest, but also continues to function as a benchmark for more recent contributions in the study of imperialism. The parameters that the 'pioneers' set and the insightful observations they made about the prevailing conditions continue to have relevance. Nonetheless, as Vivek Chibber has pointed out, aside from Hobson the theories of imperialism produced by the 'pioneers' gravitated strongly towards critical analysis of economic developments (Chibber 2004: 429). Whereas Hobson examined both the economic and political sides of imperialism, classical Marxist theorising is notable for a distinct lack of attention paid to the political aspects of imperialism. Furthermore, the simplistic or instrumentalist view of the state evident in the writing of particular classical Marxists comes in for criticism from 'globalisation-era' Marxists (as will be shown in part three). Such criticism is valid, not only for the classical Marxists but for the 'pioneers' as a whole. A further argument will be made, then, that the political mediation of imperialism (particularly the function of the state) did not receive enough attention from the 'pioneers of imperialism theory'. This primarily is due to the simplistic or instrumentalist rendering of the state by this cohort of writers. Although this is a flaw, it does not detract from the overall achievements of the 'pioneers'. The fact that 'globalisation-era' Marxists overwhelmingly direct their attention to the work of the 'pioneers' rather than the neo-Marxists is another example of the enduring nature of their early contributions to theorising.

Returning to the two approaches to imperialism sketched out above – the reformists and revolutionaries – it is possible to split the 'pioneers' evenly. Of the six writers, three of them can be categorised as reformists and three as revolutionaries. The reformists saw imperialism as either an aberration deriving from poor policy choices, the undue influence of particular interest groups such as financiers or as political and economic developments that did not require revolutionary upheaval to redress. Throughout this book the term reformist specifically refers to Hobson, Hilferding and Kautsky, and it denotes their advocacy of non-revolutionary remedies to the problem(s) of capitalist imperialism. Hobson quite easily is characterised as a reformist, because for him there was nothing fundamentally wrong with British economic and political institutions. The distortions of imperialism that he identified were correctable through judicious applications of legislation and policy. For Hilferding and Kautsky, the application of the reformist label is not quite as straightforward as in Hobson's case. Common to Hilferding and Kautsky was the experience of being involved in organising working-class political parties in Austria and Germany and getting elected representatives into parliament. The sinecure of an official, paid position within the apparatus of the Austrian and German Social Democratic Party (Sozialdemokratische Partei Deutschlands, SPD) and the daily business of party affairs also helped foster a more cautious approach to class struggle, the attainment of state power and the fight against militarism. The attraction of reformism as a business-as-usual approach therefore is understandable.

Hilferding made his name as a Marxist thinker in Vienna amongst a group that included Max Adler, Otto Bauer and Karl Renner, who collectively became known as the Austro-Marxists (Bottomore and Goode 1978: 6). He had practised as a medical doctor for five years and then again as part of his military service in World War I (Bottomore 1981: 2). Hilferding came to the attention of Kautsky as a result of his contributions to the leading Marxist theoretical journal *Die Neue Zeit*, from 1902 onwards. He was appointed to the SPD school in Berlin in 1906, and his relationship with the party continued after being given the foreign editorship of its journal *Vorwärts* (Bottomore 1981: 2–3).

On 4 August 1914, the majority of the SPD representatives in the German Reichstag voted to support war credits, effectively guaranteeing that the German war effort would be financed. Voting for war credits had far-reaching implications. It precipitated a split in the ranks of not only the peak body of working-class parties, the Second International, but also caused splits in German social democracy itself. Hilferding had taken up a minority position in opposing the voting for war credits. This watershed moment did not brand him as a reformist; rather, what did was his commitment, like Kautsky, to parliamentarism and electoral action (Bottomore 1981: 11), as well as his opposition to the Bolshevik seizure of power and the formation of the Third or Communist International. These attitudes affirm his reformist credentials.

Kautsky was a complex and contradictory figure, on the one hand believing in social revolution but on the other hand considering 'the peaceful and legal road to power within the framework of democratic representative institutions both possible and desirable' (Salvadori 1990: 41). Kautsky oscillated between the revisionists of Bernstein's ilk and the radicals such as Luxemburg and the Dutch social democrat Anton Pannekoek. After his polemics with Luxemburg in 1910 (see below), Kautsky's position hardened. He found that he was drawing closer to the arguments of the revisionists that he had battled against a few years earlier (Salvadori 1990: 149). In the highly charged atmosphere that accompanied SPD deliberations about the voting on war credits, Kautsky advocated that the party's Reichstag members should abstain from voting. When the majority of SPD Reichstag representatives refused to countenance his advice, Kautsky accepted the majority position. He felt that he could not advocate 'an outright vote against the credits, "in view of the lack of clarity" about the exact responsibility for the war' (Salvadori 1990: 182).

Kautsky's criticism of the revolutionaries Luxemburg and Lenin reflected a less than sanguine belief in the efficacy of revolution. During the upheaval that came to pass in Germany late in the war he insisted on legalism, the principle of parliamentary politics and loyal opposition. That his philosophical outlook was reformist rather than revolutionary is borne out by his most famous article on imperialism 'Ultra-imperialism' (Kautsky 1914). Here he painted a possible picture of the Great Powers chastened by the destruction that attended the war, accommodating each other to ensure the status quo. As further analysis of this article follows later, for now it suffices to note that this short piece was published in September 1914 shortly after the outbreak of hostilities in August. That he should ascribe some level of equanimity to states that had large armed forces and were prepared to use that force indicates a belief in the ongoing nature of capitalism and its political forms. According to Kautsky, the correct course of action for the SPD was to extract what could be extracted from the capitalist social system until it eventually collapsed. Kautsky by these lights was a reformist.

Hobson's analysis of imperialism and Hilferding's examination of capitalist development in the decades after Marx's death put in place the political and economic concepts that Kautsky, Luxemburg, Bukharin and Lenin would build on in their theorising of imperialism. Kautsky's contribution, though reviled by Lenin, has received some praise by the two 'globalisation-era' Marxists Panitch and Gindin. They suggest that Kautsky's notion of ultra-imperialism – an accord between the imperialist nations – indeed has come to pass under the aegis of American hegemony (Panitch and Gindin 2004). Reformists' work on imperialism and capitalist development continues to resonate due to their influence on theorists like Bukharin and Lenin, for example, and by extension through them later thinkers. Moreover, the key elements of capitalist imperialism identified by the reformists (and the revolutionaries) are observable in contemporary world affairs. It is timely, then, to begin the critical analysis of reformist writings starting with Hobson's imperialism theory, moving on to Hilferding's work and finishing with Kautsky's article 'Ultra-imperialism'.

John A. Hobson: father of imperialism theory

It has been claimed that Hobson's *Imperialism: A Study* (Hobson 1988) is a classic of political literature (Townshend 1988: [9]). There is merit in this claim, for Hobson set many of the parameters of imperialism theory. His groundbreaking study highlighted the development in capitalism that saw a shift from commodity export to the export of capital, the prominent role of financiers in the direction of state policy and the pernicious effect of imperialism on the British economy and mores. Hobson's work deserves its lofty reputation.

Born in 1858 into a family with liberal views, Hobson spent his formative years in Derby. After a brief stint teaching, he arrived in London in 1887 to take up journalism (Cain 2002: 15; Townshend 1988: [11]). Peter Cain states that Hobson 'was undoubtedly raised in an atmosphere where free market capitalism and the Gladstonian state were largely taken for granted as guarantors of individual freedom' (Cain 2002: 16). Hobson's shift to the left of the Liberal spectrum came in the 1890s under the impetus of social crises and the unfolding events in South Africa. The 1895 Jameson Raid was an unsuccessful attempt to de-stabilise the Kruger government in South Africa, at the behest of Cecil Rhodes and his fellow mining capitalists who perceived the Afrikaner government as obstructive. The unsuccessful attempt at de-stabilisation inflamed liberal opinion in Britain and also was 'a key moment in the emergence of the idea of "financial imperialism"' (Cain 2002: 60). Links between the shareholders of Rhodes' British South Africa Company, the City of London connections and members of the aristocracy revealed to Hobson the potential for these people to bring to bear political influence favourable to their business interests (Cain 2002: 60).

Hobson published a number of articles about the unfolding situation in South Africa in 1899 while based there as a special correspondent for the *Manchester Guardian*. According to Cain, what the South African experience did for Hobson was not only confirm his suspicions about the mendacity of financial interests but also the cosmopolitan nature of financial capitalism. Hobson's unravelling of the cosmopolitan nature of financial capital did not end at pointing out the national origins of the financiers. With a decidedly anti-Semitic streak, Hobson alleged that in South Africa the economy was dominated by Jewish financial interests (Cain 2002: 92).

Back in Britain, Hobson wrote up his observations and published *The War in South Africa* in 1900 (Cain 2002: 286). In 1901, he wrote six articles for the *Speaker* which, combined with another article published in early 1902, laid the groundwork for 'The Economies of Imperialism', the first part of *Imperialism: A Study* (Cain 2002: 103).

The economics of imperialism

In his introductory remarks to the 1938 edition of *Imperialism: A Study*, Hobson cited 'three fields of causation of imperialism': first were political illusions; second were the 'financial fears and mistrusts which prevented sane monetary arrangements for internal and external marketing'; and, finally, the 'tragic absurdity summarised as "poverty in plenty"', which for Hobson represented a 'refusal to make full use of existing or attainable productive resources' (Hobson 1988: [51]). One reason for the territorial expansion indulged in by advanced nation-states was found in the inherent predatory and pugnacious character of the 'animal man'. Human nature thus is a causal factor of imperialism, yet Hobson also saw a development in capitalism which was telling:

> My contention is that the system prevailing in all developed countries for the production and distribution of wealth has reached a stage in which its productive powers are held in leash by its inequalities of distribution; the excessive share that goes to profits, rents and other surpluses impelling a chronic endeavour to oversave in the sense of trying to provide an increased productive power without a corresponding outlet in the purchase of consumable goods (Hobson 1988: [51–2]).

Oversaving, accompanied by underconsumption at the other end of the socio-economic spectrum, are two sides of the same coin. The surplus of savings looking for investment opportunities and surplus population seeking employment opportunities were manipulated by interested parties, like financiers and businessmen with overseas investments, ultimately giving rise to imperialist policies. Democratic struggles within the advanced countries for more just and equitable economic outcomes were diverted by imperialism (Hobson 1988: [60]).

Perhaps the most famous trope associated with Hobson is his 'economic taproot' of imperialism hypothesis. The genesis of the 'economic taproot' was found in the work of the American Marxist H. Gaylord Wilshire (Etherington 1982: 19). Wilshire's analysis of capitalism in America in the 1890s suggested that there had been 'a relentless progression from competition to monopoly' which had blocked channels of investment. Domestically there was a surplus of capital looking for investment opportunities (Etherington 1983: 40–1). Wilshire claimed that capitalists in America at that time were greatly in need of foreign fields of investment, hence the advocacy of imperialism by the Republican Party (Etherington 1983: 41). The change in American capitalism outlined by Wilshire became the example which Hobson used to flesh out his taproot hypothesis:

> It was sudden demand for foreign markets for manufactures and for investments which was avowedly responsible for the adoption of Imperialism as a political policy and practice by the Republican party to which the great industrial and financial chiefs belonged, and which belonged to them. The adventurous enthusiasm of President Theodore Roosevelt and his 'manifest destiny' and 'mission of civilization' party must not deceive us. It was Messrs Rockefeller, Pierpont Morgan, and their associates who needed Imperialism and who fastened it upon the shoulders of the great republic of the West. They needed Imperialism because they desired to use the public resources of their country to find profitable employment of their capital which otherwise would be superfluous (Hobson 1988: 77–8).

Great Britain, Germany, Holland and France were compelled to locate larger amounts of their economic resources outside their political domains, too. Offshore investments, export of surplus capital and goods were accompanied by policies of political expansion or colonisation (Hobson 1988: 80). Following this expansion and the opening up of new markets was the extension of protection by the mother country to these new colonies and markets. Competition between the advanced countries for new territories and new fields of investment created additional imposts on taxpayers, by way of government subsidies, tariffs and costs associated with administrative and military functions. Indirect taxation was the preferred method of financing these undertakings as the burden of funding such governmental expenditures was not only concealed, but was transferred to the public (Hobson 1988: 97–8). Increasingly, imperialist financiers used state guaranteed debt or public loans to concentrate in their hands influence over governments. Not only was the holding and trading of government debt a profitable business, it also could be decisive in determining political outcomes at critical times (Hobson 1988: 108).

Summarising Hobson's views on the economic taproot of imperialism, it was the desire of highly organised industrial and financial interests to impose the security and development of their private overseas investments on the public purse and the armed might of the state. The private overseas investments spoken of here were comprised of surpluses of goods and capital. Necessary accompaniments to the economic root of imperialism – the drive to send surpluses overseas – were 'war, militarism, and a "spirited foreign policy"' (Hobson 1988: 106).

Crucially, for Hobson, the problem of oversaving and underconsumption could be alleviated by reform. At the heart of the oversaving and underconsumption nexus was mal-distribution of income. Mal-distribution of income could be overcome through the awarding of higher wages, boosting worker's consumption. Consequently, domestic demand would create new possibilities for investment in the home economy. Changes to the taxation regime meant that oversaving could be channelled into the community where it could be spent on improving consumption and living conditions (Hobson 1988: 85, 86, 88). Social reform would raise the 'wholesome standard of private and public consumption for a nation, so as to enable the nation to live up to its highest standards of production' (Hobson 1988: 88). Foreign trade still would continue, with the small surpluses of British manufactures traded for the raw materials and foodstuffs required, but the exodus of surplus capital and goods would be minimised. Imperialism, in Hobson's view, was distorted economic development which brought in its train benefits to certain interest groups or classes. States became increasingly enmeshed in imperialist policies, practices and militarism, yet the source of the policies, practices and militarism was economic.

Old imperialism, new imperialism, colonialism and liberalism's sell-outs

Hobson did not entirely disapprove of imperialism. There were positive and negative versions of imperialism, sane and insane, legitimate and aggressive (Townshend 1988: [19]). For example, imperialism in its pre-1870s guise often was more rational than the post-1870s variety, which Hobson called 'New Imperialism'. The difference came down to the type of policies implemented in the protectorates or colonies. Sane imperialism for Hobson was the implementation of policies 'devoted to the protection, education, and self-development of a "lower-race"'. In contrast, the insane version promoted the untrammelled exploitation of the resources and the 'lower races' of a colony or protectorate by white settlers (Hobson 1988: 246). To illustrate the sane imperial approach, Hobson used the example of the experience of native people in Basutoland, South Africa, under British administration from 1884. Chiefs were kept in place and Europeans were forbidden to hold land, undertake mineral exploration and work or own mines. Compared to British policy in Basutoland the attitudes displayed in Johannesburg and Rhodesia towards native peoples and resources was base and exploitative, hence the insane tag (Hobson 1988: 245–6).

Uniquely, 'New Imperialism' was a policy adopted by a number of powers. The ensuing competition between European and American powers for colonies and markets necessarily precluded the establishment of a hegemonic power. In earlier forms of empire, where inter-imperial rivalry was not a concern, hegemony conferred benefits. 'When Roman citizens, with full civic rights, were found all over the explored world, in Africa and Asia, as well as in Gaul and Britain, Imperialism contained a genuine element of internationalism' (Hobson 1988: 8). The single empire phenomenon did not disappear with the end of Imperial Rome, rather it continued through the Middle Ages in the Holy Roman Empire, appearing as the ideal of Charlemagne for Western Europe, and animating the drive for a European Empire pursued by Peter the Great, Catherine and Napoleon. Internationalism, or humane cosmopolitanism, was a product of particular political and social circumstances which, according to Hobson, were most often found in single empires. These earlier empires bestowed certain advantages on their subjects or citizens, giving them rights or inculcating a sense of connectedness (humane cosmopolitanism), a set of affairs that eventually dried up under the narrowness of nineteenth-century nationalism, which in turn had become part of the arsenal of the competing empires of 'New Imperialism' (Hobson 1988: 8–12).

In favourably comparing the old type of empire with 'New Imperialism', Hobson was not only making a value judgement, but also making moral and political judgements. Another feature of 'New Imperialism' that vexed Hobson was the annexation of new territories, with no thought given by the colonial power to the self-governability of the indigenous populations (Hobson 1988: 124). Not only would this open up administrative and political problems for the colonial power(s), it was morally wrong to integrate indigenous populations into the orbit of the advanced capitalist nations without giving them the chance to develop and advance themselves.

Like the dichotomy of older sane imperialism counterposed to bad, aggressive 'New Imperialism', Hobson asserted that colonialism also was characterised by two divergent forms. Prior to the 1870s, the British colonial experience did not drain 'the material and moral resources' of the nation because it set up 'free white democracies' which were decentralised and connected to Britain through ties of informal federation, resulting in little or no strain on the home government (Hobson 1988: 125). Yet 'New Imperialism':

> is the very antithesis of this free, wholesome colonial connection, making, as it ever does, for greater complications of foreign policy, greater centralisation of power, and a congestion of business which ever threatens to absorb and overtax the capacity of parliamentary government (Hobson 1988: 125).

The expansion of Europe in the last quarter of the nineteenth century under the auspices of 'New Imperialism' was decidedly different to the colonialism that had come before. For Britain, the European powers and America, participation in this scramble for colonial possessions came at a cost, as it did for the colonial subjects. A major cost associated with the push of Britain and the European powers into Africa and Asia was expenditure on military forces and armaments. Territorial aggrandisement, competition and thus increased tension between the powers acted as multipliers on military expenditure. The increasing drain on the public purse meant that the provision of productive public projects had to be curtailed, with future generations burdened with onerous amounts of debt. Much needed social reforms and 'the cultivation of the arts of material and intellectual progress at home' were neglected (Hobson 1988: 152).

Militarism and heightened tension between imperial powers culminated in the outbreak of wars. Colonial expansion also caused internecine fighting amongst colonial peoples. Inter-tribal animosities were fomented and the Christian civilising mission – supposedly part of the positive side of the colonial experience for the colonial subjects – was sometimes bypassed if it meant that the savage propensities of colonial peoples could be harnessed to imperial advantage (Hobson 1988: 138).

Hobson claimed that, in Britain and on the Continent, advocates of 'New Imperialism' were an eclectic group comprising:

> the city ground landlord, the country squire, the banker, the usurer, and the financier, the brewer, the mine owner, the ironmaster, the shipbuilder, and the shipping trade, the great export manufacturers and merchants, the clergy of the State Church, the universities and the great public schools, the legal trade unions and the services (Hobson 1988: 142–3).

Compelled to come together to thwart the challenge posed by the spreading of the franchise to the masses, a political development that had the potential to help alleviate inequality of economic opportunities, these sectoral interest groups supported 'New Imperialism' as a way to maintain power, property and privileges (Hobson 1988: 142–3).

Leaders of the Liberal party in Britain and their counterparts in Europe had sold out to 'a confederacy of stock gamblers and jingo sentimentalists', meaning that they had relinquished the cause of social reform, their heritage, for their business interests. The path of reform remained open. By rallying good liberals and seeking alliances with working-class political organisations, Hobson believed that 'New Imperialism' could be fought and overcome through democracy and social reconstruction (Hobson 1988: 143–5).

Acknowledging the difficulties connected with civilising the anarchy of global politics, Hobson saw evidence for the beginning of a pacific union of states in the reciprocal duties that states undertook for each other. International conferences, diplomacy, postal services, credit arrangements, railway systems that crossed state boundaries and The Hague conference on the laws of war exemplified a budding community of interests at the international level (Hobson 1988: 164–71). What Hobson was proposing, in fact, was very similar to Kant's conception of a liberal pacific union of states, first propounded in *Perpetual Peace* in 1795 (Kant 1972). Kantian political philosophy, particularly the vision of a cooperative and harmonious international state system, is recognised as being one of the cornerstones of Liberal Internationalism, which remains one of the mainstream theoretical paradigms in the discipline of International Relations. Whilst Kant is recognised as the progenitor of Liberal Internationalism, Hobson's *Imperialism: A Study*, in which liberalism and liberal political philosophy were employed to critique imperialism, has been overlooked by those working within the discipline of International Relations. Oddly, Hobson's study, as is by now well known, achieved the status of a pivotal text in imperialism theory, largely through Lenin's use of some of Hobson's findings and in the former's admiration of certain features of Hobson's work. A possible reason for the lack of recognition of Hobson's study by International Relations academics can be found in the exclusion of imperialism theory as an alternative theoretical paradigm in the discipline itself.

New Imperialism, morality and the liberal white man's burden

The advanced nations had an important role in the spreading of civilisation, and imperialism, too, was useful in lifting the 'lower races' (Hobson's term for colonial subjects and other 'less civilised' people) up where they could partake in the benefits that the metropolitan countries could confer. The involvement of a leading power in the affairs of the 'lower races' was only to be effected if it was seen to improve the safety and civilisation of the world's inhabitants and not just in the advanced nation's interests alone. Too often in the era of 'New Imperialism', the moral aspect of intervention in the affairs of others by Western powers was supplanted by the business 'deal' (Hobson 1988: 232, 241). A solution to the problem of the sort of annexationist and interventionist frenzy that characterised 'New Imperialism' was a set of principles by which the colonial governments should abide in their political and economic control of the 'backward races'. There was an absolute necessity that intervention in territories had to be conducted by governments. Such a stipulation was a consequence of the rapaciousness of private adventurers, slavers, fortune seekers in the past and mining magnates like Rhodes in South Africa just prior to the outbreak of war there. Arguing that people of the less developed areas of the world should be free to decide for themselves about how to utilise their resources was naïve. Contact with the 'white races' was unavoidable and it was 'more perilous and more injurious in proportion as it lacks governmental sanction and control' (Hobson 1988: 230–1).

Western imperialist nations had not only engaged with the predominantly 'lower races' of Africa, they also had been involved in colonial experiments and partitioning in Asia. Here was a true test of the West's imperial mission. Unlike the 'backward' peoples and countries, the East (India, China and the rest of Asia) was rich in culture, had complex societies and whilst not as advanced as the West industrially, nevertheless could not be countenanced as 'backward'. Hence the challenge, how did the 'New Imperialism' fare in Asia? The answer, according to Hobson, was clear. The ancient civilisations of the East and particularly China were damaged by European intervention:

> the violent breaking down of the characteristic institutions of Asia to satisfy some hasty lust of commerce, or some greed of power, is quite the most fatally blind misreading of the true process of world civilization that it is possible to conceive. For Europe to rule Asia by force for purposes of gain, and to justify that rule by the pretence that she is civilizing Asia and raising her to a higher level of spiritual life, will be adjudged by history, perhaps, to be the crowning wrong and folly of Imperialism. What Asia has to give, her priceless stores of wisdom garnered from her experience of ages, we refuse to take; the much or little which we could give we spoil by the brutal manner of our giving. This is what Imperialism has done, and is doing, for Asia (Hobson 1988: 327).

The damage was not confined to Africa and Asia. Imperial powers such as Britain in their pursuit of an agenda that skewed economic, social and political policies mostly for the benefit of a small coterie of financiers and assorted others, found that the harmonious development of the social, political and economic life of the nation was distorted. Implementation of imperialist policies was 'a depraved choice of national life' with governments succumbing to self-serving interests. In Hobson's view the consequences were grave. By adopting the policy of 'New Imperialism' the British government had renounced the qualities that for nations as well as for individuals elevated them above brute impulse (Hobson 1988: 368). Continuing along the same path would lead to national decay and decline. The Roman Empire was the prime example of the decay and fall of a once powerful state. With the passage of time the Roman state became over-centralised. Once renowned for the physical and moral vitality of its society, the extraction of tribute that Rome levied on its colonies eventually told on it. The rise of a moneyed oligarchy that drained the resources of both Rome and its colonial outposts, led to parasitism. Onerous taxation, usury and luxury sapped the lower orders and the aristocracy. Eventually, the parasite drains the life-blood from its host, condemning both to 'atrophy, decay, and final extinction'. This applied to the individual organism as well as nations (Hobson 1988: 366–7).

Hobson's contribution to the study of imperialism

Credit is due to Hobson for opening up the analysis of the economic, political and moral components of imperialism and establishing the parameters that subsequent thinkers followed. Also, drawing on the insightful work of Gaylord Wilshire, Hobson was one of the first to identify developments in capitalism that had occurred in the latter part of the nineteenth century. In so doing, he stole a march on most of his Marxist contemporaries.

Coming from a solid liberal background and continuing to hold on to that perspective over the course of his life, Hobson never lost his faith in the power of reform. Having witnessed first hand the machinations of people such as Cecil Rhodes in South Africa, Hobson was not a dispassionate observer. There is real feeling in his condemnation of the direction that Britain had taken when the government embraced the policy options of 'New Imperialism'. Despite this condemnation, and his recognition that there had been qualitative changes to capitalism in the last decades of the nineteenth century, 'New Imperialism' for Hobson was not a systemic problem. Throughout his study, a reformist, liberal outlook tempered his critique. The structural problems that he identified in the capitalist political economy of his day were not so great that enlightened public policy could not deal with them. Underconsumption had its solution in government social spending. The revenue for such a programme could be raised by taxing the oversaving of those that pushed for imperialist policies. All it took was political will, which, channelled through existing political institutions, would resolve problems associated with 'New Imperialism'.

The consequences of not adopting the type of reform programme advocated by Hobson were clear. The decline of the Roman Empire illustrated how increased influence of privileged aristocratic elements had inexorably led to the draining of resources and thence to parasitism. Whilst decline might not happen quickly, it unfolded with the certainty of a law of nature if not addressed.

Hobson's notion of parasitism was quite influential. Lenin, for instance, adopted it in his pamphlet on imperialism. In the latter's hands it was a symptom of the moribundity of the highest stage of capitalism, which by definition was beyond reform. The difference in the use of parasitism made by Hobson and Lenin highlights the difference between the reformist and revolutionary approaches to imperialism. Hobson always thought that the processes associated with imperialism could be curtailed or reversed.

Written at the turn of the century, Hobson's magnum opus has attracted a considerable amount of criticism. Attention has focused on particular elements of his economic arguments. Critics such as the historians D.K. Fieldhouse, John Gallagher and Ronald Robinson seized on Hobson's use of statistics and his engagement with colonialism to suggest that his theory of imperialism was economistic and therefore ill-equipped to account for the scramble for colonies that occurred after the 1870s. Cain, agreeing that some of Hobson's claims were not supported by evidence, argues that 'only small amounts of capital flowed to many of the territories acquired in the late nineteenth century' (Cain 2002: 253).

Scholars supportive of Hobson's writing have countered the dismissal of economic theories of imperialism and Hobson's theory in particular. Cain, whilst acknowledging that Hobson was loose with his use of statistics and that some of his arguments were ambiguous, contended that small amounts of investment going to British colonial possessions in Africa and the tropics did not necessarily negate the entire economic side of his theory (Cain 2002: 254). Etherington suggests that Gallagher and Robinson in their haste to dismiss what they perceived was the economic determinist essence of Hobson's theory, oversimplified his position into a flag-following-trade proposition. Effectively, Gallagher and Robinson misinterpreted Hobson, dramatically reducing the scope of his theory, tarring him with the brush of economism and Eurocentrism. Despite what Gallagher and Robinson thought, Hobson had emphasised the role of policy makers and the 'official mind' in the matters of colonial policy and 'New Imperialism'. Also, Hobson did not rule out the influence of the periphery in the decision-making process, well before Robinson and Gallagher championed the importance of the periphery in promoting colonial acquisitions (Etherington 1982: 31). Hobson's theory of imperialism was not just about economic motives. The bulk of his book explored the political and moral sides of imperialism. Nonetheless, the arguments that Hobson presented on the economic basis of imperialism have been contentious.

Also problematic was his paternalistic and racist viewpoints exemplified by his 'lower races' typology, showing perhaps his Victorian prejudices. The anti-Semitic nature of his attacks on financiers also is disturbing, as is his focus on the machinations of the latter group. Cain and Etherington express concern about the conspiratorial nature of Hobson's writing on the financiers, with Etherington suggesting that financiers were vilified by Hobson (Etherington 1984: 70). Brewer makes the point that financiers and the role they played in Victorian Britain was fundamental to Hobson's theory of imperialism. It was the conspiracy of financiers that gave Hobson's theory its explanatory power (Brewer 1990: 84). The directing role of the financiers in the export of surplus capital overseas and how their interests were furthered by 'New Imperialism', however, was not explored in any detail by Hobson (Brewer 1990: 85–6). One of the consequences of this less than rigorous approach to the function of financiers was that it was easy for Hobson to vilify them.

From a Marxist perspective, Hobson's emphasis on underconsumption and oversaving is problematic. In his preoccupation with underconsumption and oversaving as being the economic root of 'New Imperialism' Hobson oversimplified the dynamics of capitalism. What distinguishes the age of capitalism from previous epochs is not underconsumption and oversaving, which is a pre-condition for capitalist crises but the historically specific one of *overproduction* (Engels 1976: 371–2). Adopting a reform policy of redistribution of wealth to address underconsumption and oversaving will not fundamentally alter capitalist relations of production. Capitalism is predicated on and perpetuates inequalities of wealth and opportunity. Reforms may alleviate some of the harshest aspects but will leave the underlying structure intact.

As critics point out Hobson's theory of imperialism is not without flaws, yet the compelling nature of his analysis has vitality. His pioneering study of the political economy of capitalist imperialism influenced Lenin whose own book became the iconic text on the subject. Additionally, the moral and psychological impacts of imperial policies on both coloniser and colonised, which made up the bulk of Hobson's study, foreshadowed the writing of Frantz Fanon among others. Hobson's study of imperialism laid the groundwork that became the basis for later theorists' critical interventions.

Imperialism was not an inherent or systemic problem of capitalism, according to Hobson, therefore reform could address the problems that arose. For the next writer, Hilferding, imperialism grew out of changes that had occurred in capitalism since Marx's death. Like Hobson, however, Hilferding believed that imperialism could be overcome in the political realm, specifically through the advent of a social democratic majority in parliament. The imperialism, war, revolution schema was not inevitable and the seizure of power by authoritarian parties of the left or right were anti-democratic.

Hilferding's *Finance Capital* and imperialism

Hilferding was born in 1877 in Vienna into a Jewish merchant family. Having settled in Germany, following Hitler's ascension to power in 1933 Hilferding fled, residing in exile in Switzerland and France. He was arrested in the south of France by Vichy authorities, handed over to the Gestapo and died in one of their prisons in Paris in 1941. Presumably sealing his fate was the combination of his Jewish heritage and his background as a Marxist theoretician. It was *Finance Capital* (1981), first published in 1910, which established his reputation as one of the leading theorists of Marxist political economy. The book sought to 'arrive at a scientific understanding of the economic characteristics of the latest phase of capitalist development' (Hilferding 1981: 21). The concentration and centralisation of capital had proceeded at an ever-quickening pace since Marx's death in 1883. A new phase had been ushered in with 'the rapid expansion of capitalism' occurring after 1895 (Hilferding 1981: 318). Tied in with this rapid expansion were forms of ownership noted by Marx in *Capital* called joint stock companies or corporations. The major shareholders of stock in a company were able to divest themselves of responsibility for the day-to-day running of the company. Joint stock companies not only divorced the management of a business from its ownership, they also allowed the interlinking of corporations.

Hilferding examined how competitive struggle had brought about the clustering of enterprises, highlighting how cartels, trusts and syndicates formed in branches of industry and in agriculture to modify the anarchical nature of the market. A cartel made up of two or more enterprises operated to restrict 'certain kinds of competition in the sphere of circulation by establishing uniform terms and conditions of payment' (Hilferding 1981: 204–5). The modification of competition continued with monopolistic consortia entering into price agreements, setting production quotas and regulating supply. The tendency for ever greater control led from cartels, to trusts and then syndicates. Hilferding likened the progression in forms to that of the political realm; confederations, federal states and a unitary state (Hilferding 1981: 205–6). Essentially, the competitive stage of capitalism had been progressively supplanted and with it came different types of business ownership as well as forms of monopolistic association the purpose of which was straightforward: economic domination (Hilferding 1981: 206).

In Germany, which had come late to political unification and to industrialisation, the free trade approach that Britain relied on was not an option. The competitive advantage of British manufacturers could be countered only through protective tariffs. The protective tariffs implemented by the German state were initially modest, with the short-term aim of enabling German industry to get on its feet. Having established themselves, German manufacturers and agricultural producers came not only to rely on the tariffs but championed their use as an economic weapon. Hilferding claimed that the tariffs were a form of tribute levied on domestic consumers (Hilferding 1981: 308).

The changing face of capitalism one: finance capital

Hilferding brought to light two important features of German and US capitalist development. These features were important because of the influence they had on subsequent theorising of imperialism. The first of these features was the amalgam of banking, industrial and commercial capital, which Hilferding called finance capital:

> Finance capital signifies the unification of capital. The previously separate spheres of industrial, commercial and bank capital are now brought under the common direction of high finance, in which the masters of industry and of the banks are united in a close personal association. The basis of this association is the elimination of free competition among individual capitalists by the large monopolistic combines. This naturally involves at the same time a change in the relation of the capitalist class to state power (Hilferding 1981: 301).

Marx had posited three fractions of capital: industrial capital, involved directly in the production process including agriculture; financial capital, the domain of banks and associated financial entities; and commercial capital, the realm of merchants and the buying and selling of commodities (Brewer 1990: 92). Finance capital was the fusing together of the three fractions and was thus qualitatively different to financial capital.

Finance capital grew out of the rapid rate of German industrialisation with its concomitant monopolising tendencies. German banks were closely connected with the industrialisation process and were themselves bound up in monopolisation, acting to encourage cartel formation to safeguard their loans, and through competition amongst themselves reducing their own numbers from nine to six major banks. Brewer points out that there was some ambiguity in how Hilferding portrayed finance capital. At one level, it was the capital that came into the possession of industrial capitalists through the agency of the banks. On another level, it was the control over the economy exercised by the banks (Brewer 1990: 93). Notwithstanding this ambiguity, the concentration of capital evident in the German experience was such that the limited number of banks assumed a pivotal role in shaping industrial production. This was in contrast to banks in England, which in the late nineteenth and early twentieth century were not involved in long-term investment in industry (Brewer 1990: 94). The majority shareholders in the banks (the German banks being joint stock companies or corporations) increasingly became the dominant figures in both the banking and industrial spheres (Hilferding 1981: 225).

Kautsky, Bukharin and Lenin saw finance capital as a symptom of contemporary capitalist development. Whilst finance capital did assume a greater role in the economies of the advanced capitalist nations over time, *financial* capital was not as intimately connected with industry in Britain when Hilferding wrote. Also noteworthy is that, for both Hobson and Hilferding, financiers and finance capitalists had established themselves in positions of power and influence. Financiers in Hobson's purview were able to distort public policy for their own advantage, exerting a malign influence in British politics. Hilferding asserted that, through their pivotal role in industrial development, the major banks in Germany managed to gain control of the commanding heights of the national economy.

The changing face of capitalism two: the export of capital

The free trade capitalism upon which Britain had relied during its period of industrial supremacy primarily was associated with the export of commodities. With increased competitive pressure coming from newly industrialising powers such as Germany and the US, combined with the imposition of protective tariffs, the export of capital supplanted the export of commodities. The export of capital was the second feature that Hilferding identified in German and US capitalist development, which, in turn, was taken up by later Marxist writers.

British commodities that once had found their way into markets across the globe due to their cheapness now faced tariff walls that raised their prices. Surmounting the challenge of declining export profits gave impetus to the export of capital. Getting in behind tariff barriers and taking advantage of the higher prices in a foreign market prompted the setting up of manufacturing plants in that market. The industrial plants, of course, were to remain in the ownership of the parent company, with profits repatriated to the home country. German banks, too, were keen on exporting capital by setting up branches in foreign countries and extending loans:

> Thus a large German bank establishes a branch abroad, which then negotiates a loan the proceeds of which are used to construct an electrical generating plant, and the construction work is assigned to an electrical company which is connected with the bank at home ... It is the intimate connection between bank and industrial capital which is responsible for the rapid development of capital exports (Hilferding 1981: 315).

Territoriality, colonialism and the rise of the strong state

With greater concentration and centralisation of capital bringing in its train cartelisation and ultimately finance capital, the competitive struggles within national economies tended to abate. New sources of profit and new fields of investment were sought. Capital export opened up new markets, helping to moderate the effects of crises, prolonging prosperity, and boosting domestic production (Hilferding 1981: 318). With the drive to export capital becoming general, the international sphere became highly competitive with advanced nations seeking to cordon off their spheres of influence, dependencies and colonies from other capitalist powers. The simplest way to achieve this goal, for Hilferding, was through the incorporation of 'parts of the world market into the national market, through a colonial policy which involves the annexation of foreign territories' (Hilferding 1981: 325).

There were three objectives of the territorial policy of finance capital: first was the establishment of a large economic territory; second was the closure of territory to foreign interests through imposition of protective tariffs; and third was the reservation of territory for the exploitation of monopolistic combinations (Hilferding 1981: 326). In the free trade era, Britain commanded a substantial economic territory by dint of its empire. The US, too, through westward expansion had a vast economic territory. Germany, unified in 1871, did have a reasonable economic territory to exploit but through the processes Hilferding detailed, German capitalists in concert with the German state had successfully closed off their national market and sought new territories for investment and resource extraction overseas.

The free trade era, according to Hilferding, displayed an indifference to colonies whereas the new phase of capitalism was remarkable for a more active colonial policy evident amongst the advanced nations. This new form of colonialism aggravated tensions between states, requiring the deployment of armed forces to safeguard territory from rivals. The role of the state changed, too. The economic policy of finance capital – with its strong monopolistic tendencies, tariffs, capital export and revamped colonialism – demanded a strong interventionist state. In contrast, the bourgeoisie, prior to the era of finance capital, had displayed a keen dislike of strong absolutist states. A key tenet of liberalism is that the state should have a limited role in the private sphere, a principle that has its roots in the struggles against absolutist states. This was a tenet abandoned along with others:

> The old free traders believed in free trade not only as the best economic policy but also as the beginning of an era of peace. Finance capital abandoned this belief long ago. It has no faith in the harmony of capitalist interests, and knows well that competition is becoming increasingly a political power struggle. The ideal of peace has lost its lustre, and in place of the idea of humanity there emerges a glorification of the greatness and power of the state ... The ideal now is to secure for one's own nation the domination of the world an aspiration which is as unbounded as the capitalist lust for profit from which it springs ... Since the subjection of foreign nations takes place by force – that is, in a perfectly natural way – it appears to the ruling nation that this domination is due to some special natural qualities, in short its racial characteristics. Thus there emerges in racist ideology, cloaked in the garb of natural science, a justification for finance capital's lust for power, which is thus shown to have the specificity and necessity of a natural phenomenon. An oligarchic ideal of domination has replaced the democratic ideal of equality (Hilferding 1981: 335).

Whilst the conditions of finance capital necessitated a strong state, capitalists 'acquired the power to dominate the state' in two ways. First of all by virtue of the economic power that capitalists wielded and, second, by the active subordination of other classes' interests unto their own (Hilferding 1981: 337). Domination of the state was partially attributable to the alliances that urban capitalists arranged with large landowners. Having the landed gentry onside cleared the way for the domination of the state by finance capital, removing the obstacle of possible opposition by a powerful class, thereby ensuring the implementation of imperialist policy (Hilferding 1981: 342). Two points are evident here: first, for Hilferding the state was dominated by capitalists and was used as an instrument to further their political and economic ends; and, second, imperialism was a policy.

The state as instrument, imperialism as policy

Hilferding claimed that the state pursued annexationist policies and imposed protectionist tariffs at the behest of capitalists. In short, his was an instrumentalist view of the state. Such a view of the state was commonly held by classical Marxists. Hilferding obviously did not feel the need to have an elaborate theory of the state, for his central concern was analysis of late nineteenth- and early twentieth-century capitalism. The economic rather than the political developments of the conjuncture interested him, and given the relatively unsophisticated nature of the theorisation of the state at the time, perhaps it is no surprise that Hilferding opted for an instrumentalist view of the state.

Clearly for Hilferding, imperialism was a policy. Unfortunately, he was not clear in his conceptualising of imperialism. For instance, in the final part of his book, where imperialism is ostensibly discussed, there was no attempt to define the term. Imperialism was either the economic policy of finance capital, 'modern protectionist policy', or was intimately bound up with the export of capital, a strong state and the annexation of territories (Hilferding 1981: 366, 322). Ideologically, imperialism was the celebration and promotion of a strong state, militarism, war and racism (Hilferding 1981: 336, 346, 349). Thus it was a vaguely defined term that seemed to be the militaristic and expansionist tendencies inherent in finance capital coupled with an ideological side. There was, however, enough material in the final part of *Finance Capital* to enable theorists to synthesise said material and define imperialism more concisely. Bukharin was the first to take advantage of Hilferding's critical insights into capitalist development to enhance his own systematic analysis of imperialism and the world capitalist economy (Brewer 1990: 107).

Hilferding's foundational work on capitalism and imperialism

Hilferding's place as one of the founders of Marxist imperialism theory is assured because his work on revealing the shift from the competitive free trade era of capitalism to the era of finance capital opened up a host of concepts that subsequent writers adopted. Amongst these were finance capital, the export of capital (Hobson had referred to it but Hilferding gave a more detailed analysis), tariffs, cartels and the concentration and centralisation of capital tending towards monopolisation. Not only did Bukharin and Lenin draw on these concepts but neo-Marxists as well as 'globalisation-era' Marxist writers have made use of the export of capital and finance capital tropes to build their theories.

By claiming that imperialism was a policy, albeit a policy that capitalists could not avoid pursuing (Hilferding 1981: 366), Hilferding seemingly straddles the reformist/revolutionary divide that characterised the work of the pioneers. Yet, his close association with Kautsky and his commitment to formal parliamentary democracy, one of the cornerstones of Kautsky's vision for the transition to socialism, marks him as a reformist (Bottomore 1981: 11). Only in the final pages of his book – in a chapter on the proletariat and imperialism – does Hilferding offer up any political programme. The dictatorship of the magnates of capital inevitably gives rise to opposition and the proletariat must gather round it the disaffected classes of society and seize state power. Violent clashes would necessarily ensue with the masses of people exploited by finance capital arrayed against it. The dictatorship of the magnates of capital would be supplanted by the dictatorship of the proletariat (Hilferding 1981: 368–370). This brief excursus on the solution to the intractable problems associated with finance capital and imperialism appears to be revolutionary, with terms like dictatorship of the proletariat and seizure of state power. Hilferding, however, did not go beyond generalities and the appearance of these at the end of the book seems like an afterthought. When revolutions took place in Russia in February and October 1917 (culminating in the Bolshevik seizure of power through the auspices of the Petrograd Soviet), Hilferding, whilst initially sympathetic, thought that the regime would not last. Isolation, he thought, would see it off. He quickly lost his sympathy for the regime, disapproving of the Bolsheviks' authoritarian approach to dealing with Russia's problems. He rejected the use of red terror in the Civil War and criticised the crushing of dissent within the Bolshevik party. He also expressed concern about the Comintern being run from Moscow and its insistence on affiliating parties subscribing to democratic centralism. The public criticism of Bolshevik policies extended to the German Communist Party (Kommunistische Partei Deutschlands, KPD), whose adventurist tactics and divisive approach to the German worker's movement were anathema to Hilferding (Smaldone 1988: 290; 1994: 3). For Hilferding and for many German social democrats the path to socialism was inconceivable without formal democracy, key components of which were parliamentarism and electoral politics (Bottomore 1981: 11). In practice, Hilferding was committed to reformism whilst paying lip service to certain revolutionary ideas in his theoretical work.

In sum, Hilferding's theorising of imperialism as presented in *Finance Capital* made a lasting contribution to imperialism theory in general and Marxist writing on the subject in particular. It had its weaknesses in its reliance on generalities and in universalising the peculiarities of German capitalist development. In addition, due to his more circumspect/reformist approach, there were minimal practical political lessons that he drew from his analysis. This ambivalence about the tactics of the working class and its organisations regarding the overthrow of finance capital was to be made good by later Marxist theorists of imperialism such as Luxemburg and to an even greater extent Bukharin and Lenin. The strengths of Hilferding's work lies in his concerted attempt to undertake a thoroughgoing Marxist analysis of the capitalism of his day. In so doing, he popularised the concepts of finance capital, gave a more detailed analysis of the export of capital and showed how tariffs and the new forms of capitalist organisation – cartels, trusts and syndicates – indicated that the competitive era of capitalism ostensibly had passed.

Negotiating through the minefields of war, revolution and imperialism: Karl Kautsky

Kautsky, by the start of the twentieth century, had built a reputation for being one of the leading theoreticians in German social democracy. Born in Prague in 1854, he moved to Vienna and came under the influence of socialists there, becoming a convinced Marxist in his mid twenties. He was the editor of the SPD organ *Die Neue Zeit* from 1883 to 1917. Just after the commencement of hostilities in 1914, Kautsky's article 'Ultra-imperialism' appeared in *Die Neue Zeit*. Written weeks before fighting commenced, with an upcoming Congress of the Second International in mind, the outbreak of war intervened thus stopping the Congress and facilitating the collapse of the Second International (Kautsky 1914; Nettl 1966b: 612–13; Meldolesi 1984a: 1834). The German SPD was the most organised and well-supported member party of the Second International and it went through a series of crises prior to the outbreak of and during the war (Salvadori 1990: 181–225; Nettl 1966b: 601–52). At the heart of the crises and consequent splits in the SPD were the complex issues of tactics in the pursuit of the goal of socialism, overlaid by the questions of supporting the nation in time of war. In other words, the question of reform or revolution was now joined by the complex issue of nationalism versus internationalism.

In negotiating his and the party's way through these problem areas, Kautsky modified his theoretical viewpoint on war, imperialism and the role of the SPD by taking up a 'centrist' position. That is, he distanced himself from the revolutionary elements found in his polemics against Bernstein and the revisionists conducted through the period 1898 to 1903 (Nettl 1965: 68), the high point of which can be found in an essay he wrote after the 1905 Russian Revolution: 'Motor Forces and Perspectives of the Russian Revolution'. Lenin claimed that the essay vindicated the position of Russian social democrats on the strategic slogan of the dictatorship of the proletariat and peasantry, calling Kautsky 'the leader of the German revolutionary Social Democrats' (Salvadori 1990: 104). By 1910, Kautsky's ardour for revolutionary slogans had cooled and in that year he castigated Luxemburg for her continued radicalism. The exchanges between Kautsky and Luxemburg over SPD strategy precipitated Kautsky's 'centrist' line (Salvadori 1990: 140). Having eschewed revolutionary formulations he could not embrace the revisionist position that he had spent so long campaigning against, which explains his attempt to occupy the middle ground.

The 'centrist' line required the revamping by Kautsky of the basis of his theorising. By 1914, Kautsky had revisited his previous work on the agrarian question and the policies of finance capital, arriving at a new conclusion:

> Imperialism – in the sense of colonial expansion, the recourse to arms, the danger of war – is the line preferred by financial capital but is not the only policy open to it. Thus the proletariat could align itself with a progressive sector of the middle class on ultra-imperialist aims for peaceful development, which would allow power to go to social democracy in the course of time (Meldolesi 1984a: 1833).

Both in theory and in practice, Kautsky's 'centrist' line was a re-assertion of the 'inheritance' position or line, which was the belief that the SPD would inherit state power. With the growth in numbers of party members and elected Reichstag deputies, havoc would be created in the SPD's political opponents such that 'society would disintegrate and Social Democracy {would} be able to step into its place' (Nettl 1965: 82). The 'inheritance' position was Kautsky's default setting with revolutionary phrases merely surface phenomena. His writing on imperialism, which culminated in 'Ultra-imperialism', was the product of at least four years of reflection and thinking. At the end of that process his conclusion was that imperialism was not a necessary stage of capitalism but a policy that both capitalists and nation-states would eventually see as misguided.

From imperialism to 'ultra-imperialism'

Connections between industrial and agricultural sectors underpin Kautsky's version of imperialism. The product of developed industrial capitalism, imperialism was the subjugation or annexation of increasingly larger agrarian zones or spheres of influence by the advanced capitalist nation-states. The annexation of the agrarian zones took the form of colonialism. The proviso was added by Kautsky that the establishment and extension of a colonial empire could succeed only on the basis of the annexation of culturally inferior countries (Kautsky 1914: 6).

During free trade capitalism, which was based on Britain's ascendancy as industrial workshop of the world, the United Kingdom had unfettered access to an agrarian hinterland. Competition in the form of the industrialisation of the US and Germany and their imposition of tariffs forced the British to reciprocate with their own tariffs. The consequent push to divide up the remaining 'free' agricultural zones created the environment for the emergence of imperialism (Kautsky 1914: 3).

Industrial expansion, after the 1870s, had proceeded at such a rapid rate that markets struggled to keep up. Transportation methods were improved through the spread of railways in both industrial and agrarian countries. Lacking the capital to invest in railway construction, agrarian countries became the recipients of foreign capital earmarked for railway and other infrastructure projects. Capitalist nations sought to safeguard their capital exports through the power of their states. Therefore, as more capital went to the agrarian zones, greater political control over those zones ensued (Kautsky 1914: 3). Some agrarian nations, most notably Russia, were able to avoid the colonial experience, directing the incoming capital to industrial development of their own. Essentially capital export did not help in the industrialisation of agrarian nations. The combination of political control and limited development ensured that the agrarian country remained at the level of a provider of agricultural products and raw materials (Kautsky 1914: 4).

Competition for the remaining 'free' zones or spheres of influence in the world's agricultural regions was considerable causing an arms race, thence a shipbuilding frenzy, breaking out into world war. Kautsky asserted that there was no economic necessity for the continuation of an arms race after the war. Capitalists could see that the capitalist economy was threatened 'by the contradictions between its states' (Kautsky 1914: 4). Not only capitalists could see the problems that the policy of imperialism caused. Opposition to imperialism arose in the more developed agrarian zones as well as amongst the proletariat in the industrial countries, chafing under the tax burdens imposed on them due to the costs of the arms race and colonial expansion:

> Imperialism is thus digging its own grave. From a means to develop capitalism, it is becoming a hindrance to it. Nevertheless, capitalism need not yet be at the end of the line. From the purely economic standpoint, it can continue to develop so long as the growing industries of the capitalist countries can induce a corresponding expansion of agricultural production (Kautsky 1914: 5).

According to Kautsky, imperialism was only one mode of expansion of capitalism. At the end of the World War, there was the possibility that the great imperialist powers would come to some arrangement, desisting from the arms race and like cartels, reaching agreement about the coordination of their foreign policies. He predicted that the cartelisation of foreign policies and the materialisation of a federation of powers would usher in a new phase, that of ultra-imperialism (Kautsky 1914: 6).

Ultra-imperialism and the role of social democracy

Ultra-imperialism, then, was the dawning recognition that the violent form of capitalist expansion – the preferred policy of finance capital – was too costly and too disruptive. The power politics of the years before the outbreak of war had to be superseded lest another conflagration arose. Kautsky expected that statesmen would heed the lessons. He saw that the concept of a federation of central European states, which had been floated prior to the outbreak of war, had positive ramifications. Kautsky thought that the integration of different communities into a collective one – a confederation of states – was 'an appropriate formula for [a] large empire whose capitalism needs to reach its last and highest form, in which the proletariat will assume power' (Meldolesi 1984a: 1838). Such a multinational entity should be based on equal rights, with democratic conditions applying in each member nation.

German capitalist development, observed Kautsky, required a larger internal market, hence his critical approval of a confederation of central European states. The political union of the 'United States of Europe', whilst at that time only a possible future scenario, nevertheless was a programme that social democracy should support in the post-war era. Undoubtedly, this was support of capitalism and potential political forms arising from a capitalist economic base, but in Kautsky's mind that support, though conditional, was warranted. By critically supporting capitalism and its political forms, social democracy would help deliver the expansion of industrial production and more harmonious political forms, the latter being both democratic and egalitarian. By not supporting the rapacious and conflictual policies of imperialism, which produced arms races and world war, social democracy would help ensure that the capitalists and the political leaders would eventually turn their back on those policies (Meldolesi 1984a: 1838–9).

The aim of social democrats in the post-war phase of ultra-imperialism was to act as a pressure group, encouraging the further development of the means of production whilst countering imperialist policies. Unlike Bukharin and Lenin, for example, Kautsky did not see imperialism as the final phase of capitalism. Instead, he considered imperialism the violent extension of spheres of influence or outright annexation of agrarian zones by industrialised capitalist powers. It was not the definitive crisis of capitalism and therefore did not require the revolutionary seizure of power and the smashing of the bourgeois state (Salvadori 1990: 202).

Hilferding's influence on Kautsky

Hilferding's analysis of finance capital was a seminal influence on Kautsky's theorising. Both the export of capital and the confluence of banking and industrial capital that formed finance capital were concepts that Kautsky adopted and adapted. Especially insightful for Kautsky was Hilferding's work on cartels. The confederation of powerful capitalist states, a configuration that Kautsky predicted would come into being after the war, reaching accord about political and economic arrangements, was the extension of Hilferding's findings about cartels, trusts and syndicates to the domain of International Relations (Meldolesi 1984b: 1878). The positing of a syndicate or cartel of states and the perceived weakness of the labour movement in Germany were the grounds that Kautsky used to promote the tactics of passivity associated with the inheritance position. In his view, the capitalist states would still be powerful after the war, coming to their senses and making arrangements amongst themselves for the peaceful exploitation of their own spheres of influence (ultra-imperialism). Parties like the German SPD, because of the less than fortuitous social, political and economic conditions, had to act prudently.

Kautsky: right after all?

A number of assumptions underpinned Kautsky's vision of an ultra-imperialist future. Given that Kautsky's writing on ultra-imperialism has been the subject of renewed interest, it is important to tease out these assumptions. According to 'globalisation-era' Marxists Panitch and Gindin, Kautsky's ultra-imperialism corresponds closely to the framework of post-Cold War international relations (see also Donald 1993: 205). Such is the nature of American hegemony and the intimate connection between the US state and the states of other advanced capitalist nations that Lenin's assertion about inter-imperialist rivalry now is effectively rendered obsolete. They go further and assert that the reason for Lenin's scorn towards Kautsky's analysis of imperialism was that, fundamentally, he had the temerity to claim that:

> all the major capitalist ruling classes, after 'having learned the lesson of the world war', might eventually come to revive capitalist globalization through a collaborative 'ultra-imperialism' in face of the increasing strength of an industrial proletariat that nevertheless still fell short of the capacity to effect a socialist transformation (Panitch and Gindin 2004: 9).

Rehabilitating ultra-imperialism uncritically, however, is problematic because it was based on a set of assumptions that proved to be not simply wrong but, moreover, 'politically incoherent' (Salvadori 1990: 203).

The political incoherence stemmed from Kautsky's claim that capitalism would be rejuvenated after the war and the SPD and other social democratic parties would be able to take up where they left off. He made this claim shortly before the catastrophic voting for war credits by SPD Reichstag deputies, which opened a chasm in the ranks of the SPD. Kautsky did not rescind this claim, allowing publication of his article on ultra-imperialism to go ahead after the outbreak of war. Kautsky's reformism, which had become more prominent after 1910, ruled out any extra-parliamentary opposition to the policies of the German government, an attitude that infuriated the revolutionaries Luxemburg, Bukharin and Lenin.

The SPD underwent a series of splits towards the war's end, and Kautsky joined one of the new (short-lived) splinter parties the Independent Social Democratic of Germany (Unabhängige Sozialdemokratische Partei Deutschlands, USPD). The establishment of the Weimar Republic following the war, and revolutionary upsurges in Berlin and various other German cities and regions between November 1918 and January 1919, gave the lie to an easy resumption of political roles (Donald 1993: 204–5, 214). The history of the Weimar Republic shows that the inheritance strategy underpinning Kautsky's ultra-imperialism did not bring about socialism.

What particularly attracted the ire of Lenin was Kautsky's proposal that, at the end of the war, there would be a coming together of the great imperialist powers that would see them reach an accord whereupon they would drop the conflictual policies that caused the Great War. This scenario did not come to pass. The Versailles Treaty, which imposed onerous reparations and other conditions on Germany courtesy of the victorious nations, laid the groundwork for World War II. In the aftermath of the war, notes Hobsbawm, 'every party in Germany, from the Communists on the extreme left to Hitler's National Socialists on the extreme right, concurred in condemning the Versailles Treaty as unjust and unacceptable' (Hobsbawm 1998b: 36). Kautsky's identification of imperialism as primarily a relationship between the industrialised nations and the agrarian nations was rebuffed by the conditions placed on Germany subsequent to the signing of the Armistice in 1918. The occupation of the Ruhr by the French in 1923 was a further example of how imperialism was not just an exploitative relationship between industrial and agrarian countries. French capitalists and bourgeois politicians, it has been suggested, had an eye on the Ruhr as a 'political prop for French domination in Europe' (Broué 2006: 686).

Kautsky's reformist ideology shaped his conceptualising of imperialism and his predictions for future geopolitical and capitalist development. It is a risky exercise to suggest that the insights found in 'Ultra-imperialism' are more in tune with the current conjuncture because, for one thing, inter-imperialist rivalry appears to be superseded. Panitch and Gindin, in resurrecting Kautsky's assertion about collaboration amongst ruling classes in advanced capitalist nations, extract ultra-imperialism from its social, political and economic context. Additionally, the reformism and problematic assumptions that lay at the heart of the theory are overlooked. Despite these concerns, the harking back by Panitch and Gindin to Kautsky's ultra-imperialism is an example of the continued interest that classical Marxist theories hold for contemporary Marxist thinkers.

'Ultra-imperialism', Kautsky's enduring legacy

Kautsky's contribution to imperialism theory is most notable for the reactions it has engendered. On the one hand, it came in for scathing criticism from Luxemburg, Bukharin and Lenin as we will see in the next chapter. Interestingly, for more recent Marxist writers Panitch and Gindin, ultra-imperialism has been vindicated decades after it was first proposed. Imperialism, for Kautsky, was the policy of violence pursued by industrial nations, usually in connection with the securing of sources of raw materials and agricultural products. Kautsky was convinced that imperialism was not the final stage of capitalism and its excesses would be toned down or reformed by the ruling classes. Capitalists and bourgeois politicians would, Kautsky assumed, come to see the political and economic short-sightedness associated with imperialist policies. As the leading theoretician of the German SPD and one of its key figures, Kautsky helped shape that party's response to imperialism and war. In his view, opposition to both imperialism and war had to be tempered by knowledge of the strength of the bourgeois state and weaknesses of social democracy respectively. Consequently, he thought that, once the war concluded, conditional support had to be given to capitalist expansion and the political processes and institutions in advanced capitalist nations. These were appropriate tactics for social democratic parties to implement given the power imbalance between states and working-class parties. In Kautsky's mind, the revolutionary seizure of the state could be countenanced only as an extreme last resort.

'Ultra-imperialism' was Kautsky's attempt to demonstrate that reform remained the best strategy that the SPD and kindred parties could adopt both at the time and just after the war. His theory of imperialism was a reflection of his political outlook. This is something that we will see also in the writing of the revolutionaries; political outlook colouring theoretical perspective. It is important to highlight this as criticism has been directed Lenin's way for his 'proclivity for over-politicizing theory' (Panitch and Gindin 2004: 9). Classical Marxist writers as a cohort were involved in the day-to-day activities connected with political parties, whether legal or illegal. Therefore political lessons, strategies and tactics usually shaped and reflected their analyses.

The aftermath of the Great War, the Bolshevik revolution, the failure of the German revolutionary uprisings and subsequent German social, political and economic developments made Kautsky's offering on imperialism redundant. 'Ultra-imperialism' probably would have faded from view entirely if it had not been vilified by Lenin in his pamphlet. It is, perhaps, one of the ironies of history that elements of Kautsky's conceptualising of ultra-imperialism have been rehabilitated in the post-Cold War world. Ironic, but also deeply problematic, because the social, political and economic contexts as well as Kautsky's reformist outlook all have been overlooked by those interested in the partial rehabilitation of his theory.

Conclusion

The reformists Hobson, Hilferding and Kautsky produced the concepts and insights that the revolutionary theoreticians Luxemburg, Bukharin and Lenin used to construct or refine their own theories of imperialism. Hobson's seminal book set out the political, social, moral and economic boundaries of imperialism theory. Hilferding, whilst not creating a fully elaborated theory of imperialism himself, nevertheless presented a Marxist analysis of capitalist development in the decades after Marx's death revealing many important changes, particularly in the economies of Germany and the US. Tropes such as the export of capital, finance capital, financiers, cartels, syndicates and trusts, and stages of capitalist development came from the reformists and found their way into the writing of the revolutionaries.

Hobson, Hilferding and Kautsky saw imperialism as a major issue intimately linked to capitalism. Yet, they did not consider imperialism as something unavoidable nor that it was an inevitable product of capitalism. Political systems in Britain and Germany, according to the reformists, were sufficiently robust and politicians were astute enough to deal with the excesses of imperialism. Revolutionary upheaval was unnecessary and, according to Hilferding and Kautsky, may well have been counter-productive for the organised working-class movement.

A problem with the analysis of imperialism undertaken by the 'pioneers' is the paucity of the political theory evident in their writing. This problem is especially evident in the output of classical Marxists. We saw this in Hilferding's *Finance Capital* where the capitalist class used the state as an instrument. The instrumentalist view of the state also appears in Bukharin's and Lenin's analyses as discussed in the following chapter.

Theorising of imperialism by the reformists set out the parameters for much of the analysis of imperialism that was to follow. Aspects of their work continue to have contemporary relevance. Panitch and Gindin argue that Kautsky's conceptualising of ultra-imperialism foreshadowed the contemporary global political situation, with one major imperialist power setting the ground rules for the other imperialist powers. Whilst it was found that such a view of Kautsky's ultra-imperialism hypothesis de-contextualised it, nonetheless, Panitch and Gindin furnish proof of the continued relevance of the work of the 'pioneers'. A stronger case for the continued relevance of classical Marxist theories of imperialism can be made about the revolutionaries and it is to their work that attention now turns.

CHAPTER 2

IMPERIALISM AS UNAVOIDABLE CONSEQUENCE OF CAPITALIST DEVELOPMENT

THE REVOLUTIONARIES: LUXEMBURG, BUKHARIN AND LENIN

Introduction

Taking the view that imperialism was a necessary consequence of capitalist development were the revolutionaries Rosa Luxemburg, Nikolai Bukharin and Vladimir Lenin. Luxemburg was an active participant in the struggles against revisionism in the German SPD and a staunch critic of any move to dilute the revolutionary heart of Marxist social theory and practice. She railed against the nationalist fervour and the rising tide of militarism that took hold of Wilhelmine Germany and her opposition to the war led to her incarceration (Broué 2006: 58, 62). Along with another 'new radical' Karl Liebknecht – who also received a jail term for his outspoken resistance to the war (Broué 2006: 60) – Luxemburg helped bring into existence the Spartacus group that emerged from meetings of disgruntled SPD officials, activists and trade union leaders between June 1915 and March 1916 (Broué 2006: 64). The Spartacists, as they became known, sought to re-direct the German labour movement away from the reformism/revisionism that marked the SPD. In 1913, the year before the outbreak of war, Luxemburg published *The Accumulation of Capital* (1971). This book was a considered response to the Bernsteinian thesis that capitalist crises had not brought about the collapse of capitalism that Marx had predicted. Eduard Bernstein and fellow revisionists had claimed that Marxism needed to be revised in light of capitalism's continued existence and the problems associated with orthodox Marxist theory such as value theory and the theory of wages (Howard and King 1989: 72–7).

Luxemburg believed that she had uncovered the reasons for capitalism's non-collapse in the increasing incorporation of the colonial world into the structures of capitalist accumulation. Imperialism was the method whereby capitalist nations had forestalled their imminent collapse. She believed Marx's *Capital* contained errors, especially his reproduction schemas found in *Capital Volume Two* (Marx 1978), which she asserted was premised on a closed system (Mommsen 1981: 40). By tackling this perceived problem, Luxemburg sought to counter revisionism and account for the significant expansion of capitalism and its colonial development from the late nineteenth century onwards. The positioning of imperialism as a necessary by-product of what essentially is a flawed analysis of Marx's reproduction schemas does not detract from the positive fruits of her labours. Luxemburg, for instance, first brought to light the use of militarism as a subsidiary means of capital accumulation. 'Defence expenditure', according to Mommsen, 'acted as an additional method of realizing surplus value – an idea which has been adopted in various forms by later Marxist thinkers' (Mommsen 1981: 44).

Luxemburg's Marxist contribution to imperialism theory arguably has been underappreciated. Certainly the focus of *The Accumulation of Capital* is not primarily on imperialism. Her understanding of the subject nonetheless led her to argue that, whilst imperialism was 'the historical method for prolonging the career of capitalism', any such continuation would not prove indefinite. There would be a reckoning and the 'mere tendency towards imperialism of itself takes forms which make the final phase of capitalism a period of catastrophe' (Mommsen 1981: 43). The 'final phase of capitalism' pre-empted Lenin's 'last or highest stage of capitalism', with Wolfgang Mommsen observing that Lenin owed much to Luxemburg's analysis of imperialism without ever actually acknowledging it (Mommsen 1981: 47).

Such has been the influence of Lenin's book that Bukharin's contribution (for which the former penned an introduction) has been largely overlooked. Bukharin's insightful views on imperialism, however, received a ringing endorsement from Alex Callinicos who, amongst other things, acknowledged Bukharin's central concept of the world economy in the title of his own work *Imperialism and Global Political Economy* (Callinicos 2009: 19). Bukharin's *Imperialism and World Economy* (Bukharin 1973) points out the high level of development attained by capitalism in the opening years of the century. He saw in imperialism the intertwined and interdependent nature of capitalism and the state, a nexus that had developed in the monopoly stage of capitalism. Bukharin believed that states had become so intimately tied up in the capitalist accumulation process he coined the phrase 'state capitalist trusts' to describe the relationship. State capitalist trusts were dependent on the territorial space of the nation-state and the subordination of the state to the interests of 'its' capitalists. Countering these national features was the increased internationalisation of the capitalist accumulation process. The contradiction between the national and the international in the political and economic nexus of capitalist imperialism arguably is Bukharin's most important addition to imperialism theory.

Interestingly, Bukharin, like the reformists, saw imperialism as a policy to which *finance capital* resorted, in other words a policy of conquest (Bukharin 1973: 114). Lifted straight from Hilferding, finance capital was the amalgamation of industrial and banking capital, a feature of German industrial development. At first glance, it appears that Bukharin reified finance capital, attributing policy making capabilities to a set of social relations. Bukharin's argument, according to Brewer, was that capitalism had become so organised under the aegis of finance capital that there was unification of the capitalist classes of each national bloc. Such was the unification of interests that the state no longer had to arbitrate over competing fractional interests and thus could be seen as simply reflecting the policies, values and ideals of the magnates of capital (Brewer 1990: 115). Brewer rightly points out that Bukharin's treatment of the state was 'over-simple' (Brewer 1990: 114).

Unlike the reformists, Bukharin did not think it was possible to circumvent international tensions and the inevitable wars that were the very essence of imperialism, through policies and legislation. Imperialism was not amenable to reform and Bukharin dismissed

Kautsky's ultra-imperialism as a pipe-dream. The only solution to the Gordian knot of imperialism was proletarian revolution.

Prior to 1917 and the Bolshevik seizure of power in Russia, Lenin was in the minority of social democratic leaders still advocating the revolutionary line in Europe and in Russia. One purpose that Lenin had in mind when writing on imperialism was to demonstrate that reformists like Kautsky were wrong in their appraisal of the conjuncture. It was wrong for reformists to think that the excesses of imperialism – such as the horrendous war that was then ravaging Europe – could be avoided or reformed away so long as capitalism continued to exist. *Imperialism: The Highest Stage of Capitalism* (Lenin 1973) was not merely some excursus in painstaking academic research; it served political and polemical ends as well.

It is important to make this point because two latter-day Marxist critics tax Lenin with over-politicising theory. Panitch and Gindin make a series of strong criticisms of classical Marxist theorists. They claim, *inter alia*, that the elevation of the particular circumstances that applied to late nineteenth- and early twentieth-century European development and especially the intense rivalries between the Great Powers became an *idée fixe* for classical Marxist theorists (Panitch and Gindin 2004: 9). Panitch and Gindin, in criticising Lenin's response to Kautsky, abstract out the intense struggles over strategy and tactics that these theorists *and* political leaders were compelled to undertake in reaction to the tumultuous events of their times. Reform or revolution was the burning question of the era. In part three, where 'globalisation-era' Marxist offerings are accorded more detailed analysis, Panitch's and Gindin's combined offering on twenty-first-century imperialism is examined in more detail. Here it suffices to state that one of their criticisms of Lenin's work – his over-politicising of theory – is illustrative of the type of misunderstanding that Lenin's treatise on imperialism has attracted and continues to attract.

The above should not be taken as wholehearted endorsement of Lenin's theory of imperialism. It is untenable either to dismiss his work completely or to make the assertion that his tract remains the definitive last word on imperialism (Churchward 1959: 76). Unlike Bukharin, Lenin did not propound an overtly instrumentalist view of the state in his study of imperialism. There was minimal analysis of the political aspects of imperialism in his book, due to Lenin's desire to avoid Tsarist censorship (Lenin 1973: 1). Criticism raised by Panitch and Gindin concerning the lack of political theory in the theorising of imperialism by classical Marxists applies to Lenin's work.

Although there are problems with Lenin's theory of imperialism as critics have rightly pointed out, there is much that remains relevant. Certain features of the world that Lenin identified early in the twentieth century are readily observable today. Global capitalism is as pervasive as ever and still prone to crisis. Amidst great wealth there exists great poverty and international politics still is marked by the 'might makes right' approach synonymous with *Realpolitik*. Conflicts continue to occur, though admittedly not at the level of the conflagrations that marked the first half of the twentieth century. Hence the ongoing interest in and relevance of Lenin's tract; it is not the final word on imperialism theory, nor is it a painstakingly assembled theoretical excursus. Nonetheless, it holds contemporary significance because the major features of global capitalism and geopolitics Lenin identified in 1916 are discernible in the new millennium, albeit in modified forms. An examination of Lenin's writing on imperialism brings this to light.

This chapter presents two key arguments. First, the analysis of imperialism by the revolutionaries provided benchmark theories that continue to have contemporary relevance. The revolutionaries built on the work of reformists, but deviated from the reformists' analyses over the question of the inevitability of imperialism. Luxemburg, Bukharin and Lenin produced empirically rich theories, with each providing cogent definitions of capitalist imperialism, noteworthy because they were the first to do so. The work of the revolutionaries has been and continues to be highly influential, with contemporary Marxist intellectuals referring back to the writing of Luxemburg, Bukharin and Lenin to shape their work on twenty-first-century imperialism. The second argument concerns the paucity of political analysis evident in the writing of the revolutionaries. Criticisms of Panitch and Gindin about the omission of state theory and/or the instrumentalist rendering of the state in classical Marxist imperialism theory is important. By relying too heavily on the economic analysis of imperialism, the theories of imperialism produced by revolutionaries, especially Bukharin and Lenin, were rather one-sided.

Rosa Luxemburg and the necessity of non-capitalist regions for capitalist accumulation

Born in Poland in 1871 and later adopting German citizenship, Rosa Luxemburg was one of the SPD's stalwart 'leftists' and a leading theorist in the party. There was no question of her commitment to the revolutionary side of Marxism and her opposition to reformists in the SPD's ranks. From 1910 onwards, she had locked horns with Kautsky over the issue of the mass strike and the role of revolution in the supplanting of capitalism and the building of socialism (Nettl 1966a: 414–50). Luxemburg's *The Accumulation of Capital* was published in the year prior to the outbreak of World War I. The last section of that book, it has been argued, was 'the first comprehensive theory of imperialism sculpted by a Marxist' (Lee 1971: 847).

The book was ostensibly written about the perceived problem of accumulation and expanded reproduction in Marx's *Capital*. According to Luxemburg, the problem with Marx's modelling of reproduction in Volume Two of *Capital*, predicated as it was on an economy composed of capitalists (and assorted hangers on) and workers only, could not account for the increase in consumer or producer goods that each production cycle poured on the market. There was no possibility for expanded reproduction as consumption of consumer and producer goods remained static (Lee 1971: 847). Luxemburg's solution to the problem was straightforward; the reproduction process of capitalism was expanded by incorporating non-capitalist territories into Western capitalist economies. A number of phases were associated with this incorporation process, the last of which was imperialism. Hence her definition of imperialism: 'Imperialism is the political expression of the accumulation of capital in its competitive struggle for what remains still open of the non-capitalist environment (Luxemburg 1971: 446).'

Luxemburg's biographer has suggested that she did not go to the lengths that Lenin did three years later in his pamphlet spelling out the five distinctive features of imperialism. Luxemburg preferred to view imperialism as a general set of effects, amongst which were:

> Militarism closely connected with colonialism, protectionism and power politics as a whole ... a world armament race ... colonial robbery and the policy of 'spheres of influence' all over the world

> ... in home and foreign affairs the very essence of a capitalist policy of national aggression (Nettl 1966b: 524).

For Luxemburg, what distinguished imperialism from capitalism was not so much the changed nature of capitalism but rather the increased negative effects that imperialism had on society and social democracy. By emphasising that imperialism was a combination of effects, Luxemburg studiously avoided fixating on one special feature such as militarism. Her SPD colleague Karl Liebknecht, for instance, had become almost single-minded in his anti-militarism (Liebknecht 1972). Luxemburg's view of imperialism and how social democracy should respond to it was clear. The task of social democracy was to highlight all the aspects of imperialism, showing that it was a universal condition that required universal opposition by social democracy (Nettl 1966b: 524–5).

Intriguingly, for one whose outlook was revolutionary there is not much in the way of political analysis and strategising evident in Luxemburg's *The Accumulation of Capital* (1971). Peter Nettl states that within the book there is a rigorous theoretical analysis of imperialism's economic causes, yet there is only the 'physiognomy' of its political manifestations (Nettl 1966b: 535). By physiognomy Nettl means that the political manifestations of imperialism were outlined rather than defined by Luxemburg. His conjecture is that Luxemburg's reason for not drawing out political manifestations could be found in her effort to assert that imperialism was capitalism 'writ large'. By painting a picture of the overall rapaciousness of imperialism, Luxemburg was angling for a much stronger response from the SPD, rather than another 'anodyne by ballot' that Kautsky had proposed (Nettl 1966b: 536).

Luxemburg argued that imperialism was a product of the intrinsic economic problems of capitalism. When the accumulation processes in capitalist nations came up against the limits imposed on them by domestic markets, non-capitalist regions were assimilated into the capitalist global economy so that the realisation of surplus value could continue. Accumulation, then, was not just 'an internal relationship between the branches of capitalist economy; it primarily [was] a relationship between capital and a non-capitalist environment' (Luxemburg 1971: 417). Like other revolutionary theorists Bukharin and Lenin, Luxemburg saw imperialism as the final historical stage of capitalism. She viewed this phase or stage as characterised by 'lending abroad, railroad constructions, revolution and wars' (Luxemburg 1971: 417, 419).

International loans as lever: opening up the non-capitalist regions

Lending in the form of international loans was a particularly powerful instrument for shaping the economic development of nascent capitalist countries. Additionally, loans were crucial levers in prising open and supplanting the natural economies (that is, agricultural based economies) of the non-capitalist regions. In the first instance, newly emergent capitalist countries tapped into sources of finance to fund their industrialisation, state building and infrastructure. With the acceptance of the loan or loans, however, the recipients found themselves in the position of supplicants. As creditors, the old capitalist states exerted pressure on young states' foreign and commercial policies, finances and customs, in the process opening up new fields of investment and capital accumulation. The negative side of this opening up of new fields of investment and accumulation was the creation of new competitors for capitalists in the old capitalist states (Luxemburg 1971: 421).

The prime example of the invidious nature of foreign loans that Luxemburg cited was the Egyptian experience, starting with the projects of modernisation begun under the auspices of the 'the founder of Modern Egypt . . . Mehemet Ali' (Luxemburg 1971: 429). Over the course of the last half of the nineteenth century, during which time the Suez Canal was built by foreign companies and financed through a series of loans, Egypt became enmeshed in European capitalism. The combination of international loans, large speculative projects, the Suez Canal scheme and the exploitative use of the *fellaheen* (peasants) on whose shoulders was fastened a long-term tax burden effectively brought to an end the natural economy (agricultural, peasant-based economy) of Egypt, opening the way for a commodity-based economy. The indebtedness of Egypt to European capital resulted in the increased direct involvement of Europeans in the financial, economic and political life of the country. The Egyptian state, once it had performed its function of leeching the blood of the *fellaheen* through taxation in order to pay interest on the loans, was manipulated by the British and French into deposing Ismail Pasha, the Khedive, in June 1879. A mutiny in the Egyptian army and a popular revolt in Alexandria were the pretext for the British military occupation of Egypt in 1882. The transformation of Egypt from natural economy to a commodity economy and thence to capitalist economy could not occur fast enough and had to be completed under the direct control of international capital. Militarism acted as an executor of capitalist interests involving railway construction, irrigation systems, the Suez Canal project and international loans (Luxemburg 1971: 434–9).

Free Trade, tariffs and imperialism

Extending her historical analysis of capitalist development, Luxemburg traced the switch from Free Trade to protectionism, the latter being a characteristic of the developed phase of imperialism. Britain was able to promote and defend Free Trade as it was the oldest capitalist nation and boasted an extensive empire. Access to non-capitalist hinterland, which was extensive in area and rich in resources, gave Britain a huge advantage over many other European capitalist states. The empire afforded British capitalists 'almost unlimited opportunities for capitalist accumulation' (Luxemburg 1971: 451).

Free Trade, and its corresponding ideal of a harmony of interests, grew out of a specific set of circumstances. Luxemburg contended that the Free Trade ideologues of the Manchester school based their theoretical considerations on the mistaken assumption that the accumulation of capital was built solely on commodity exchange. She was similarly critical of the idea of a harmony of interests existing between commodity producing nations and between capital and labour. The ascendancy of the doctrine of Free Trade was short lived, taking in the decades of the 1860s and 1870s. Even before this, in the 1840s, the harmony of interests of the commercial nations was shown to be chimerical when the opening up of China (courtesy of the Opium Wars) brought about a system of spheres of interest (Luxemburg 1971: 446–7). Free Trade precepts did not express the interests of capitalist accumulation in total and they were abandoned when industrial capital established itself in the major European countries (Luxemburg 1971: 450).

The passing of the era of Free Trade, however, was not solely due to the imposition of protective tariffs by industrialising European countries in reaction to Britain's industrial dominance. Reasons for the decline of Free Trade were more complex, involving competition from American industrial and agricultural products, competitive pressure on European states on each other and the growth in influence of big industrial capital. Protective tariffs heralded both the end of Free Trade and the heightening of competitive struggles amongst European capitalist powers. For Luxemburg, the crucial arena of competitive struggle hinged on the securing of access to the non-capitalist regions (Luxemburg 1971: 447–50). Such competition did not bode well for the world.

> With the high development of the capitalist countries and their increasingly severe competition in acquiring non-capitalist areas, imperialism grows in lawlessness and violence, both in aggression against the non-capitalist world and in ever more serious conflicts among the competing capitalist countries ... Though imperialism is the historical method for prolonging the career of capitalism, it is also a sure means of bringing it to a swift conclusion. This is not to say that capitalist development must be actually driven to this extreme: the mere tendency towards imperialism of itself takes forms which make the final phase of capitalism a period of catastrophe (Luxemburg 1971: 446).

Tariffs were a symptom of the heightened competition amongst capitalist powers. Intimately bound up with all this was a particular form of colonial expansion, backed up by military might, particularly naval power. Luxemburg summed up the main methods employed by capitalist powers in their relationships with non-capitalist regions, these being 'colonial policy, an international loan system – a policy of spheres of interest – and war'. Brazenness attended the behaviour of capitalist states in their dealings with non-capitalist countries: 'Force, fraud, oppression looting are openly displayed without any attempt at concealment' (Luxemburg 1971: 452). Tellingly, the relationships and behaviours described grew out of the accumulation process. That is, for Luxemburg political phenomena such as foreign policy as well as war and militarism had their basis in and were determined by the accumulation process: 'In reality, political power is nothing but a vehicle for the economic process' (Luxemburg 1971: 452).

Militarism as a weapon and as province of accumulation

Militarism played an important part in every phase of the accumulation process. Acting as executor or enforcer, the armed might of a state helped enormously in the first stages of European capitalism, which Marx called the 'process of primitive accumulation'. The conquering of the New World and the subjection of the Indian subcontinent came about through extensive use of the military. Order was maintained in the colonies and primitive means of production were forcibly appropriated, so commodity exchange and the commodity based economy could be imposed on those countries 'where the social structure had been unfavourable to it' (Luxemburg 1971: 454). The proletarianisation of the native people came about through compulsion, behind which stood armed force. Spheres of influence were carved out, loan conditions were enforced and railway concessions were wrung from backward countries courtesy of military might. Militarism also was pivotal in the competitive struggles for the division of non-capitalist regions amongst capitalist powers (Luxemburg 1971: 454).

Luxemburg, furthermore, made the interesting claim that militarism was a special province of accumulation. Principally, funding for militarism came via indirect taxes levied on workers and peasants. For capitalism and the state, a number of benefits ensued. The 'normal standard of living for the working class' was lowered, with funds diverted from wages (variable capital) and into the coffers of the state. These funds were invested by the state in armaments manufacture. In pooling these revenues, the state amassed large amounts of purchasing power, creating a new field of accumulation for capital. The concentration of revenue enabled the state to place large orders on an ongoing basis, giving stability to capitalists in the armaments industry. There appeared to be a rhythm and regularity to the growth of the armaments industry, which made it seem like it had the potential for unlimited expansion. Luxemburg claimed that the manufacture of armaments and militarism in general, and its regularity and rhythmic movement of production, all were controlled by capital. This control was achieved through legislature and by the moulding of public opinion by the press (Luxemburg 1971: 464–6).

Militarism, like the accumulation process, was predicated on the depression of the living standards of the workers and peasants, and therefore must eventually undermine the basis for its existence:

> The more ruthlessly capital sets about the destruction of non-capitalist strata at home and in the outside world, the more it lowers the standard of living for the workers as a whole, the greater also is the change in the day-to-day history of capital. It becomes a string of political and social disasters and convulsions, and under these conditions, punctuated by periodical economic catastrophes or crises, accumulation can go on no longer (Luxemburg 1971: 466–467).

The political gap in Luxemburg's imperialism theory

To avoid disasters, convulsions and catastrophes, it was necessary for the international working class to revolt and act to implement socialist principles (Luxemburg 1971: 467). The advocacy of revolution put Luxemburg at odds with Kautsky and other reformists in the SPD. Luxemburg was one of Kautsky's most vociferous opponents in the Party, so it is somewhat surprising that Luxemburg did not seize the opportunity for political strategising in *The Accumulation of Capital*. The oversight possibly was deliberate, with her intention being to show that the accumulation process had reached its limits, visiting not only decline, impoverishment and catastrophe on the non-capitalist regions but also on the capitalist heartlands themselves (Nettl 1966b: 536). Bold action, then, was needed rather than the tactics of passivity and compromise that marked the reformists in the SPD.

There is no doubt that Luxemburg took a revolutionary position regarding imperialism, seeing it as the final stage of the history of capitalist accumulation. Responding to criticism of her work by Otto Bauer she castigated him and, by extension, the 'experts' in the SPD for their rhetoric about social revolution and their compromising with the German state regarding the August 1914 voting for war credits. She claimed that such bankruptcy had 'handed leadership over to imperialism' (Luxemburg and Bukharin 1972: 149). That Luxemburg had strong views on the political response to imperialism that in her mind the SPD should have adopted is evident in a number of her other writings. Her advocacy of revolutionary tactics and the mass strike as weapon of choice for the German working class prior to World War I was apparent throughout her pamphleteering and journalism published in the SPD party press (Nettl 1966b: 864–917). In the Spartacist uprising during the post-war revolutionary tumult in Germany, she paid the ultimate price of her commitment to revolutionary politics. Luxemburg and Karl Liebknecht were murdered by members of the paramilitary Freikorps on 15 January 1919 (Broué 2006: 255–7; Nettl 1966b: 772–3).

Luxemburg's contribution to the theory of imperialism

Luxemburg's portrayal of imperialism in *The Accumulation of Capital* was something of a mixed bag. For her, imperialism was not a policy or set of policies, rather it was a phase of capitalism. Imperialism had its genesis in what Luxemburg claimed was a problem of accumulation requiring non-capitalist countries as purchasers of surplus commodities. Despite the claim made by Lee (1971) that Luxemburg's was the first comprehensive theory of imperialism by a Marxist, it was not comprehensive, omitting a number of features that both Hobson and Hilferding had identified in their works. For example, finance capital, the export of capital and the impact of monopolies received little attention in her book. Given Luxemburg's revolutionary credentials and outspoken opposition to reformists/like Kautsky in the SPD, perhaps the most puzzling aspect of her book is its minimal engagement with the political side of imperialism. Her focus was to account for problems in Marxist economic theory and presumably she thought that she had covered the political aspects of imperialism extensively enough elsewhere.

Critics identify a number of problems in Luxemburg's examination of the accumulation process and imperialism. Her key premise, namely that accumulation could expand only with non-capitalist regions taking up the surplus of commodities produced by the capitalist nations, is flawed. There was no absolute compulsion for non-capitalist regions to act as outlets for excess commodities. The system was not as closed as Luxemburg assumed. Underpinning her outlook about capitalist production was the teleological belief that production in general should have a purpose. Individual capitalists have purposes but the capitalist system as a whole does not; it is anarchic, with profit its only motive. Selling means of production and other commodities to other capitalists for profit was not only possible but actually happened, helping to expand accumulation (Brewer 1990: 60–6; Howard and King 1989: 106–14).

Consequently, Luxemburg's definition of imperialism suffered. Central to it was the struggle for the securing of non-capitalist regions by capitalist nations as guarantors of expanded reproduction. Brewer insightfully remarks that Luxemburg may not have proved that capitalism needed a non-capitalist environment, but her stressing of the appearance and growth of capitalism in a non-capitalist environment nonetheless was commendable (Brewer 1990: 66).

The theme of the absolute necessity of non-capitalist regions for capitalist accumulation and imperialism would find its echo in the neo-Marxist dependency theory of Andre Gunder Frank. A crucial difference observable in Luxemburg's study and neo-Marxist dependency theory was that the former stressed the active role of European capitalist accumulation in the relations between capitalist and non-capitalist regions.

Recent commentators have been influenced by Luxemburg's account of Western capitalism's forays into the non-capitalist world. Harvey and Wood, two 'globalisation-era' Marxists, acknowledge her work in passing. Harvey, in fact, develops Luxemburg's trope about the use of force and predation to inform his 'accumulation by dispossession' concept (Callinicos 2009: 40–1). Another praiseworthy insight of hers was the positing of militarism as a province of accumulation. There had been work on militarism by SPD theorists (with Liebknecht writing a book on the subject), but Luxemburg was the first classical Marxist to explicitly make the link between militarism, the accumulation process and imperialism. Later Marxists followed up her groundbreaking work in this area (Mommsen 1981: 44).

The descriptions that she gave of the travails of Egypt, Turkey and China at the hands of imperialist powers were powerful indictments of imperialism. In the struggle against the excesses that accompanied the final stage of capitalism not only did Luxemburg write, agitate and organise, helping to create a new political party (Spartacusbund), she also gave her life. Her example as a committed revolutionary and insightful and iconoclastic Marxist theorist continues to inspire.

World economy and imperialism: Bukharin's systematic analysis

Unlike Luxemburg's study, Bukharin's work on imperialism qualifies as a comprehensive account. Born in 1888, Bukharin joined the Russian Social Democratic Labour Party in 1906 and established a reputation as one of the party's leading theoreticians before eventually falling victim to one of Stalin's purges in 1938. Drawing extensively on Hilferding's seminal book, Bukharin extended that work by treating imperialism as the 'policy of finance capitalism'; indeed, a policy that finance capitalism could not avoid following (Brewer 1990: 111; Bukharin 1973: 114; Cohen 1970: 439; Howard and King 1989: 246). Hilferding's theory of imperialism was a by-product of his central analytical concern, which was updating Marx's critique of capitalist political economy. A similar claim can be made about Luxemburg's account of the subject in *The Accumulation of Capital*, where her primary focus was not on imperialism. To Bukharin, then, goes the distinction of being the first of the classical Marxists to construct a comprehensive theory of the subject.

Bukharin went further than simply building on Hilferding's insights into finance capital, asserting that imperialism was the 'most essential element' of modern capitalism. Imperialism was an inevitable historical category that appeared at a specific stage – the last – in the development of capitalism (Cohen 1970: 439). The strong emphasis on inevitability received its impetus from Bukharin's opposition to the 'imperialism as policy' approach found in official social democratic circles. Prefiguring Lenin's assault on Kautsky's notion of ultra-imperialism, Bukharin argued that to project a future with no wars in the epoch of imperialism was a 'deeply harmful Utopian fantasy' symptomatic of reformism. In other words, Kautsky had relied on a 'sunny' view of capitalism, which whilst pointing out its adaptability, glossed over its inherent contradictions (Bukharin 1973: 142–3).

In Bukharin's mind, a defining element of early twentieth-century capitalism was the centrality of the world economy. Here his outlook contrasted with Hilferding's, whose focus was the economies of the advanced nations. According to Bukharin, the advanced national economies functioned as units of the world economy and were subject to the laws of the global market (Howard and King 1989: 245). Not only were the national economies of advanced capitalist states subject to the laws of the world market, such had been the changes to capitalism – monopolisation, cartelisation, concentration and centralisation, state intervention – that the law of value did not operate within national economies. The law of value only operated at the international level. Bukharin was able to arrive at this conclusion because capitalism had transcended the competitive turmoil of its early existence; competitive capitalism was superseded by monopoly capitalism, which in turn had formed the basis of an 'organised' state capitalism (Howard and King 1989: 246).

Basing his work on the contradictions between the national and international aspects of organised capitalism, Bukharin constructed *Imperialism and World Economy* (1973). Summarising Bukharin's overall contribution to imperialism theory, Howard and King suggest that there are three principal contributions that he made to the classical Marxist corpus: first was the systematising and radicalising of Hilferding's theorising, culminating in Bukharin's shifting of focus from national economies to the world economy; second was his argument about the 'national centralisation of capital [moving] beyond finance capital to form . . . quasi-totalitarian state capitalisms' (Howard and King 1989: 246); third and finally was his recognition that the nature of the state in the imperialist era – the 'new Leviathans' – militated against the use of the state by any revolutionary party aiming to build socialism. The state had to be smashed (Howard and King 1989: 248).

Bukharin's world economy: lynchpin of a theory

Bukharin defined the centrepiece of his analysis as '*a system of production relations and, correspondingly, of exchange relations on a world scale*' (Bukharin 1973: 26 emphasis in original). The world economy was subject to the same anarchical, non-regulated conditions that had plagued national economies in the era of competitive capitalism. Being expansive, capitalism eventually linked all parts of the globe through processes of exchange and production. The combination of division of labour and the uneven development of productive forces playing out at the national and international levels created different types of economies and production spheres, increasing the social division of labour (Bukharin 1973: 20). A cleavage of entire countries on the basis of industrial versus agricultural forms of production was evident, replicating the 'town and country' bifurcation on a global scale. Having once been the pinnacle of capitalist development, national economies had become units of the world economy.

Bukharin drew attention to the depth and breadth of capitalist development in the world economy, with more extensive connections on the one hand and more intensive, thicker networks on the other hand (Bukharin 1973: 28). Those extensive connections facilitated the drawing of non-capitalist regions into the capitalist world economic system, where intensive networks strengthened existing capitalist relations of production.

Helping propel the prodigious growth of turn-of-the-century capitalism was the qualitative improvement in the production processes courtesy of technical progress. The application of electricity, internal combustion motors, turbines, chemical discoveries and the intertwining of science and industry to a high degree caused a rapid qualitative leap in the productive forces of world capitalism (Bukharin 1973: 28–9). Noteworthy here and throughout the text is Bukharin's use of statistical tables to support his arguments. He employed empirical evidence from heavy industry, such as coal, iron ore, cast iron, copper and gold, supplemented by tables for foodstuff production, railroad tracks laid, shipbuilding and immigration amongst others to bolster his claims (Bukharin 1973: 30–1, 33–5, 37, 39, 40, 42–5). Compared with the offerings of Hilferding, Kautsky and Luxemburg, Bukharin's contribution is empirically richer.

Following in Hilferding's footsteps, Bukharin traced the increased international connections established by Germany's large 'national' banks. German banks were not alone in this regard, with British, French and Dutch banks expanding their branches in their colonies, too. Finance capital, the amalgamation of banking and industrial capital, had consolidated its central position in the national economies of Europe and had extended its reach internationally. The impact of rapid technological progress in the production process, combined with the increased international linkages of industry and finance capital and the growth of monopolies, had moulded industry progressively 'into one organised system' (Bukharin 1973: 52).

Organised capitalism came in the wake of the elimination or subordination of weaker competitors and the powerful influence of finance capital on the organisation and direction of investment and production. National economies had been transformed from an arena of competing capitals into an entity where there were organisational connections in all branches of production. National capitalist economies had come to be organised not through policy directives but through the inexorable unfolding of the law of capitalist competition.

The next step Bukharin identified was the incorporation of the state into the national accumulation process. State power became enmeshed with banking and industrial capital forming a 'state capitalist trust'. Out of this nexus came 'state capitalism':

> The most striking feature of modern capitalism was for Bukharin the new interventionist role of the state. As the term state capitalism was meant to indicate, the state had ceased to be merely the political instrument of the ruling class (or classes), the disinterested adjudicator of *laissez faire* economic competition between groups of the bourgeoisie; it had become, through the agency of finance capital, a direct organizer and owner in the economy, 'a very large share-holder in the state capitalist trust' and its 'highest and all-embracing organizational culmination' (Cohen 1970: 441).

The wartime German state exemplified the model of a 'state capitalist trust'. Immersed in every facet of the economy, regulating and militarising, directing production, the German state showed how economic needs and requirements determined state functions (Bukharin 1973: 63). Crucially, for Bukharin, state capitalism was the product of the economic, social and political conditions of the two decades leading up to the Great War, just as *laissez faire* had been for the period of competitive 'pluralistic' capitalism.

Through the operation of cartels, setting up of tariffs, the coming together of finance capital and the state, culminating in state capitalist trusts, organised capitalism virtually eliminated competition at the national level. Not so for the world economy, however, where competitive struggles played out in greater intensity. So great was the intensity of these political and economic struggles that militarism and conflict were unavoidable. Prior to the outbreak of war, it was the peoples of colonies who had witnessed the barbarous, wasteful and destructive activities of imperialism at first hand. Now the same destructive forces that had visited colonial peoples were experienced by the toilers in the capitalist heartlands on a much larger scale. No advantages that had accrued to the European proletariat through colonial policy, the 'few pennies', the nationalism, and the limited connections with the imperialist state could compensate for the 'millions of butchered workers ... to the vandalism of plundered productive forces, to [the] high cost of living and starvation' (Bukharin 1973: 167).

The choice was clear for the working classes of Europe. Imperialism was the cause of the Great War and would be the cause of more wars. The state capitalist trusts of each nation were implicated equally in the carnage. In advocating support for their particular state capitalist trusts, social democratic parties (such as the SPD in Germany) not only had bankrupted the Second International but also had shown how the programme of patient progress through parliamentarism and reform was a charade. Kautsky was the representative of the reformist SPD who, with his concept of ultra-imperialism, epitomised all that was wrong with the reformist tradition:

> But is not the epoch of 'ultra-imperialism' a real possibility after all, can it not be affected by the centralisation process? Will not the state capitalist trusts devour one another gradually until there comes into existence an all embracing power which has conquered all the others? This possibility would be thinkable if we were to look at the social process as a purely mechanical one, without counting the forces that are hostile to the policy of imperialism. In reality, however, the wars that will follow each other on an ever larger scale must inevitably result in a shifting of the social forces. The centralisation process, looked at from the capitalist angle, will inevitably clash with a socio-political tendency that is antagonistic to the former. Therefore it can by no means reach its logical end; it suffers collapse and achieves completion only in a new, purified non-capitalist form. It is for this reason that Kautsky's theory is by no means realisable. It looks upon imperialism not as an inevitable accompaniment of capitalist development, but as one of the 'dark sides' of capitalist development ... His concept implies a slurring over of the gigantic contradictions which rend asunder modern society, and in this respect it is a reformist concept (Bukharin 1973: 142–3).

Problems with Bukharin's handling of the state and state capitalism

Two main criticisms have been made about the treatment of the state and the concept of state capitalism found in Bukharin's *Imperialism and World Economy*. First, he elided the complex interactions that take place between the state and civil society. The state became completely bound up in the accumulation process as part of state capitalist trusts and thence state capitalism. Such a claim took the formulation found in *The Communist Manifesto* about the 'executive of the modern state [being] . . . a committee for managing the common affairs of the whole bourgeoisie' to another level (Marx 1973: 69). Namely, the common affairs of the entire bourgeoisie had crystallised into the economic affairs of the state capitalist trusts and thence state capitalism. State capitalism, as Bukharin formulated it, was a case of the economic base determining the political superstructure not in the final analysis, but from the outset:

> The fact is that the very foundation of modern states as definite political entities was caused by economic needs and requirements. The state grew on the economic foundation; it was only an expression of economic connections; state ties appeared only as an expression of economic ties (Bukharin 1973: 73).

Questions about the legitimacy of the state and its functions apart from the economic – such as the social and political – were given short shrift. With the advent of organised capitalism, the tensions between capitalist class fractions had largely been overcome. Thus, parliament, traditionally *the* bourgeois political arena where the bourgeoisie had battled against the monarchy and feudal landed interests and resolved conflicts amongst fractions of its own class, faced a crisis of legitimacy. In the era of imperialism, parliament was a 'decorative institution' with the function of passing on the decisions made by businessmen's associations, sanctioning formally, 'the collective will of the consolidated bourgeoisie as a whole' (Bukharin 1973: 128). By subordinating the political to the economic – through the mechanism of state capitalism and showing that parliament had been de-legitimised – Bukharin was able to dispense with the reformist reliance on parliamentarism. The purpose here was to undermine Kautsky's favoured political strategy.

Bukharin's formulation of state capitalist trusts and state capitalism had its problems. His treatment of the state was 'over-simple' (Brewer 1990: 114). He was not alone in this regard. As Chibber points out, what marks classical Marxist writings on imperialism is the omission of 'the political mediation of the deep economic forces that [were] taken to be driving imperial projects' (Chibber 2004: 429). Moreover, Chibber's crucial insight about the minimal level of engagement with the state seen in Luxemburg's and Lenin's writing on imperialism holds for Bukharin and Hilferding. That is, they all assumed that 'the state did not figure as an independent factor in explaining imperialism, mainly because they functioned with a fairly simple notion of the state-capital relation' (Chibber 2004: 429). The 'reductionist and instrumentalist treatment of the state' is one of the major failings of classical Marxist theories of imperialism (Panitch and Gindin 2004: 6). There is no question that the state and its relationship with capitalist imperialism were treated simplistically by Bukharin.

The second main criticism of Bukharin's work is directed at his concept of state capitalism. One of the assumptions underpinning state capitalism was that the competitive struggles amongst capitalists within national boundaries had been largely overcome. It was over the issue of national capitalism that Bukharin's and Lenin's views diverged. Both writers stressed there had been the transformation of *laissez faire* capitalism into monopoly capitalism, though Lenin did not see monopoly capitalism as monolithic. Within advanced capitalist countries, monopolisation produced a variegated picture; a mixture of monopoly and free competition. Consequently, monopolies and trustification did not abolish internal crises (Cohen 1970: 448–9). On the contrary, internal crises in individual capitalist economies were exacerbated by the partiality of the monopolisation process. There were conflicts of interest between the monopolistic and competitive sectors, for example, which showed that competitive pressures still existed. State capitalism as propounded by Bukharin was problematic because it did not take into consideration the uneven development of capitalism both within nations and in the capitalist world economy as a whole. Uneven capitalist development caused changes in the relative strengths of the capitalist powers and formed a crucial part of the economic basis of the military rivalries between the great European powers (Howard and King 1989: 249). Lenin's emphasis on the continuing competition within national economies contrasted with Bukharin's shifting of the key problem area to the world economy. Their divergent views on the nature of capitalist development at that particular juncture remained a point of contention between Bukharin and Lenin (Buchanan 1976: 69; Cohen 1970: 449; Howard and King 1989: 249).

Weighing up Bukharin's theory of imperialism

These criticisms of two aspects of Bukharin's exposition highlight his tendency to ignore or simplify some of the complexities attending the political and economic components of imperialism. Despite these concerns, Bukharin produced the first comprehensive Marxist account of imperialism. Gathering together Hilferding's insights found in *Finance Capital* such as the product of industrial and banking capital – finance capital, organised capitalism, cartelisation and capital export amongst others – Bukharin created a coherent and logically consistent theory of imperialism. It emphasised the importance of the capitalist world economy not only for the accumulation process but as an integral element of imperialism. Relationships between the international and national economies – of superordination and subordination respectively – were provocative and thought inspiring. Noteworthy, too, is Bukharin's marshalling of empirical evidence to support his arguments. Of the 'pioneers of imperialism theory', Hobson, Bukharin and Lenin stand out for their use of statistics to bolster their theses. Intriguingly, 'globalisation-era' Marxists Harvey and Wood (as well as the writing by many other Marxists including Hardt and Negri) have been criticised for the lack of empirical evidence found in their work on imperialism (Sutcliffe cited in Callinicos 2009: 19; Fuchs 2010: 222).

Bukharin sought to provide a theory that would account for the outbreak of war that drew in the major European powers and, like Luxemburg and Lenin, underscore the connections between monopoly capitalism, capitalist expansion, the state, inter-imperialist rivalry and war. Unlike reformists such as Hobson and Kautsky, who saw imperialism as a policy or set of policies subject to reform, Bukharin saw imperialism as an unavoidable and unreformable policy of finance capital. The only way to overcome the ruinous policy of imperialism was by smashing the state and replacing the 'dictatorship of finance capital' with the 'dictatorship of the revolutionary proletariat' (Bukharin

1973: 170). Any other course was either liberalism, dangerously utopian or misleading. Kautsky, in particular, was the focus of Bukharin's ire regarding the former's predictions and prescriptions in 'Ultra-imperialism'. In this and in other respects, Bukharin's book mapped out several of the concerns found in Lenin's tome published a year later in 1916. Accordingly, it remains an important part of the classical Marxist *oeuvre* on imperialism.

Pinnacle of classical Marxist imperialism theory? Lenin's *Imperialism*

Lenin's small book on imperialism has been the subject of high praise and sharp criticism since its publication. Such has been its standing that it is impossible to ignore. Firmly in the camp of the revolutionaries, one of Lenin's aims was to counter Kautsky's concept of ultra-imperialism. A further aim was to explain why the Great Powers had gone to war. Another aim was to account for the bankruptcy of the Second International, brought about by the capitulation of various social democratic parties to supporting their national governments on the morrow of the Great War. *Imperialism* (Lenin 1973) had strong polemical elements and consequently has been criticised for 'over-politicising theory' (Panitch and Gindin 2004: 9). Criticism of this sort overlooks how the political complexity of war, collapse of the Second International and societal unrest informed Lenin's work on imperialism. The theory of imperialism that Lenin propounded has been considered to be the most authoritative, hence the sniping from both enemies and 'misguided adherents of Marxism' (Bagchi 1983: 2).

Lenin, born Vladimir Ilich Ulyanov (1870–1924) in Simbirsk to a government official and his teacher wife, came to revolutionary politics early in life. By the time he penned his book on imperialism Lenin had led the Bolshevik faction of the Russian Social Democratic Labour Party for over a dozen years, most of that time in exile. In his preface for the 1917 publication of the book, Lenin trusted that his pamphlet would enable 'the reader to understand the fundamental economic question, viz., the question of the economic essence of imperialism, for unless this is studied, it will be impossible to understand and appraise modern war and modern politics' (Lenin 1973: 2). He had deliberately avoided discussing the political side of imperialism too much so as to avoid Tsarist censorship. Despite this constraint, political and geopolitical developments were canvassed – albeit minimally – in the pamphlet, as they, too, were integral to Lenin's understanding of imperialism.

Concentration leading to monopolisation

Acknowledging his debt to Hobson and Hilferding, Lenin developed his theory of imperialism based on some of their core findings. Starting with the concentration of production and monopolies, Lenin provided empirical evidence of the growth of large corporations in the US and Germany. Using these figures he concluded that:

> at a certain stage of its development, concentration itself . . . leads right up to monopoly; for a score or so of giant enterprises can easily arrive at an agreement, while on the other hand, the hindrance to competition, the tendency towards monopoly, arises from the very dimensions of the enterprises (Lenin 1973: 14).

The transformation of competition into monopoly, according to Lenin, was an important feature of contemporary capitalist development. Hilferding had been the first classical Marxist writer to highlight this feature.

The concept of 'combination' was another feature of modern capitalism that Hilferding had identified and Lenin agreed was significant. Here, what were separate fields of the production process were unified under one corporate entity. In other words, different branches of industry were grouped under a single enterprise such as in the processing of raw materials in the production of pig iron or even steel making (Lenin 1973: 14). Combination conferred benefit, ensuring a more stable rate of profit as the vagaries of trade fluctuations were either levelled out or removed. In periods of depression, combination strengthened the position of those enterprises compared with non-combined enterprises (Hilferding cited in Lenin 1973: 15).

Concentration and combination was so powerful in Germany that large enterprises in various industries were coming together to form giant enterprises. These giant enterprises were 'backed up and directed by half a dozen big Berlin banks' (Lenin 1973: 16). The experience of concentration was not confined to the emergent capitalist countries Germany and the US. Britain, too, felt the effects of concentration due to the size of the enterprises and the great investment of capital within those enterprises, which thwarted competition. Unlike German and American capitalist development, where the formation of cartels had been facilitated by protective tariffs, British monopolist alliances came about when competition had reduced the number of chief competing enterprises to a dozen or so (Lenin 1973: 17).

Concentration of production, asserted Lenin, was a fundamental and general law of capitalist development. Differences discernible in national approaches to the question of protective tariffs or free trade, for example, did not alter the unfolding of this general law. Qualitatively capitalism had changed with the supersession of free competition by monopoly capitalism occurring at the beginning of the twentieth century (Lenin 1973: 18). The transition to monopoly capitalism from free competition took place over three stages. In the 1860s, monopoly was in an embryonic stage, with free competition the general rule. The crisis year of 1873 marked the formation and steady development of cartels. The late nineteenth-century boom and subsequent crisis of 1900–3 saw cartelisation become one of the foundations of economic life. The transformation was complete, capitalism had metamorphosed into imperialism (Lenin 1973: 20).

Cartels and trusts, the organisational phenomena that Hilferding analysed, had fostered the organisation of capitalism in Germany and the US to the extent that agreements over market share and employment of skilled labour, for example, were routine. However much the monopolisation process had organised and socialised the production process, it could not entirely rid capitalism of the chaos that attended production driven by the profit motive alone: 'On the contrary, monopoly which is created in *certain* branches of industry, increases and intensifies the anarchy inherent in capitalist production *as a whole*' (Lenin 1973: 28 emphasis in original). This contrasts with Bukharin's proposition about how the organisation of capitalism under conditions of state monopoly capitalism had eradicated competition within advanced capitalist countries, shifting the competitive struggles to the world economy. According to Cohen, the divergence between Bukharin and Lenin over crises in national economies and the phenomenon of state monopoly capitalism became the basis of a 'series of disagreements' starting in 1917 and extending into the 1920s (Cohen 1970: 449).[1]

Banks were intimately connected with the processes of concentration, cartelisation and monopolisation. In the monopoly stage of capitalist development, banks not only played a pivotal role in accelerating the processes of concentration and cartelisation, they also were subjected to these same processes. From humble beginnings 'as middlemen in the making of payments' (Lenin 1973: 31) they became bigger in size and smaller in number.

Banks and monopoly capitalism

Banks, according to Lenin, played a conspicuous role in the shift from capitalism to capitalist imperialism, in the process growing:

> into powerful monopolies having at their command almost the whole of the money capital of all the capitalists and small businessmen and also the larger part of the means of production and of the sources of raw materials of the given country and in a number of countries (Lenin 1973: 31).

Mention already has been made of the close connections between giant enterprises in Germany and the leading half-dozen banks based in Berlin (Lenin 1973: 16). Leaving aside the data that Lenin provided on the increased holdings of German banks (Lenin 1973: 32, 34–5), the conclusion drawn was straightforward. With:

> the rapid expansion of a close network of canals which cover the whole country, centralizing all capital and all revenues, transforming thousands and thousands of scattered economic enterprises into a single national capitalist, and then into a world capitalist economy ... [There had been the] subordination of an increasing number of formerly relatively 'independent' or rather, strictly local economic units, to a single centre. [Rather than decentralisation, what the German banking system experienced at the end of the nineteenth and the beginning of the twentieth century was] ... *centralization*, the enhancement of the role, the

importance and the power of monopolist giants (Lenin 1973: 35 emphasis in original).

The German banking experience regarding the breadth and depth of networks was replicated in Britain, Ireland and France. Also common to the capitalist countries' banking systems was the powerful position of a handful of banking monopolists. They had recourse to the exact financial position of various capitalists and were able to manipulate and control them through extension or limitation of credit (Lenin 1973: 37). So powerful had these banking monopolists become that they effectively subordinated to their wills the commercial and industrial operations of their nations.

Regarding the connections between the banks and industry, it was in these relationships that the details outlined above are most conspicuous. The combination of bank and industrial capital was effected through share acquisition, the appointment of bankers to the boards of industrial and commercial enterprises and reciprocal appointments of industrialists and other businessmen to the boards of banks. Lenin, using the figures of German economist O. Jeidels, illustrated the extent of the concentration of capital and enterprises:

> Six of the biggest Berlin banks were represented by their directors in 344 industrial companies; and by their board members in 407 others, making a total of 751 companies. In 289 of these companies they either had two of their representatives on each of the respective Supervisory Boards, or held the posts of chairmen. We find these industrial and commercial companies in the most diverse branches of industry: insurance, transport, restaurants, theatres, art industry, etc. On the other hand, on the Supervisory Boards of these six banks (in 1910) were fifty-one of the biggest industrialists, including the director of Krupp, of the powerful 'Hapag' (Hamburg-American Line) . . . From 1895 to 1910, each of these six banks participated in the share and bond issues of many hundreds of industrial companies (the number ranging from 281 to 419) (Lenin 1973: 45).

The result, as Bukharin observed, was the coalescence of bank and industrial capital (Lenin 1973: 48). There was no doubt in Lenin's mind that the twentieth century ushered in the era of finance capital.

Finance capital and the financial oligarchy

Paying close attention to Hilferding's analysis of finance capital, and noting Bukharin's emphasis on the coalescing of bank and industrial capital, Lenin added considerable empirical detail that served to illuminate the extent of the concentration of the banks and the interconnections between them and industrial enterprises. Hilferding had defined finance capital as capital controlled by banks but employed by industrialists. Crucially, for Lenin, Hilferding passed over how monopoly had become a factor also in finance capital (Lenin 1973: 52).

Through the floating of companies, stock issues and loans to the state, a small number of people in the upper echelons of finance capital exerted enormous influence. These few were the financial oligarchy. International loans in the form of bond issues were coveted by the international financial oligarchy as they generated astonishing rates of profit. The command of these staggering sums of money by finance capital and, by extension, the financial oligarchy, allowed these interests to penetrate every sphere of public life, irrespective of the form of government (Lenin 1973: 67). Characteristically, the financial oligarchy, under changed conditions of early twentieth-century capitalism, distanced themselves from the production process. That is, members of the financial oligarchy were content to act as rentiers, living off the income generated by money capital. The separation of the financial oligarchy and, indeed, finance capital from the production process was widening and was symptomatic of this stage of capitalist development. With the domination of finance capital came the 'predominance of the rentier and of the financial oligarchy' (Lenin 1973: 69). The process of concentration did not stop there; a small number of financially powerful states were discernible.

The financially powerful states in 1910 were Britain, France, Germany and the US. Of the 575–600 billion francs worth of securities then current in the world, some 479 billion francs – almost 80 per cent – were owned by these four countries. On this basis, Lenin concluded that 'nearly the whole of the rest of the world is more or less the debtor to and tributary of these international banker countries, these four "pillars" of world finance capital' (Lenin 1973: 71–2).

Export of capital

In his discussion of capital export Lenin relied on the pioneering work of Hobson and Hilferding among others (see footnote in Lenin 1973: 74). Marx's critique of capitalist political economy had as one of its foundational claims the proposition that commodity production was the hallmark of capitalism. This proposition, asserted Lenin, remained true. In fact, capital export encouraged commodity export as loans often stipulated the purchase of commodities from the creditor nation's manufacturers (Lenin 1973: 77). Nevertheless, there had been a qualitative change to capitalism at the turn of the century and commodity export, whilst still important, was overshadowed by the export of capital.

The lure of high profits by exporting capital to backward countries was too enticing a prospect. Due to a combination of scarcity of capital, the relatively low price of land, cheap raw materials and low wages, big returns on capital invested overseas could be had. Furthermore, some of the older capitalist countries were experiencing 'overripe' capitalism. That is, they could not find fields for 'profitable' investment at home, hence the heightened export of capital (Lenin 1973: 73–4).

The export of capital undertaken by the principal exporting countries followed different paths. The British exported capital primarily to their colonies, whereas the French concentrated most of theirs in Europe, especially in Russia. Around 1910, the Germans had only a small colonial presence and their capital exports were divided evenly between the US and Europe (Lenin 1973: 75–6). With their zones of capital export delineated, and with colonies tied in subservient fashion to their respective colonial power, Lenin argued two things about capitalism and the imperialist powers: first, cartels, syndicates, trusts and monopolist capitalist combines had divided up the world between them economically; second, the Great Powers had divided up the territory of the world between them, geopolitically (Lenin 1973: 79, 89).

Capitalist combines and the economic division of the world

The concentration of capital that manifested in the form of cartels, syndicates and trusts did not stop at national boundaries. Having tied up industries in the home markets, the monopolist combines extended their reach to the world market. So, with the increasing export of capital, the widening of 'spheres of influence' and more intimate and intricate connections between colonies and foreign countries, it was logical that the next step was movement 'towards an international agreement among these combines and towards the international formation of cartels' (Lenin 1973: 79).

Using the examples of the electrical industry in the US and Germany, mercantile shipping and the steel industry amongst others, Lenin demonstrated the inexorable drive to divide up the world market. The electrical industry in Germany was comprised of seven or eight groups, around which were some twenty-eight companies. In turn, they received financial support from a number of banks. During the four-year period 1908–12, the seven or eight groups merged into two, cooperating to divide up the market for electrical goods both in Germany and in various other countries. The two major companies that emerged from the mergers were A.E.G. and Siemens & Halske-Schuckert. A.E.G. alone had control over 175 to 200 companies and thirty-four direct agencies in more than ten countries, making it a huge combine. Mirroring the German electrical combine, the US witnessed the coming together of companies in the electrical industry, culminating in the General Electric Company. The US and German giant trusts reached an agreement in 1907 that apportioned the American and Canadian markets to the General Electric Company and to A.E.G. went the markets of Germany, Austria, Russia, Holland, Denmark, Switzerland, Turkey and the Balkans. Competition between the two trusts ceased. So big were these electrical giants that they dominated the industry and could stifle any nascent competitors. Lenin issued a caveat to the effect that division of the world amongst combines like the electrical giants did not preclude the redivision of markets or market share, in the event of bankruptcy, war, uneven development or other circumstances. In other words, the division of the globe economically was subject to fluctuations contingent upon the economic might of the respective corporations (Lenin 1973: 80–2).

Various examples from other industries used to support Lenin's claim regarding the economic division of the globe make the same point and therefore can be passed over. In the course of showing how the partitioning of the world market by the powerful combines unfolded, Lenin took the opportunity to upbraid Kautsky who thought that the concentration and organisation of capitalism provided an object lesson for bourgeois politicians. He predicted that the cartelisation of the foreign policies of capitalist countries was a possibility in the post-war world. Ultra-imperialism, Kautsky argued, could pave the way for not only the peaceful division of the world's markets but also peace between imperialist powers. Lenin was adamant that ultra-imperialism was both theoretically absurd and in practice amounted to sophistry and the 'worst opportunism' (Lenin 1973: 88). This was just the opening shot in a torrid salvo that Lenin fired at Kautsky (see below). The conclusion that Lenin drew regarding the division of the world amongst the capitalist combines was that the latest stage of capitalism threw up these relationships as a matter of course. The process of concentration led to monopoly and the generation of giant combines, which in turn stifled competition. Ultimately, combines entered into agreements concerning market share and the location of markets. The economic division of the world by giant combines was matched in the geopolitical arena by the sewing up of the world's territories by great powers.

The geopolitical division of the world by great powers

Lenin asserted that the partitioning of the globe had been completed by 1900, with colonial powers having seized virtually all unoccupied territories (Lenin 1973: 90). Whilst partitioning of territories had finished, repartitioning was not precluded. The prominent feature of late nineteenth-century geopolitics was the intensification of struggle over the partitioning of the globe.

Citing Hobson's figures as proof of the intensified scramble for colonies and territorial possessions in the period 1884–1900, Lenin contrasted British opposition to colonial policy in the decades between 1840 and 1860. In this period, when British manufacturing dominated the world and the Free Trade mantra resonated near and far, bourgeois politicians decried colonial possessions and the pursuit of colonies (Lenin, 1973: 92). There was a sea change in colonial policy in the decades after, though, promoted by the machinations of mining capitalists and financiers like Cecil Rhodes and politicians of the ilk of Joseph Chamberlain. Cynically, certain British bourgeois politicians began to hail imperialism as the answer to social problems like overcrowding, surplus population and unemployment. It was the cynical political manipulation of types like Rhodes that infuriated Hobson and which Lenin alluded to when quoting an exchange between Rhodes and a journalist friend in 1895, to the effect that to avoid civil war, Britain needed to adopt imperialist policies (Lenin 1973: 93–94).

Lenin acknowledged that colonial policy and imperialism existed before capitalism. With the coming into being of monopolies and the dominance of finance capital in the advanced capitalist countries, however, there was an attendant change in the nature of colonial policy and imperialism. Social economic systems determined the form and nature of both imperialism and colonial policy and 'the capitalist colonial policy of *previous* stages of capitalism is essentially different from the colonial policy of finance capital' (Lenin 1973: 97–8 emphasis in original).

As part of the intense striving to tie up all sources of raw materials the monopolist capitalist combines were keen supporters of colonial acquisition by their respective national governments. Colonial possessions were a guaranteed way for the giant combines to have access to raw materials and through the auspices of the state, to deny resources to competitors, sometimes achieved through the creation by legislation of state monopoly (Lenin 1973: 98). Not content with securing access to existing sources of raw materials, acquisition of areas with *potential* sources of raw materials also impelled the scramble to carve up the globe.

It was in examining the experiences of Argentina and Portugal that Lenin showed some sophistication in his political analysis of imperialism. Argentina, a politically independent nation, was the recipient of substantial amounts of British capital. Through the strong connections established with British finance capital by the Argentinean bourgeoisie, it was not hard to see how control of the political and economic life of the South American state was shaped. Similarly, Portugal was a politically independent state boasting colonies of its own. Like Argentina, it had strong connections with Britain, having enjoyed political and financial ties for two centuries. Portugal became a protectorate of Britain, which enabled the British to export goods and capital to Portugal and its colonies with ease. The semi-colonial relationship that Portugal had with Britain was not novel; what was novel was that in the latest stage of capitalism these relationships had become part of a general system, part of the totalising drive of the process of partitioning and re-partitioning of the world (Lenin 1973: 101–3).

Because the globe had been parcelled out between the Great Powers, leaving them with little or no room for manoeuvre, for Lenin conflict was the necessary result:

> The question is: what means other than war could there be *under capitalism* of removing the disparity between the development of productive forces and the accumulation of capital on the one side, and the division of colonies and 'spheres of influence' for finance capital on the other? (Lenin 1973: 118 emphasis in original).

Great Power rivalry, asserted Lenin, must lead to war, hence there was no way out of the impasse save for world revolution and the building of socialism. Clearly reforms could not address the fundamental political and economic problems engendered by the latest stage of capitalism.

Analysis of the politics of imperialism was not Lenin's primary concern. The role of the state in imperialism was passed over, leaving Bukharin as the only classical Marxist writer to address the state at any length in his theorising of imperialism. Lenin did examine the function of the state in the imperialist epoch, most notably in *The State and Revolution* but not in the 'classic' text under review. As pointed out by Churchward, Lenin was not trying to explain international relations in his theory of imperialism, nor was he ignorant of the role of power politics and political factors, despite ostensibly ignoring them. His aim was more modest, hoping his pamphlet would be of assistance to enquiries into the economic essence of imperialism and in evaluating the war (Churchward 1959: 77). Consequently, the level of analysis of international and domestic politics in *Imperialism* was nominal. Panitch's and Gindin's criticism about the paucity of state theory in classical Marxist analyses of imperialism holds for Lenin's book as well.

Five features and a definition

Lenin, though mindful of what he called the 'conditional and relative value of all definitions', arrived at a definition of imperialism by succinctly summarising its five essential features (as outlined above). His definition states:

> Imperialism is capitalism in that stage of development in which the dominance of monopolies and finance capital has established itself; in which the export of capital has acquired pronounced importance; in which the division of the world among the international trusts has begun; in which the division of all territories of the globe among the biggest capitalist powers has been completed (Lenin 1973: 105–6).

More succinctly, then, according to Lenin imperialism was 'the monopoly stage of capitalism'. Albeit somewhat tersely stated, Lenin's working definition of imperialism nonetheless was based on a wealth of evidence. Relying on the work of Hobson, Hilferding, Bukharin, a host of bourgeois economists (perhaps even Luxemburg, though unacknowledged), and, as negative example Kautsky, *Imperialism* argued that the latest stage of capitalism inevitably led to war. Lenin also established that the unfolding of capitalist development necessarily transformed the free competition that had been characteristic of early capitalism into monopoly capitalism. The processes that culminated in the imperialist stage of capitalism could not be fundamentally altered by recourse to parliamentarism and attempts at reform, because states were connected with and did the bidding of finance capital. Thus revolution was the only strategy that working-class parties should employ to overcome the horrors of imperialist war and embark on the building of socialism.

One of the chief merits of Lenin's book is his definition of imperialism. It is a concise and coherent summation of the main features of what he and some other 'pioneers of imperialism theory' regarded as a new phase in capitalism. Compared with other pioneers (except for Bukharin whose definition of imperialism as a policy of finance capital was quite succinct), Lenin's definition was both logically consistent and unambiguous. Conversely, he did not offer up his definition as the last word on imperialism, noting the 'conditional and relative value of all definitions' (Lenin 1973: 105).

Parasitism, decay, stages and Kautsky

'Parasitism' was another proposition about imperialism Lenin adopted and adapted from Hobson. With the advent of finance capital, at the apex of which stood the financial oligarchy (Hobson's financiers) there existed a further subset – the social stratum of rentiers who were content to live off the proceeds of their investments. The increased importance of capital export enabled such a parasitical approach to be adopted by rentiers. They were completely removed from the production process and it was the appearance of these people that 'set the seal of parasitism' on the countries that exported capital and thus lived off the labour of those in the colonies and overseas (Lenin 1973: 120).

Citing Hobson to the effect that financiers or rentiers were not the sole beneficiaries of the parasitical policies of imperialism, Lenin took it a step further and suggested that a labour aristocracy had been created. The parasitism of capitalist imperialism engendered monopolist profits, some of which were used to buy the acquiescence of the lower classes (Lenin 1973: 122). Opportunism accompanied the rise of the labour aristocracy (often in occupations Hobson had identified, such as those connected with naval shipbuilding, government contractors and so on). What was meant by opportunism was the acceptance by sections of the proletariat of capitalism and bourgeois ideology, leading to acceptance of nationalism or what Lenin called social chauvinism (Lenin 1973: 123–4, 129, 130–1).

Opportunism in the working classes denoted that the parasitism and decay of monopoly capitalism had spread to all the social classes. The parasitism of imperialism, through opportunism, also had infected social democratic parties, the proof of which came in the collapse of the Second International and in the case of Germany SPD parliamentarians voting for war credits.

The exemplar of opportunism was Kautsky. In 'Ultra-imperialism' Kautsky effectively was offering up not Marxism but rather:

> a most reactionary method of consoling the masses with hopes of permanent peace being possible under capitalism, by distracting their attention from the sharp antagonisms and acute problems of the present times, and directing it towards illusory prospects of an imaginary 'ultraimperialism' of the future (Lenin 1973: 143).

Tellingly, for Lenin, Kautsky glossed over the fundamental contradictions of imperialism refusing to see that, even if there were periods of international calm, these were just lulls before new storms. Kautsky was endeavouring to preserve at all costs the crumbling unity of the opportunists in European social democracy (Lenin 1973: 143–8).

Monopoly capitalism essentially was moribund capitalism. Within it, though, were the seeds of a new social system. Therefore, monopoly capitalism was a social system in transition, hence the claim that imperialism was the last stage of capitalism (Lenin 1973: 153). Evidence of the moribund nature of monopoly capitalism – or imperialism – could be found in the catastrophe of the war then raging amongst the Great Powers. Lenin, however, concluded that capitalism would not implode, leaving an inheritance of state power for the representatives of opportunist working-class parties. Imperialism could not be reformed into something less offensive, it had to be overcome by a worldwide proletarian revolution. Imperialism, according to Lenin in 1920, represented the eve of the proletarian social revolution (Lenin 1973: 10).

Some critiques of Lenin's *Imperialism*

The elevation of Lenin's pamphlet on imperialism to canonical text certainly contributed to a hardening of attitudes towards it. For critics, Lenin had focussed too much on the economic side of imperialism. Furthermore, by relying on Hobson and to a lesser extent Hilferding, his understanding of imperialism suffered a number of defects. Critics, such as the historians D.K. Fieldhouse along with John Gallagher and Ronald Robinson, argued that both Hobson and Lenin had constructed a poor model of imperialism, a model given the sobriquet 'economic imperialism'. As understood by these three historians, economic imperialism conflated the theories of imperialism advanced by Hobson and Lenin. In exclusively focussing on British expansion and utilising statistics on British capital exports, colonial acquisitions and alluding to his analysis of the 'imperialism of the last three decades', in 1902 Hobson had 'made imperialism synonymous with colonialism' (Stokes 1969: 288–9).

Lenin wrote about colonialism and colonial policy, but these were only of secondary interest to him in his analysis of imperialism. Primarily, he 'was concerned not to provide a theoretical analysis of the scramble for colonies in the last three decades of the nineteenth century but of the genesis of war in Europe after 1900' (Stokes 1969: 291). Furthermore, Lenin's arguments in *Imperialism* were tailored to address 'tactical exigencies, and his writing was slanted to condemn the errors of "reformism" and "social democrat opportunism" symbolized for him in the person of "the renegade Kautsky"' (Stokes 1969: 296). Understanding Lenin's pamphlet depends on acknowledging that it was designed not only to analyse imperialism from a revolutionary Marxist perspective, but that it sought to demonstrate the economic essentials of monopoly capitalism and be a polemical exercise. Lenin's aims in writing the book were relatively modest, and he certainly was not attempting to provide a general theory of imperialism (Churchward 1959: 77).

Howard and King insightfully identify a number of problems in Lenin's conceptualising of imperialism. They recognise that various elements of imperialism adumbrated by Lenin were only loosely connected and that vagueness marked his exploration and exposition of the forces behind the export of capital.[2] The economic analysis of monopoly capitalism undertaken by Lenin (and by Bukharin) suffered from superficiality (Howard and King 1989: 259). The creation of a bribed or bought-off section of the working class – the labour aristocracy – and the impact of imperial expansion on the European labour movements giving rise to reformism or opportunism, also was problematic. Howard and King concede that generally there is nothing amiss in the claim that the fruits of imperial exploitation and participation in parliaments may have more deeply integrated the European working classes into capitalism. Where they find fault with Lenin (and Bukharin) is in the assumption by the latter two that only a minority of the labour movement had been affected and that the revolutionary integrity of the proletariat was unchanged. How had the labour aristocracy been incorporated or integrated into capitalism? What were the mechanisms? These were issues that Lenin had not addressed when offering his explanation for opportunism in the labour movement (Howard and King 1989: 260). Brewer, in his examination of the issue of the labour aristocracy, concluded that both Lenin and Bukharin were right to emphasise the stratification that had occurred in the proletariat. Some workers' living standards had risen, especially those living in the pre-eminent capitalist nations. Sectional and nationalistic sentiments influenced the working classes and, moreover, had a material basis. It is to Lenin's and Bukharin's credit that they teased out this in their writing on imperialism (Brewer 1990: 128).

A claim Lenin made that has generated a considerable amount of angst is that Great Power rivalry, or as it later came to be known inter-imperialist rivalry (Lenin did not use this term in his book), inevitably led to war. He arrived at this conclusion on the basis of his analysis of the economic features of monopoly capitalism and on the basis of arguing against Kautsky's reformist policy of ultra-imperialism.

We have seen criticisms levelled at Lenin by Panitch and Gindin in the section on Kautsky above. They charged Lenin and the classical Marxists, *inter alia*, with elevating 'a conjunctural moment of inter-imperial rivalry to an immutable law of capitalist globalization' (Panitch and Gindin 2004: 5). Others have made more nuanced criticisms suggesting that Lenin and Bukharin were aware of capitalism's adaptability and acknowledged that there could be periods of peace and even domination by a single capitalist power, though ultimately Lenin and Bukharin stressed the inevitability of ongoing imperialist wars. Having laid too much emphasis on the inevitability of war both writers 'failed to predict the long period of peace between the major capitalist powers in the second half of the twentieth century under US hegemony' (Howard and King 1989: 261). Brewer argues that the polemics Lenin and Bukharin directed against Kautsky may have had some validity, but their arguments against him were not theoretically decisive and they overstated their cases. Somewhat peculiarly, given that it undercuts his foregoing criticism, Brewer concedes that both world wars are, indeed, strong evidence that inter-imperialist rivalry was a dominant tendency of the time leading to wars (Brewer 1990: 133).

Recognising that the dominant geopolitical tendency of the first half of the twentieth century was war between major powers is a crucial factor when making an assessment of Lenin's claim about imperialism necessarily giving rise to great power rivalry and war. When Lenin and Bukharin wrote, imperialist rivalry *had* plunged the advanced capitalist (and numerous other) nations into a conflagration of unprecedented savagery. The years leading up to World War I were not conflict- or tension-free, either, with small-scale wars, militarism and arms races attracting the attention of the 'pioneers of imperialism theory'. Therefore, it was not hard to make the argument that imperialism in the early twentieth century was demonstrably connected with Great Power rivalry and war. The inevitability aspect of Lenin's argument was common to the analyses of contemporary capitalism and imperialism undertaken by revolutionary Marxists such as Luxemburg and Bukharin. The revolutionaries highlighted the economic characteristics of capitalism believing these to be the determining features. Consequently there was a downplaying of the political features of imperialism evident in their work, leading to a tendency to simplify the complexities associated with anything other than the economic side of capitalist imperialism. In hindsight, Lenin overstated the case about inter-imperialist rivalry necessarily leading to war between great powers.

Aside from the privileging of the economic giving rise to the overstatement or simplification in question here, there were other mitigating factors at play. First, there was a need to counter the reformist strategies of Kautsky and others. Also, practical political activities in times of war and revolutionary upheaval perhaps were not conducive to the systematic working out of the niceties of political theory. Marxist critics writing from the vantage point of the second half of the twentieth century and even into the new millennium have tended to berate Lenin not only for oversimplifying, but also for not having foreseen post-World War II developments. The latter criticism, not having foreseen the *pax Americana* of the last half of the twentieth century, is to tax Lenin with not being prescient. Furthermore, whilst there has been no rivalry between capitalist powers to match the situation as it stood in the first half of the twentieth century, there have been enough conflicts in the second half of the century to suggest that the connection between war and imperialism has not been severed.

Perhaps the most telling criticism made of Lenin's imperialism theory concerns its lack of political analysis. It was not possible to 'deduce imperial domination from capital export or capitalist rivalry from the logic of uneven development without additional arguments connecting the evolution of national social formations to the world accumulation process' (Willoughby 1995: 328). Lenin did not discuss how the state functioned with regard to the accumulation process nor did he address the complex relationships found in the realm of the international state system in his book. As previously noted, the classical Marxist accounts of imperialism paid little attention to the capitalist state, and, for one critic at least, Lenin was the most guilty of reductionism in his subordination of the political to the economic (Willoughby 1995: 328). Whilst the latter claim is debatable given Bukharin's treatment of the state in his state capitalist trusts and state capitalism formulations, the criticism is valid not only for the classical Marxists but for the 'pioneers of imperialism theory' as a whole (Callinicos 2009: 70–1, where he focusses on some of the classical Marxists only; Chibber 2004: 429; Panitch and Gindin 2004: 6, where they criticise the classical Marxists and exclude Hobson; Willoughby 1995: 330, though he excludes Kautsky from this criticism).

Lenin's imperialism theory: a summary

Having been accorded the status of iconic text by sections of the left for a large part of the twentieth century, Lenin, if he had lived to witness it, perhaps would have been bemused by such veneration. He was astute enough to qualify his contribution to imperialism theory, declaring that he was simply presenting a 'popular outline'. Understandably, the status of the text has polarised opinion about the theorising of imperialism contained within its pages. Critics of Lenin's *Imperialism* have sometimes railed against what they perceive it to be about; for example, the critics of economic imperialism – Fieldhouse, along with Gallagher and Robinson – conflate Hobson's and Lenin's theories of imperialism and, additionally, through a case of 'mistaken identity', misconstrue what Lenin was trying to do in his analysis of imperialism. For such critics, the concept of imperialism had become an *idée fixe* promoted by the international socialist movement, with Lenin being the leading exponent of imperialism theory (Stokes 1969: 285–9).

More recently, as discussed above, critics have pointed out shortcomings in Lenin's tract. There is no need to revisit these critiques. It suffices to say that there are, indeed, problems in Lenin's analysis of imperialism. Nonetheless, some of these criticisms made by Marxists overlook both the (deliberately) limited scope of the book and some of the historically specific conditions that informed Lenin's analysis of imperialism. Amongst those historically specific conditions were World War I, the collapse of the Second International and the struggle against reformism/revisionism. Also, the fact that Lenin was principally a political leader and strategist often gets overlooked. Theorising was not conducted for the sake of theory alone; for Lenin theory had to serve a political end.

Lenin's *Imperialism* was not intended to be the last word on the subject, rather it was a contribution to an understanding of the economic essence of imperialism. On the positive side it was a logical and lucid explication of what Lenin thought were the main economic features of a new stage of capitalism. Moreover, Lenin's analysis is empirically rich, drawing extensively on bourgeois and Marxist sources. His insights into the constitutive elements of imperialism – the five features – continue to resonate.

Evidence of the continuing relevance of Lenin's imperialism theory for those currently engaged in writing about the subject is not hard to find. Alex Callinicos, in one of his interventions into imperialism theory, not only casts a critical eye over classical Marxist theories but uses as his theoretical template a synthesis of Bukharin's and Lenin's theories of imperialism (Callinicos 2009: 25–66). Christian Fuchs suggests that Lenin can be used as 'a theoretical and methodological model for contemporary critical globalization studies' (Fuchs 2010: 223). Furthermore, Fuchs argues that some of the contemporary discussions of new imperialism, empire and global capitalism have been notable for their imprecise understanding of what constitutes imperialism, denoting a lack of grounding in classical Marxist theories – especially Lenin's. To come to terms with contemporary political economic development it is necessary to re-engage with Lenin's imperialism theory, update his theoretical arguments and flesh them out using the same rigorous empirical approach that he himself employed (Fuchs 2010: 222–3). Other Marxist thinkers may not be as sanguine about Lenin's theorising as Callinicos and Fuchs, but these two examples indicate that Lenin's insights about imperialism still strike a chord.

To conclude, Lenin's *Imperialism* is not the pinnacle of imperialism theory. Yet it has provided sufficient conceptual and empirical material on which later thinkers could draw. What it lacks in political theory, for example, is balanced by the wealth of data used by Lenin to support his arguments and by the clear definition of imperialism he offers. It is fair to say that it has not only been highly influential, but that it continues to be an important theoretical resource.

Conclusion: the legacy of the 'pioneers'

From the foregoing critical analysis of the writing of the 'pioneers of imperialism theory' a number of points can be made. First, the 'pioneers' all perceived that qualitative changes to capitalism had occurred on the cusp of the twentieth century. These qualitative changes were seen by some of the writers as marking a transition from one stage of capitalism to another. Transition from the competitive capitalism that had been the hallmark of Britain's domination of the global economy through much of the nineteenth century was largely attributable to the industrialisation of the US and Germany. The industrialisation of these two countries was achieved through the use of protective tariffs, cartels, the concentration and centralisation of capital and the direct intervention of the state in the economy as opposed to the *laissez faire* approach officially adopted by British governments. These developments in Germany and the US were taken by Hilferding to be emblematic of not only industrialisation but also a new stage of capitalism, where finance (and financiers) had become immensely important and influential. It was further assumed by Kautsky, Luxemburg, Bukharin and Lenin that Hilferding had uncovered a blueprint that other countries would follow on their path to industrialisation and subsequent immersion in the capitalist social system. Second, the qualitative changes to capitalism had important consequences in the international arena. Colonialism, which had existed for hundreds of years, had been transformed according to Hobson. A new level of rapaciousness was apparent, seen in the treatment of China and the Chinese by the British, as outlined by Hobson, had debilitative effects not only on the Chinese but on British politics and society as well. Luxemburg, too, drew on the Egyptian experience at the hands of the British and French financiers in addition to the Chinese and Turkish experiences of European 'beneficence' to underline how ruthless the European states and business interests were in their dealings with less developed countries. The predatory nature of interstate relations also was evident in relationships between the advanced capitalist countries. All the 'pioneers' were aware of the heightened levels of bellicosity, militarism and arms spending indulged in by the Great Powers, which ultimately led to World War I.

There was a causal link or links between the changes to capitalism that had occurred in the closing decades of the nineteenth and opening years of the twentieth century and the predatory and rapacious character of international relations. For this cohort of thinkers, imperialism was a historically specific phenomenon associated with the expansiveness of capitalism, its contradictions and its symbiotic relationship with domestic and global politics. Whilst a consensus about the essential elements of imperialism existed, there were fundamental differences of opinion about how to correct its excesses. On one side were the reformists who maintained that imperialism was capable of correction through policy or legislative changes. On the other were the proponents of revolution – Luxemburg, Bukharin and Lenin – who argued that imperialism was not amenable to reform as it was determined by the dynamics of capitalism.

Out of all this a definition that addressed a number of imperialism's key characteristics eventually emerged. Drawing on the groundbreaking work of Hobson, Hilferding, Bukharin (and perhaps even Luxemburg) and using Kautsky's concept of ultra-imperialism as a whetstone to sharpen his own understanding, Lenin's definition of imperialism, despite his reluctance to offer it up as such, became definitive. It was the five key features of imperialism and the stipulation that capitalism had reached its highest stage – in short, the conciseness of Lenin's definition – that helped establish its popularity. A number of the next cohort of Marxist thinkers that engaged with imperialism – the neo-Marxists – used Lenin's imperialism theory as the default or common-sense position. Such was the case for Paul Sweezy and Samir Amin, for example, as discussed in part two.

A number of later thinkers, then, have used Lenin's conceptualising of imperialism as the standard. Others have extolled the individual contributions to imperialism theory of Hobson (Cain 2002; Etherington 1984), Hilferding (Bottomore 1981), Luxemburg (Lee 1971), Kautsky (Panitch and Gindin 2004) and Bukharin (Cohen 1970). Whilst all the 'pioneers of imperialism theory' contributed to the foundational literature, some contributions carried more weight. Hobson's contribution was and is noteworthy. His critique of the political, economic, social and even moral aspects of late Victorian British development established parameters that others were to follow to a greater or lesser extent. For his part, Hilferding was the first Marxist to seriously attempt to update Marx's analysis of capitalism, observing that finance capital, capital export, cartels and syndicates, tariffs and the concentration and centralisation of capital were indicators of a modified capitalism. Bukharin and Lenin both systematised Hilferding's insights (as well as aspects of Hobson's and others) to arrive at clear definitions of imperialism, supported in both instances with impressive amounts of empirical data. The work of these four writers did most to establish and consolidate the theorising of imperialism in the first of three distinct phases in Marxist engagement with the subject.

The influence of the 'pioneers', and particularly Lenin's work, continues to be felt. Mention has been made of recent forays into critical examination of the global capitalist economy, imperialism and globalisation by Callinicos and Fuchs in the section on Lenin above. Fuchs, for example, argued that an understanding of Lenin's canonical text on imperialism was necessary for critical globalisation studies. He made use of Lenin's five key features of imperialism, adding new data which served to support his contention about the continued relevance of Lenin for an understanding of contemporary capitalism and geopolitics (Fuchs 2010: 215–45). Those more critical than Callinicos and Fuchs of the classical Marxist legacy, such as Panitch and Gindin, nonetheless have gone back to the product of earlier thinkers rather than engage with the neo-Marxists because the classical Marxists produced the benchmark for imperialism theory. By using classical Marxist theories as negative example, Panitch and Gindin in their own way confirm that status.

Much has changed in the world since the 'pioneers' theories were published. The warring between advanced capitalist states, a feature of the first half of the twentieth century, has seemingly passed. Contemporary international politics is shaped by a single hegemonic power, which sits at the head of a hierarchy of advanced capitalist states; a different scenario to that which exercised the minds of the pioneers. Capitalism has changed in significant ways, too. Continuities, however, are evident as well. The capitalist accumulation process has broadened and deepened, but has not fundamentally altered. Processes of concentration and centralisation have continued with phases of mergers and acquisitions apparent, while capital export continues. Since the end of the Long Boom in the West, finance or financiers, and even finance capital, have assumed such a powerful position that states have been compelled to de-regulate. Moreover, in the wake of the Global Financial Crisis of 2008, they effectively have been forced to prop up this sector in countries like the US, Britain and other European nations. The invasions of Iraq and Afghanistan by the US and a small supporting cast of subordinate states are a clear indication that militarism and war continue to be part of the agenda of rich and powerful countries, albeit directed at less powerful states rather than at each other. Many of the characteristics of the capitalist accumulation process and the rapacious and war-like nature of international relations highlighted as symptomatic of capitalist imperialism by the pioneers years ago have not disappeared. Therefore, the imperialism theories of the pioneers remain useful and can be said to have contemporary relevance.

The major shortcoming of the collective output of this group was the lack of attention paid to the political aspects of imperialism. The sharpest criticism regarding this shortcoming has come from 'globalisation-era' Marxists. These critics suggest that the political mediation of imperialism, particularly the function of the state, did not receive enough attention from the 'pioneers of imperialism theory'. This criticism is valid and examples can be seen in the simplistic or instrumentalist rendering of the state by Bukharin and Lenin for instance. Despite the problems, the 'pioneers' left a rich theoretical resource for future writers. It is now appropriate to move to the next phase of theorising, that of the neo-Marxists.

CHAPTER 3

PAUL SWEEZY AND PAUL BARAN

THE FOUNDERS OF NEO-MARXIST IMPERIALISM THEORY

Introduction

Paul Sweezy and Paul Baran were prominent non-orthodox Marxist theorists whose work on monopoly capitalism and imperialism influenced radical scholarship and revolutionary politics across several continents, especially during the upheavals of the 1960s and 1970s. *Monopoly Capital* (Baran and Sweezy 1968) has been described as a 'masterly popularisation of Marxian theory that has been more influential than any other work in radical political economy' since its publication in 1966 (Howard and King 2004: 411). The work of Sweezy and Baran was disseminated not only through scholarly publications, but also in *Monthly Review*, with Sweezy remaining an editor from its inception in May 1949 until his retirement in 1997 (Howard and King 2004: 413). This journal has helped to develop critical Marxian scholarship for more than sixty years. A major concern shared by numerous *Monthly Review* contributors through the 1960s and 1970s was the *under*development of the colonial and newly independent countries, understood to be the direct result of monopoly capitalism. For the two theorists, monopoly capital became *the* defining element of twentieth-century capitalism, so much so that in their co-authored book *Monopoly Capital* imperialism almost completely disappeared.

Transformations in the global political and economic conditions that informed the analyses of Sweezy and Baran were remarkable. After the upheavals of the Great Depression and World War II, the relative political, economic and military strengths of the advanced capitalist states had been radically altered. The anti-colonial struggles after World War II were given some succour by the rise to dominance of the US, which adopted an official anti-imperialist, anti-colonial stance. This heralded a change in the political appearance of the system of states: 'It was not through formal empire, but rather through the reconstitution of states as integral elements of an informal American empire, that the international capitalist order was now reorganized and regulated' (Panitch and Gindin 2004: 17). Part of the process involved in creating an informal empire was the anti-colonialism of the US, pursued through what was termed the 'Open Door' policy. The 'Open Door' policy sought to open up the non-colonised countries to US trade and investment, and apply pressure on the remaining colonial empires to give equal access to American businesses for trade and investment in their colonies. This policy commenced with Roosevelt's 'New Deal' and its initial purpose was to undermine the preferential treatment afforded businesses from Britain throughout its empire (Magdoff 1969: 125).

The most important driver of the de-colonisation process was the struggle for national liberation in many of the colonies. This period of resistance had a powerful influence on the social and political structures of the world, including the United Nations General Assembly where the number of newly independent nations swelled the ranks of member states from fifty-one in 1945 to 127 by 1970. The General Assembly, from the late 1950s to the early 1960s, was dominated by the issue of colonialism, in particular the developments in Namibia, Rhodesia, the Congo and South Africa, which reflected the voting-power of the newly independent states of the Third World (Luard 1979: 47).

Political independence, however, did not seem to lead to a noticeable improvement in the economies of many of the former colonies. This problem exercised the minds of a number of critical thinkers including Sweezy and Baran and it formed the basis for much subsequent neo-Marxist writing. Indeed, so much emphasis was placed on the 'relationships of dependency, exploitation, and oppression' that, for the new school of Marxist scholarship, imperialism was 'defined as the exploitation of the less-developed countries by the advanced capitalist countries of the West' (Polychroniou 1991: 87).

This chapter argues that both Sweezy and Baran helped shift critical analysis of imperialism from the European 'core' states to the undeveloped 'peripheral' states of the Third World that subsequent writers took up and expanded upon. The impact that capitalism and imperialism had on the countries of the periphery became a hallmark of neo-Marxist critiques. Sweezy, in particular, but also Baran, through their writings and the auspices of the *Monthly Review*, helped raise interest in this problem area. Thus they were the founders of neo-Marxist imperialism theory. The second argument concerns the trajectory of Sweezy's and Baran's conceptualising of imperialism. Starting with Sweezy's *The Theory of Capitalist Development* (1970) and finishing with *Monopoly Capital*, there was a noticeable modification of (and even a movement away from) aspects of Marxist political economy by both writers. Such a shift away from key aspects of Marxist political economy influenced how both writers conceived and theorised imperialism. By the time *Monopoly Capital* was published, there was scarcely a reference to the term.

This chapter commences with a critical textual analysis of *The Theory of Capitalist Development* followed by Baran's *The Political Economy of Growth* (1976). A section devoted to examining Sweezy's and Baran's uses of three economic concepts that contributed to the decline in their interest in imperialism then follows. The chapter finishes with a textual analysis of *Monopoly Capital* and some concluding remarks.

Sweezy and *The Theory of Capitalist Development*

Born in 1910 into a Wall Street banker's family and educated at Harvard University and the London School of Economics, by the 1930s Sweezy had become convinced of the explanatory power of Marxist political economy. He maintained a commitment to Marxism until his death in 2004. In 1942, he consolidated his reputation as an eminent Marxist thinker with the first publication of *The Theory of Capitalist Development*.

The question of imperialism is taken up in Part Four of Sweezy's book. Two chapters (XVII and XVIII) are of particular interest. The first of these chapters canvasses five interlocking and overlapping themes: nationalism, militarism, and racism; imperialism and classes; imperialism and the state; wars of redivision; and the limits of imperialism. The second contained some important insights on the connections between fascism and imperialism. Chapter XVII starts with a basic recapitulation of Lenin's definition of imperialism, with minor modifications (Sweezy 1970: 307). Sweezy posited five features of imperialism as a stage in the development of world economy:

> (a) several advanced capitalist countries stand on a competitive footing with respect to the world market for industrial products; (b) monopoly capital is the dominant form of capital; and (c) the contradictions of the accumulation process have reached such maturity that capital export is an outstanding feature of world economic relations. As a consequence of these basic economic conditions, we have two further characteristics: (d) severe rivalry in the world market leading alternatively to cutthroat competition and international monopoly combines; and (e) the territorial division of 'unoccupied' parts of the world among the major capitalist powers (and their satellites) (Sweezy 1970: 307).

Sweezy, in summarising the nature of imperialism, suggested that the 'international antagonisms of imperialism are fundamentally the antagonisms of rival national capitalist classes' (Sweezy 1970: 308). A further claim was that, 'since in the international sphere the interests of capital are directly and quickly translated into terms of state policy, it follows that these antagonisms assume the form of conflicts between the states and thus, indirectly, between whole nations' (Sweezy 1970: 308). What is being alluded to here is the concept of inter-imperialist rivalry, and the summary itself does not diverge from a classical Marxist perspective on imperialism. Sweezy, furthermore, suggested that the nature of nationalism and militarism under imperialism had changed in comparison to the functions they had performed under the previous phase of capitalism. They had now become 'weapons in the world struggle among rival groups of capitalists' (Sweezy 1970: 308).

Militarism, according to Sweezy, had risen to a position of permanent importance in 'all the imperialist nations'. This had 'far-reaching economic consequences' in that it fostered:

> the development of a group of specially favoured monopolists in those industries, like steel and shipbuilding, which are most important to the production of armaments. The munitions magnates have a direct interest in the maximum expansion of military production; not only do they benefit in the form of state orders but also they are afforded safe and lucrative outlets for their accumulated profits. Hence it is these elements of the capitalist class which take the lead in calling for an aggressive foreign policy (Sweezy 1970: 309).

Sweezy's insights on militarism owed its provenance in part, if not wholly, to Luxemburg, Hobson and German social democrats like Karl Liebknecht who had written on militarism prior to the outbreak of World War I (Liebknecht 1972). The expenditure on armies and navies, Sweezy asserted, operated as an offsetting mechanism 'to the tendency to underconsumption' (Sweezy 1970: 309).

A relationship also existed between imperialism and racism. As Hilferding and Hobson had pointed out, the notion of 'racial superiority' formed part of the ideological armoury of imperialism. The usefulness of racism was not limited to rationalising foreign conquest. It also was useful to the ruling classes for diverting attention away from class struggle. Racial antagonism and discrimination against racial minorities could and did lead to the depression of wages of the disadvantaged, with 'favoured sections of the population ... [reaping] substantial material rewards' (Sweezy 1970: 311).

There was a merging of interests between the large landowners and industrialists under conditions of advanced capitalism. Conflicts between the two groups – so commonplace during capitalism's early years – had diminished and there was a concomitant unification of the interests of the working classes. Workers became more aware that organisation and co-operation were the primary means of achieving their class objectives, such as shorter hours, higher wages and better working conditions. This provided the impetus for the formation of trade unions and political parties to promote working-class policies and programmes (Sweezy 1970: 312).

Sweezy described an array of middle groups that stood between the ruling classes and the working classes. Some of those associated with these middle groups had declined in importance such as independent farmers, many of whom had turned into property-less tenants, wageworkers, or in a minority of cases, had turned into capitalist farmers (Sweezy 1970: 313). Addressed here were perceived changes to the composition of the middle class with some such as 'industrial and governmental bureaucrats, salesmen, publicists, dealers ... professionals and teachers' becoming part of a 'new' middle class (Sweezy 1970: 313–14). These last were brought into being by rising living standards, the growth of monopoly and the centralisation of capital (Sweezy 1970: 313). In short, in advanced capitalist countries some fractions of the middle class declined in importance, whereas others grew in numbers and influence. Sweezy's analysis of classes was conventionally Marxist, positing two main classes with the middle class, though more numerous than in previous stages of capitalism, squeezed between the 'extortions of monopoly capital' and the 'demands of the working class' (Sweezy 1970: 314).

In his synopsis of the impact imperialism had on classes, Sweezy established a direct link between the interests of the propertied class and monopoly capital's expansiveness and its reliance on state protection and assistance (Sweezy 1970: 314). The impact of imperialism on the working class was problematic. Sweezy agreed with Lenin's argument about the rise of a labour aristocracy. He suggested that:

> in so far as foreign trade and capital export make possible the importation of cheap wage goods and enlarge the profits of the capitalist class, it is clear that opportunities are opened up for the workers to improve their standard of living without necessarily arousing the bitter hostility of their employers (Sweezy 1970: 315).

The working classes adopted a live and let live approach towards their class rivals, for that arrangement was mutually beneficial.

Once inter-imperialist rivalry escalated and competition for markets increased, capitalists then moved to force wages down in order to maintain their profits. It was then that the interests of the working class and the ruling or propertied class diverged (Sweezy 1970: 316). The divergence of interests was reinforced when the working class realised that the end product of imperialism, war – the culmination of inter-imperialist rivalry – showed that they had much to lose and little to gain under imperialism. Regarding the middle classes, Sweezy stated that it was difficult to generalise their relationship with imperialism. Some fractions within this class would lose and others would gain. Nonetheless, the powerful ideological factors of nationalism and racism could be and were used on the middle classes (and sections of the working classes) in order to swing the middle classes behind an imperialist agenda. Sweezy asserted that 'the net result of imperialism is to bind the middle classes closer to big capital and to widen the gulf between the middle classes and the working class' (Sweezy 1970: 317).

Concerning the relationship between imperialism and the state, two main points are discernible. First, imperialism, through the rise of empires, the centralisation of capital and the growth of monopoly and militarism, ensured an increase in the power of the state and an ongoing enhancement of its functions: 'contradictions of the accumulation process in the epoch of imperialism provide additional grounds for increased state activity, particularly in the economic sphere' (Sweezy 1970: 317). Second, Sweezy asserted that imperialism, whilst bringing about the enhancement of the powers of the state, also resulted in the reduction of the power of the legislature compared with the executive. He contrasted the role of parliament in the early modern period, where it was used by the nascent capitalist class to fight the power of the centralised monarchies, with the role of parliament during the epoch of imperialism:

> In the period of imperialism, however, a sharp change occurs. With the tightening of class lines and the increasing severity of social conflict, parliament becomes more and more a battleground for contending parties representing divergent class and group interests. While on the one hand parliament's capacity for positive action declines, on the other hand there emerges an increasing need for a strong centralized state ready and able to rule over distant territories, to direct the activities of fleets and armies, and to solve difficult and complex economic problems. Under the circumstances, parliament is forced to give up one after another of its cherished prerogatives and to see built up under its very eyes the kind of centralized and uncontrolled authority against which, in its youth, it had fought so hard and so well (Sweezy 1970: 319).

The final sections of Sweezy's chapter on imperialism examine wars of redivision and the limits of imperialism. His comments on wars of redivision were a recapitulation (with some minor updating) of Lenin's proposition that, as a consequence of European expansion, the world had been divided up between the colonial or imperialist powers. What remained was the struggle amongst these powers for the redivision of the world, not the claiming of or 'owning' of an unoccupied part of the world. Sweezy also drew attention to what he claimed was the glaring weakness of Rosa Luxemburg's theory of imperialism, namely the notion that annexation was confined to the agrarian or backward parts of the globe. Like Lenin, Sweezy affirmed that the annexation of new markets and sources of raw materials would be pursued by imperialist nations in both agrarian and highly industrialised sectors of the world (Sweezy 1970: 320–1).

Of real interest is Sweezy's characterization of World War II as *not* being a simple case of inter-imperialist struggle. Rather, Sweezy saw it as three distinct wars merged into one: first was a war of redivision on the World War I pattern, with Germany, Italy and Japan on one side and Britain and the US on the other; second was a war between capitalism and socialism, with Germany on one side and the Soviet Union representing socialism on the other; and third was the anti-imperialist war of national independence waged by China against Japan. This meant that the inter-imperialist rivalry that was the cornerstone of World War I had been joined by *anti*-imperialist struggle, thus modifying and limiting the impact of imperialism (Sweezy 1970: 324).

In the final section of the chapter Sweezy identifies two fundamental limits to imperialism. First is the internal development of the imperialist nations themselves, which led to increases in class struggle and the rise of militarism. The increased likelihood of inter-imperialist rivalry leading to war, in turn, caused an upsurge in revolutionary fervour and social upheaval (Sweezy 1970: 324–6). Sweezy's argument here was that the internal contradictions of imperialism would limit its development, an argument that was in keeping with Lenin's viewpoint. The second fundamental limit to imperialism is the relationship between metropolis and colony, a theme neo-Marxist theorists subsequently took up with much vigour. It was claimed that the:

> development of the colonial economy was not well balanced [with the consequence] that under ... imperialism, industrialization advances very slowly, too slowly to absorb the steady flow of

> handicraft producers who are ruined by the competition of machine-made products from the factories of the advanced regions (Sweezy 1970: 326).

Furthermore, the ruined handicraft producers were thrown back into the ranks of the peasantry, creating more pressure on the land and forcing down the living conditions of the mass of the peasantry. According to Sweezy, the answer to these problems was a concerted improvement in the land system, increased production in agriculture, reduction of peasant numbers, and a high rate of industrialization (Sweezy 1970: 326). The nature of imperialism precluded these developments.

Powerful interests opposed colonial development. Colonial landlords did not support land reform and metropolitan manufacturers opposed protective tariffs in the colonies, which resulted in inhibited industrial development in the colonies and stagnant economies (Sweezy 1970: 326). Apart from the landlords and 'a few relatively small groups which are in effect agents of imperialist rule' (Sweezy 1970: 327), for the great majority in the colonial countries living standards declined.

By making the claim about the stifling of colonial industrial development and economic stagnation, Sweezy modified an assumption held by classical Marxist theorists like Bukharin and Lenin. Both these thinkers assumed that there would be industrial development in the colonies. The industrial development would be uneven, with some sectors developing rapidly whilst others lagged, the whole process determined by profits and the prospect of profits in typical capitalist fashion. Nonetheless, the assumption was that the colonies would industrialise. Sweezy's analysis led him to conclude that this assumption had not been borne out by the midpoint of the twentieth century. The themes of metropolitan/colonial relationships, economic stagnation and lack of development of the colonial world in *The Theory of Capitalist Development*, became some of the central concerns of subsequent neo-Marxist theorising on imperialism. Sweezy is the founder of neo-Marxist imperialism theory.

Connections between fascism and imperialism: Sweezy's view

Sweezy devoted chapter XVIII to the problem of fascism. He linked the rise of fascism in Germany and Italy with the wars of redivision typical of the imperialist epoch. Whilst connecting fascism and imperialism was not unusual for the time, it did represent an updating of Marxist theorising on imperialism. The conditions that gave rise to fascism were described in a brief but succinct passage:

> A nation, the economic and social structure of which is seriously disrupted as the result of an imperialist war of redivision, may, failing a successful socialist revolution, enter a period of class equilibrium on the basis of capitalist relations of production. Under such conditions, the intensification of the contradictions of capitalism leads to a severe internal crisis which cannot be 'solved' by resort to the normal methods of imperialist expansion. This is, so to speak, the soil in which fascism takes root and grows (Sweezy 1970: 332).

The foundations of fascism, according to Sweezy, were to be found in the middle classes who had been squeezed between organised labour and the ruling classes. The middle classes showed a marked hostility towards the other classes, though the former's hostility to the ruling classes was assuaged by appeals to 'race', nationalism, war and foreign conquest, in short, fascist ideology. As well as the middle classes other societal elements were attracted to fascism, such as criminals, unorganised labour, the unemployed, independent farmers and disaffected youth, especially when fascist parties were seen to be making political headway (Sweezy 1970: 333). The attitude of capitalists towards fascism changed over time, starting with suspicion, stemming from the strident early attacks on finance capital by the German Nazis and their 'national socialist' rhetoric, giving way to acceptance. Once fascism had shown that it was a force to be taken seriously, capitalists thought they could use fascism and fascists as allies in the struggle against the organised working class and foreign capitalists (Sweezy 1970: 334). A corollary of the rise to power of fascist parties in Europe was the authoritarian state.

Under fascism the means of production retained the form of capital, and exploitation still took the form of the production of surplus value (Sweezy 1970: 339). It followed, therefore, that even with the advent of fascism, the ruling class still would be the capitalist class, notwithstanding the fact that its personnel may have altered. In Germany, for instance, Jewish capitalists had their assets and capital expropriated, whilst fascist functionaries leveraged themselves into positions of power in industry. New members of the ruling class, however, still were compelled to preserve and expand capital (Sweezy 1970: 339). Fascism was not a novel social order, it grew out of the ashes of the nations that were ravaged or defeated in inter-imperialist struggle, where the capitalist structure had been severely injured but not overthrown (Sweezy 1970: 346). Fascism was an extreme form of political rule based on monopoly capitalism, which used racism, nationalism and foreign conquest, militarism and war as part of its *modus operandi*. Thus fascism was and is intimately connected with imperialism.

Sweezy, imperialism and *The Theory of Capitalist Development*

Sweezy started with a definition of imperialism that relied on a slightly modified version of Lenin's five basic features of imperialism. He then visited themes that had been treated previously by the 'pioneers of imperialism theory', including militarism, nationalism, monopoly capitalism, classes and their relationships with imperialism, the role of the state in imperialism and racism as an ideological tool.

Sweezy's analysis of the social, political and economic conditions of the mid twentieth century produced three important contributions to Marxist imperialism theory. The first was in his unraveling of the relationship between fascism and imperialism. The second came in his interesting analysis of World War II, and the third was Sweezy's focusing on metropolitan/colonial relationships that helped bring about the lack of development or stagnation of the colonial world. Exploring the links between fascism and imperialism was a significant updating of Marxist imperialism theory. His investigation revealed new political forms ushered in by the fascist era and connections between fascism and imperialism, as well as illuminating the relationships that various classes had with fascism in general. Similarly, his presentation of World War II as being three conflicts rolled into one was an interesting and insightful addition to the body of Marxist writing on that war and imperialism. Here, too, Sweezy's contribution can be read as an updating of the canon rather than a fundamental challenge to existing theories. Most significant were the concepts of colonial underdevelopment, the lack of industrialisation and stagnation that was arguably the lot of the majority of the world's nation states. This focus on the Third World and its lack of development was, indeed, a clear change of emphasis, which formed the focal point for subsequent neo-Marxist theorists in their analyses of imperialism.

The next point to be made about *The Theory of Capitalist Development* (and this moves the analysis momentarily away from Sweezy's theorising on imperialism) is that Sweezy had real reservations about aspects of classical Marxist political economy. Specifically, Sweezy did not agree with Marx's transformation of values into prices, a problem that Marx tackled in volume three of *Capital*. According to Sweezy, Marx's calculation of a system of prices from a system of values had 'set the stage for a final vindication of the labor theory of value, the solid foundation of his whole theoretical structure', but Marx's handling of the transformation of values into prices was unsatisfactory (Sweezy 1970: 123). For Sweezy this was not a major difficulty, though it was problematic enough to require a resolution. The final vindication of the labour theory of value was to be achieved by recourse to the efforts of Ladislaus von Bortkiewicz to find an alternative problem solution (Sweezy 1970: 115–30). It has been noted by critics that von Bortkiewicz's analysis, first presented in 1907, has formed the basis of many attempts to either reform or repudiate the labour theory of value (Mandel 1976b: 289–91; Mandel and Freeman 1984: ix–x, 141–63). Whilst there has been and continues to be much dispute about the 'transformation problem' and, by extension, the labour theory of value, the important point that comes from this reservation of Sweezy was that it was an indication of a willingness to engage critically with Marxist political economy. Critical engagement with Marxist political economy was and is a positive development, helping to keep it from ossifying. Furthermore, insights gained from other economics 'schools' cannot be dismissed out of hand by Marxists. Nonetheless, Sweezy and Baran have attracted criticism for going too far with their reservations about central elements of Marxist political economy. In particular, their substitution of a cornerstone of Marxist political economy – surplus value by the less precise concept of economic surplus – was deemed to be problematic (Brewer 1990: 142). Mention is made of this here because, as will be argued to a greater extent in a later section, the tendency of Sweezy and Baran to substitute important Marxist political economic concepts such as surplus value led to the obscuring of the relationship between capitalism and imperialism. With the passage of time, Sweezy's and Baran's theorising of imperialism became less insightful and virtually disappeared from their analysis.

Baran, the nature of imperialism and *The Political Economy of Growth*

Baran was born in 1910 in Nikolaev, Russia, into a family that had strong connections to the Menshevik side of the Russian Social Democratic Party. After much movement between the Soviet Union, Germany and the US, he eventually settled in the US in the 1930s, attaining a professorship at Stanford University in 1951. Baran was not a prolific writer, with his major works *The Political Economy of Growth* (1976) and the co-authored *Monopoly Capital* both produced in the last decade of his life (Foster 1992: 24). He died in 1964.

In the preface to the first edition of *The Political Economy of Growth*, Baran wrote that one of the book's main objectives was to examine 'the "unreformed" nature of contemporary imperialism and its inherent animosity towards all genuine initiative at economic development on the part of the undeveloped countries' (Baran 1976: 13). Furthermore, a succinct indication of what Baran thought was the principal problem associated with imperialism can be found in his claim that 'economic development in underdeveloped countries is profoundly inimical to the dominant interests in the advanced capitalist countries' (Baran 1976: 120).

The first phase of industrialisation of the West had almost run its course by the end of the nineteenth century, culminating in tremendous changes in 'the structure of the capitalist economies' (Baran 1976: 113). There had been a marked increase in the concentration and centralisation of capital, which was accompanied by the displacing of small firms by large-scale enterprises, with the latter assuming centre stage in the economic life of the advanced capitalist countries. Large-scale enterprise became the foundation of monopoly and oligopoly, one of 'the characteristic features of modern capitalism' (Baran 1976: 113). The era of European expansion, armaments races, political crises and war from the middle of the nineteenth century through to the early decades of the twentieth century was 'the epoch of imperialism, wars, national and social revolutions' (Baran 1976: 113–14). A summary of Western capitalist development and political events such as this was in keeping with classical Marxist imperialism theory.

World War II and ensuing global events challenged the position of global capitalism. According to Baran, the rise of China after 1949, combined with the growth of the socialist bloc of states and the upsurges in the colonial and dependent countries, caused alarm in the metropolitan heartlands. The international arena from the 1940s through to the late 1950s had as its pre-eminent feature a 'momentous movement to do away with the entire edifice of imperialism, to put an end to the backwardness and prostration of the overwhelming majority of the human race' (Baran 1976: 117).

There was opposition to that 'momentous movement'. For the underdeveloped world, economic and social progress was blocked by the economic and political order of capitalism and imperialism. Advanced capitalist countries had their own bottlenecks to development with private investment and consumption coming up against the constraints found in the drive for profit maximisation, conditioned and underpinned by monopoly and oligopoly (Baran 1976: 118–19). The prospect for these countries probably was 'the continuous re-emergence of the grim dilemma between war-induced bursts of output and depression-induced floods of unemployment' (Baran 1976: 119).

Imperialist powers resisted the economic and social development of their colonial dependencies, which, when confronted with national liberation struggles, hardened into a counter revolutionary alliance of the imperialist powers (Baran 1976: 120). Statements favouring economic development in the underdeveloped world were part of the political and ideological stratagems used by Western powers in the late stages of the colonial era. Aid from the developed world was earmarked for progressive improvements of the living standards of backward areas, with a view to lessening popular pressure for industrialisation and undermining the movement for economic and social progress (Baran 1976: 121).

Another stratagem that Baran identified was the advocating of political independence in order to avoid the appearance of old-fashioned imperialism. The old ties of dependence that a colony felt with its metropolitan centre were crucially modified if not completely severed with the advent of political independence. Yet dependence was maintained in a new form through the mechanism of economic infiltration, the preferred method of American imperialism (Baran 1976: 123).

Baran's conception of imperialism was circumscribed. He made little attempt to give it a clear definition. He referred to the conditions needed for economic development in both advanced and less developed nations coming up against the barriers of 'the economic and political order of capitalism and imperialism' (Baran 1976: 118). Imperialism was an integral part of the political and economic order of capitalism, which had as one of its central features a system of international domination. The domination of imperialist powers over undeveloped nations necessarily meant the lack of industrialisation and the stagnation of the economies of the undeveloped world. Here was the core of imperialism, the essence that Baran identified in the opening part of his book.

Financiers, the state and imperialism

Baran adapted Hobson's insights on how small groups associated with finance and industry were able to sway statesmen and political cliques into adopting the foreign policy interests that they wished to see pursued. Though Hobson's claims about the ideological appeal of a civilising mission and the strong influence of elites on foreign policy are important and insightful, they were not sufficient to explain the intricacies of imperialism:

> What has been decisive in promoting monopolistic business's spectacular success in rendering the body politic of advanced capitalist countries a willing tool of its foreign interests is the fact that these policies are not merely and not even primarily based upon obfuscation of the masses, upon corruption of officials, and upon treachery of politicians. That the policy of imperialism may be actually of benefit to the ordinary man in an imperialist country was clearly realized by Lenin, who drew attention to the existence of a 'labour aristocracy' sharing in the extra-profits of monopolistic business (Baran 1976: 245).

The fruits of imperialism accrued not only to the plutocratic summit of the advanced capitalist countries, with residual benefits flowing to retainers and dependants, but the existence of the whole of society was affected by imperialist policies (Baran 1976: 245). There was more to imperialism than a mere duping of the populace with appeals to the white man's burden and associated rhetoric about racial superiority.

Furthermore, imperialist policies, when viewed in their entirety, accounted for substantial amounts of a nation's gross national product. The loans and grants extended to friendly governments, military expenditure, financing of propaganda, subversion and espionage apparatuses in dependent areas as well as in 'other competing or "uncertain" imperialist countries' saw the costs to an imperialist power escalate (Baran 1976: 246). The outlays associated with imperialism usurped a substantial amount of what Baran termed the economic surplus – distinct from Gross National Product – which benefited not only elite interests but also helped form and maintain a labour aristocracy. These outlays became 'the central core of . . . government intervention on behalf of "full employment" . . . [and indeed, it was this form of expenditure that was] . . . the one form . . . fully acceptable to monopoly capital' (Baran 1976: 247). Via the mechanism of this government spending, large scale enterprise was favoured and militarism became an essential element of society, by binding together disparate 'classes, groups, and strata whose jobs and income depend on the resulting maintenance of high levels of business activity' (Baran 1976: 247). A harmonising of interests became discernible between the population as a whole and monopolistic business. The uniting formula was the concept of 'full employment', which appealed to the labour movement, satisfied the farmers, contented the 'general public' and circumvented all opposition to monopoly capital's regime (Baran 1976: 247).

Imperialism, militarism, military spending, war and the decline of inter-imperialist rivalry

Military spending, for Baran, was central to the stability of monopoly capitalism. The preservation of prosperity, high employment, profits and popular support relied on that spending (Baran 1976: 258–9). In turn, militarism and military spending required an ideological 'processing' of the population, in order to secure support for monopoly capitalism (Baran 1976: 259). This ideological 'processing' entailed a system of propaganda and indoctrination that kept the populace of advanced capitalist countries in line. When this failed to keep people attuned to the needs of imperialism, however, incidents were 'provoked' (Baran 1976: 260). There was no difficulty in producing incidents as the imperialist nations were surrounded by dependent and colonial nations, who challenged their dominance and authority. War, fear, militarism and a populace indoctrinated by imperialist ideology were essential features of imperialism.

The rise of the US after World War II was a new factor in geopolitics. With the advent of a dominant imperialist power, war between imperialist powers became less likely:

> Even formerly proud imperialist empires tend to descend to the status of satellites of the dominant imperialist country, with the latter assuming more and more the role of supreme arbiter within the imperialist camp. While wars among lesser imperialist countries or among combinations of imperialist countries remain a possibility, the possibility is rather remote (Baran 1976: 260).

Two factors, according to Baran, militated against inter-imperialist wars: the socialist bloc; and the destructive potential of nuclear weapons. The socialist bloc acted as a brake on military adventurism in Asia and Africa. Nuclear weapons were a formidable deterrent:

> It is one thing to mobilize popular support for imperialist policies and armaments with the help of high employment and psychological warfare, it is an altogether different thing to be assured of popular co-operation in the face of atomic retaliation (Baran 1976: 261–2).

One of the consequences of the development of nuclear weapons was the constant need to maintain and increase arms, leading to the arms-race, a key feature of the Cold War (Baran 1976: 262–3).

Only two further sections in Baran's book engaged directly with imperialism. In the first of these sections, he argued that the capitalist system had changed from being 'a once mighty engine of economic development' into a hindrance or hurdle to advancement (Baran 1976: 402). This was especially evident in the undeveloped world. Even though it was supposedly admitted by bourgeois writers that a change to a more rational economic organisation was indeed necessary, the economic status quo would remain because of the rule of monopoly capital and imperialism (Baran 1976: 403). The final section concerned with imperialism examined the role of anti-Soviet ideology in forcing governments in both developed and undeveloped countries to devote resources to military spending. This spending was a 'prodigious waste' designed not to face an external danger such as the Soviet Union, but primarily attuned to suppressing 'internal popular movements for national and social liberation' (Baran 1976: 413). In undeveloped countries, this spending helped ensure that they were not able to break out of their economic backwardness and dependency. For socialist states, military spending in the West prompted increases in defence spending that could otherwise have been used to bolster living standards. Such were the costs of imperialism to the people in the less developed countries and 'to the peoples in the socialist countries' (Baran 1976: 416).

Summary of Baran's theorising of imperialism

Baran made a clear connection between monopoly capitalism and imperialism. Imperialism grew out of the political and economic order of capitalism and the domination of the less developed countries by the powerful capitalist states of the West was one of its central features. Other central features of imperialism were the lack of economic development and the stagnation of the economies of the undeveloped countries brought about by the advanced capitalist countries.

Baran utilised key elements of Hobson's and Lenin's offerings, though unlike the latter he never provided a definition of imperialism. The influence of Hobson's work is discernible in Baran's claim about financial and industrial elites swaying governments into adopting imperialistic foreign policies and the role of the civilising mission as integral parts of imperialism. Use also was made of Lenin's notion of a labour aristocracy to modify Hobson's claims about elite interests being the only ones to benefit from imperialism. Baran acknowledged the important role of the state in maintaining and promoting the policies, both domestic and foreign, of monopolistic and oligopolistic business concerns. In addition, he explored the connections between imperialism, war, militarism and inter-imperialist rivalry, as well as putting forward the proposition that there had been a change to the political forms favoured by imperialist powers especially the US. That is, the favoured approach for the new imperialist power was political independence backed up by economic infiltration.

Following World War II, and with the advent of the Cold War, imperialism was constrained. Two antagonistic blocs – the US-led capitalist states and the socialist bloc of states led by the Soviet Union – acted to curtail inter-imperialist rivalry. Another factor that modified imperialist behaviour was the increase and improvement in atomic weaponry.

Baran's understanding of imperialism evident in this book displayed the same acceptance of the foundational theorising of the 'pioneers' as Sweezy's earlier effort. Whilst there is no definition of imperialism, Baran identifies a direct link between imperialism, monopoly capitalism and the domination of the less developed countries by the advanced capitalist nations. Like Sweezy, Baran added important insights and updates to imperialism theory and at this stage of his writing imperialism was an unavoidable feature of global capitalism and international politics.

Sympathetic critics: Sutcliffe and Griffin and Gurley on Baran

Sutcliffe claims that Baran contributed to Marxist theory by clarifying and synthesising previous Marxist work on monopoly capitalism and adding Keynesian insights about the short-term working of capitalist economies (Sutcliffe 1976: 99). Baran was able to point out the limitations of the Keynesian approach taken over the long-term. Regarding Marxist theories of imperialism, Sutcliffe argued that there were two things that Baran added to them. The first was 'a powerful restatement of Lenin's theory of imperialism' with Baran acknowledging Lenin's connecting of growth of monopoly with capital export and the subsequent partition of the world amongst the imperialist powers, flowing into inter-imperialist rivalry, militarism and war (Sutcliffe 1976: 99). The second aspect was the fuller and more complete overview of the operation of the system of imperialism in the undeveloped regions (Sutcliffe 1976: 99). Sutcliffe claimed that the emphasis on stagnation that occurred in the undeveloped countries had its basis in ideas implicitly held by previous Marxist writers. Sutcliffe specifically cited Marx, Hilferding and Luxemburg as partial and implicit proponents of the stagnation thesis.

Baran's work is not just a re-statement of Lenin's theory of imperialism. Like Sweezy, Baran demonstrates a willingness to engage critically not only with Marxist political economy but also classical Marxist theories of imperialism. As a result:

> Baran's insights have had an enormous influence on radical economists [and his work] ... encouraged writers to explore the possibility of self-reliant development, to cast doubt on the importance of foreign aid and foreign borrowing, to measure the sizes of the surpluses ... to investigate ways in which the surplus is siphoned off to the rich countries, and to examine links among the domestic class structure, international dependency, and capital accumulation (Griffin and Gurley 1985: 1112).

Sweezy and Baran used three economic concepts in their analyses: underconsumption; the stifling of competition by monopolies; and the economic surplus, which it is argued ultimately led them to a modified understanding of imperialism and of its place in the Marxian theoretical firmament. Sweezy's and Baran's theorising of imperialism moved from acceptance of the parameters established by the 'pioneers' to one that was less clearly elaborated and which saw imperialism subsumed under the rubric of monopoly capital.

Underconsumption, stifling of competition under conditions of monopoly and the economic surplus

Sweezy and Baran relied upon the notion of underconsumption to help explain what they saw as the chronic lack of demand and stagnation that was endemic to monopoly capitalism. Brewer considers that their use of this concept is remarkably similar to Hobson's usage (Brewer 1990: 137). Underconsumption first appears in Sweezy's *The Theory of Capitalist Development* (162–89, 216–36), then Baran's *The Political Economy of Growth* (209–14), before forming part of their joint work (Brewer 1990: 138). In their collaborative work it was assumed that production revolves around the production of consumer goods:

> The flaw in the argument (which is exactly the same as Hobson's) is obvious; Sweezy [and by extension Baran] assumed that means of production are only used to produce consumer goods, but investment also goes into the industries that produce means of production ... The prospect of profit drives capitalism, not the expansion of consumption (Brewer 1990: 138).

The underconsumption hypothesis, in its simplest form, is the contention that by boosting the share of wages and thus increasing consumption, demand will bring about increased investment in home markets. This, in turn, will force the pace of growth and curtail the export of capital. As Brewer points out, the prospect of profit drives capitalism and if greater profits can be had from the export of capital, then investment in the home market will be passed up. Implicit in the underconsumption hypothesis is the notion that the worst aspects of capitalist crises or stagnation could be overcome by more enlightened social policy, for example, wage increases. Increases in wages that were significant, however, would automatically impinge on the rate of profit.

The orthodox Marxist position regarding the contradictions of capitalism that originate in the production sphere cannot be overcome by policies of reform centred in the sphere of circulation. Additionally, the caveat that Engels applied to underconsumptionist theses is just as pertinent for Baran and Sweezy as it was for Hobson. Engels claimed that underconsumption was apparent throughout history and still was to be found in capitalism, but with the advent of the latter came the historically specific phenomenon of overproduction (Engels 1976: 371–2).

Brewer identified another aspect of Baran's and Sweezy's argument about monopoly capitalism that he thought was dubious, which was the notion first advanced by Baran of the stifling of competition by monopolies. Brewer suggested that:

> There is a noticeable shift here from the classical Marxist position. The classical Marxists regarded the tendency towards monopoly as a factor intensifying competition, not suppressing it, although it is true that they were not wholly consistent in this. Baran and Sweezy by contrast, argued that the competitive struggle virtually vanishes when there are only a few large firms operating in each

> market, since they will generally adopt a 'live and let live' policy towards each other (Brewer 1990: 139).

This proposition is troublesome because the 'main weight of the argument ... falls on the claim that monopolies restrict the expansion of output to protect monopoly profits {which is} ... a static argument applied to an essentially dynamic problem' (Brewer 1990: 141). The dynamism alluded to concerns the disturbances, the competitive ebbs and flows of capitalism that occur even in its monopoly stage. Humphrey McQueen has observed that a 'company is never too famous to be merged or acquired' (McQueen 2001: 115). Pressures felt by monopolistic corporations compel them to try to undermine their rivals in order to improve market share and maximise profits. Competition was not necessarily stifled by monopolies.

The concept of economic surplus was first used by Baran in *The Political Economy of Growth* where it was divided into the *actual* and *potential* economic surplus. The *actual* economic surplus is 'the difference between society's *actual* current output and its *actual* current consumption' (Baran 1976: 132 emphasis in original). The *actual* surplus is thus 'identical with current saving or accumulation, and finds its embodiment in assets of various kinds added to society's wealth during the period in question'. He then lists the assets as 'productive facilities and equipment, inventories, foreign balances, and gold hoards' (Baran 1976: 132). Importantly for the argument that is to follow, Baran claimed that actual economic surpluses had been the by-product of all socio-economic formations, with differences in the structure and size of the surplus, depending on the level of development of the formation in question. Also noteworthy is that surplus, 'a central idea in Baran's treatment of imperialism', is more a classical economics concept rather than a Marxian one (Howard and King 1992: 169).

The *potential* economic surplus was 'the difference between the output that *could* be produced in a given natural and technological environment with the help of employable productive resources, and what might be regarded as essential consumption' (Baran 1976: 133 emphasis in original). It would appear that the concept of the *potential* economic surplus was used by Baran to highlight the possibility of the transcendence of the capitalist social order, via the rational planning and control of the *potential* economic surplus. Under monopoly capitalism there existed a 'discrepancy between [the] technical potential and the actual realised benefits, limited by the restricted purchasing powers of workers, wasteful consumption by the idle rich, unproductive activities, and the inefficiencies wrought by monopoly' (Freeman 1996).

According to Alan Freeman, it is possible to discern two main problems from an economic theory standpoint, with the combined work of Baran and Sweezy in *Monopoly Capital*. The first problem is:

> the shifting of attention from the profit rate to the magnitude of profit and reformulating this magnitude as an ill-defined 'physical surplus' instead of surplus *labour*, [which] quietly set aside the prospect of an endogenous process through which a decline in the profit rate provoked by a rise in the organic composition of capital, could provoke an internal crisis (Freeman 1996).

The reason for dropping or ignoring the tendency of the rate of profit to fall as one of the possible causes of crisis within capitalism perhaps can be found in the historical context within which both Baran and Sweezy wrote. When they wrote there was a post-war boom in capitalism, which seemed to preclude declining profit rates, even crises; what seemingly remained to be theorised by Marxists in this 'golden age of capitalism', suggested Freeman, were problems of realisation and the rational use of resources (Freeman 1996).

The second problem with *Monopoly Capital* was that, by establishing monopoly as the primary focus, it bypasses the question of whether the capitalist market system could sustain indefinite growth (Freeman 1996). Both shortcomings identified by Freeman had as their basis a predilection shared by Baran and Sweezy for reforming or sidestepping vital components of Marxist political economy, such as the tendency of the rate of profit to fall and the inevitability of capitalist crises. When they wrote during the 'Long Boom' of post-war capitalism, it is plausible that rather than argue about capitalist crises, which appeared to have been overcome, the case for socialism was best argued for on the basis of the potentially more rational direction of the economy.

Having established that these three economic concepts employed by Sweezy and Baran were indeed problematic, there remains the question of how one of these particular concepts influenced our two writers' views on imperialism. According to their claims about the economic surpluses of advanced capitalist countries, Baran and Sweezy suggest that the economic surplus only could be absorbed in general in three ways: '(1) it can be consumed, (2) it can be invested, and (3) it can be wasted' (Baran and Sweezy 1968: 87). A large part of *Monopoly Capital* looks at how the economic surplus of the US was absorbed. One of the favoured means of surplus absorption was through the associated phenomena of militarism and imperialism.

Militarism, imperialism and surplus absorption in *Monopoly Capital*

Chapter Seven of *Monopoly Capital* – the only chapter in the book concerned with imperialism – starts by posing the question of why the US oligarchy felt the need to maintain a huge military machine, when, in the past, a substantially smaller military had sufficed (Baran and Sweezy 1968: 178). What followed was an extensive analysis of militarism under conditions of monopoly capitalism and specifically US militarism. There was little attempt made by the authors to explicitly connect militarism and imperialism (what was used in the opening part of the chapter was the term empire, with imperialism rating a mention in a footnote or two throughout the chapter as a whole), and nor did they undertake any definitional work regarding imperialism.

Reference was made to Lenin's brief definition of imperialism being the monopoly stage of capitalism (Baran and Sweezy 1968: 17), and Lenin was lauded for having attempted to move Marxian theory on from its superseded involvement with the competitive model that informed Marx's economic theory. Both Baran and Sweezy, however, claimed Lenin and those writing after him had failed to pay enough attention to monopoly and its impact upon capitalist economies (Baran and Sweezy 1968: 18). Baran and Sweezy set about redressing this perceived lacunae together. Their intent was clear; monopoly capitalism, its contradictions and consequences, was their primary concern. This was reflected in their treatment of imperialism, which almost disappeared from their work – either subsumed under monopoly capitalism or militarism.

Baran and Sweezy provide an overview of the structure of 'the hierarchy of nations that {made} up the capitalist system' (Baran and Sweezy 1968: 179). This structure of states was characterised as essentially exploitative with those states at the top of the hierarchy exploiting to varying degrees those in the lower layers, with the pattern cascading down through the layers. The least powerful states were unable to exploit other states:

> Thus we have a network of antagonistic relations pitting exploiters against exploited and rival exploiters against each other. Disregarding juridical categories, we can call those at or near the top of the hierarchy 'metropolises' and those at or near the bottom 'colonies'. The sphere of exploitation of a given metropolis, from which rivals are more or less effectively excluded, is its 'empire' ... Now it is obvious that all nations – except the dependent and defenceless ones at the bottom – have a need for armed force to maintain and if possible improve their positions in the exploitative hierarchy. How much a given nation needs at a given time depends on its position in the hierarchy and on the pattern of relations in the hierarchy as a whole at that particular time (Baran and Sweezy 1968: 179–80).

Changes that characterised the US drive for expansion and empire have been noted. The new approach to empire, called neo-colonialism, was attributable to the US's own experience as a former colony. Consequently, the US relied on indirect forms of exploitation rather than direct political and economic control as per the European colonies (Baran and Sweezy 1968: 182). Here the engagement with imperialism in the book, indirect as it was, concluded.

Connections between absorption of surplus, militarism and imperialism were not really explored. This gets down to the issue of the economic surplus, which shifted the principal contradictions of capitalism from the production process, with its relations of production, to the realm of markets, exchange and trade. The fundamental problem for Baran's and Sweezy's position on capitalism was not the *production* but the *realisation* of the surplus, and by extension 'the utilisation of the surplus [which generated] such obnoxious items as advertising, government expansion, armaments, imperialism and war' (Mattick 1978: 192, 195).

Baran and Sweezy, according to Paul Mattick, were not employing a Marxian analysis of capitalism whether in its competitive or monopolistic phases, in their insistence on the substitution of surplus for surplus value. In Baran's and Sweezy's endeavour to reconfigure or renew Marx's analysis of capitalism in the era of monopoly capitalism, they made the assertion that Marx had written before monopolisation had transformed capitalism, thus rendering his analysis obsolete. This meant for Baran and Sweezy that the laws Marx had identified (such as the tendency of the rate of profit to fall and the labour theory of value, with its associated concept of surplus value) were in need of rejuvenation or rejection. A serious error:

> By treating surplus-value as 'surplus', Baran and Sweezy manage to look upon capitalism as if it were something other than itself. 'The size of the surplus,' they write, 'is an index of productivity and wealth, of how much freedom a society has to accomplish whatever goals it may set for itself' ... This is to see society in the abstract, not as a specific society; at any rate, not as a capitalist society (Mattick 1978: 203).

The problem identified by Mattick concerning the substitution of surplus for surplus value, was that a less concise formulation took the place of a still valid Marxian concept. In the process Baran and Sweezy dropped terms such as value and surplus value and took up 'the amalgam national income, the concept of "effective demand", and the Keynesian remedies for capital stagnation' (Mattick 1978: 191–2). Mentioned above was Baran's recognition that surpluses, or to be precise *actual* surpluses, were the by-product of all socio-economic formations (Baran 1976: 133). What needed to be ascertained by Baran and Sweezy was how, why and where the surpluses in the historically specific socio-economic formation of capitalism were generated.

Surplus *value*, generated in the production process, was and is pivotal to capitalism be it competitive or monopolistic. Baran and Sweezy made a terminological and categorical modification with their substitution of surplus for surplus value and suggested that *realisation* –that is, market relations – were where the principal contradictions of monopoly capitalism lay. In the process they gradually managed to shift attention: away from production relations, or class struggle; away from the production process; away from problems of profitability and the associated tendency of the rate of profit to fall; away from the internal contradictions of capitalism necessarily leading to crises; away from issues such as the export of *capital*; and, finally, away from the classical Marxist notion of imperialism being intimately connected to capitalism. What happened with Baran's and Sweezy's analysis of capitalism, monopoly capitalism and imperialism was that by importing neo-classical and Keynesian concepts into their analyses, such as the surplus, and dropping key elements of Marxist political economy their theorising of capitalism and imperialism became less rigorous and more problematic. This culminated in *Monopoly Capital* (1968) where imperialism and its connection with capitalism (or even monopoly capitalism) was not explored in any depth and the term imperialism itself featured only as a footnote in the chapter ostensibly concerned with that subject. By dropping or sidestepping certain Marxist political economic categories and concepts, Baran and Sweezy were compelled to focus on what they considered was the more important configuration of monopoly capitalism, rather than say imperialism being a stage of capitalism. The consequences for their theorising of imperialism were profound culminating in the virtual disappearance of the latter from their analysis.

Conclusion

Throughout this chapter, three key works by Paul Baran and Paul Sweezy have been critically reviewed. Their theorising of imperialism shifted away from the 'pioneers' (particularly the classical Marxist theories). The trajectory of their theorising of imperialism outlined here portended a trend that some neo-Marxists followed, namely the dissipation of interest in the subject and consequent decline in the quality of theorising associated with imperialism. Notwithstanding this, through their work they helped to draw attention to the effects of imperialism on the undeveloped world and suggested that stagnation, not development, was the necessary consequence of monopoly capitalism/imperialism. This line of thinking helped re-kindle interest in Marxism and spawned spirited debates amongst interested observers, activists and intellectuals. Furthermore, their work formed the embarkation point for a number of subsequent neo-Marxists, the so-called dependency theorists. The work of one of the latter, Andre Gunder Frank, is the subject of analysis in the following chapter.

CHAPTER 4

ANDRE GUNDER FRANK

UNDERDEVELOPMENT, DEPENDENCY AND DISENCHANTMENT

Introduction

Andre Gunder Frank was one of the first theorists to seriously take up Sweezy's and Baran's hypothesis that capitalism caused stagnation as opposed to development. Gunder Frank was one of a group of writers who subscribed to what have been called 'dependency theories'. Dependency theories posited the capitalist world system as being divided into a centre and a periphery – core and periphery, or metropolis and satellites, are other terms used – with the centre, that is the advanced capitalist states developing at the expense of the periphery (less developed or underdeveloped states, or neo-colonies) (Brewer 1990: 161). The peripheral nation-states remained dependent for any economic development on the advanced capitalist nations at the centre or core. Gunder Frank put forward a Metropolis-Satellite model to explain the dependent position of much of the Third World and Latin America in particular. Over the course of his life's work, Gunder Frank's theoretical interests encompassed not only the dependent status of Latin America, but also he sought, along with Immanuel Wallerstein and others, to situate political and economic problems of development in a long-term, holistic framework – what became known as World Systems theory. His writing in the last years of his life saw him more concerned with the 'Eurocentric' bias of much of Western historiography and social theory. Consequently, he shifted his theoretical position away from Wallerstein's position and also Marxian analysis overall. Three distinct phases can be identified in Gunder Frank's writing: first, an early phase that saw him employ Marxist concepts such as imperialism to explore and explain the dependence of the Third World; a second phase characterised by a shared commitment with Wallerstein and others to the analysis of the social, political and economic connections between regions over long time frames – World Systems theory; and, finally, a third phase that emerged from reservations he had developed about World Systems theory, Marxism and Western social theory in general.

This chapter argues that Gunder Frank's early work concentrating on the dependence of Latin America on the European and US metropolises helped bring concepts of dependency and underdevelopment to the fore of imperialism theory. Gunder Frank's theorising of imperialism built on and extended Sweezy's and Baran's claims about stagnation and underdevelopment being the outcome for the economies of the less developed countries. For Gunder Frank, underdevelopment was the necessary result of integration in the capitalist world economy. He advanced this thesis to counter two views of development. One view which he opposed came from mainstream theories of economic development and industrialisation. The other viewpoint was the orthodoxy emanating from Latin American communist parties, which was that Latin America had to progress from so-called feudal relations of production, through the stage of capitalism and thence to socialism (Gunder Frank 2000a:189). This 'stagist' version of development generated considerable argument and discussion, with dependency theory being one response. In turn, dependency theory came in for criticism regarding its relationship with imperialism theory in particular and Marxism in general (Chilcote 1982: 3–15; Howard and King 1992: 168–9, 175–6).

An essential element of Gunder Frank's early writing was his use of the concept of economic surplus, which he borrowed from Sweezy and Baran. Underdevelopment was caused by metropolitan countries siphoning off the surpluses of colonies, former colonies and less developed countries. The problem was that surplus extraction had been a feature of the economic relationships between European powers and peripheral regions since the start of the colonial era. In his reliance on economic surplus as a central element of his theory of underdevelopment and economic dependency, a problem arose in how Gunder Frank theorised imperialism, colonialism, mercantilism and capitalism. He could not clearly define any of these terms, nor could he clearly establish what the relationship was between capitalism and imperialism.

Unlike Sweezy and Baran, by the end of his life Gunder Frank had become disenchanted with much of Marxist thought and Western social theory. This was largely due to his immersion in questions of macro-historical systemic change. An argument made towards the end of the chapter is that Gunder Frank's second and third phases of writing saw him not only drop imperialism theory but also Marxism. This disenchantment with Western social theory, and Marxism in particular, was informed by Gunder Frank's concerns about the origins of capitalism and 'Eurocentrism'.

The first section of this chapter gives a brief overview of the genesis of dependency/development theories and their historical background. Gunder Frank's early work on imperialism is the subject of the next section. The third section provides a brief exposition of Gunder Frank's understanding of economic surplus and Ernesto Laclau's critique of Gunder Frank's use of the concept. The chapter then explores Gunder Frank's involvement with World Systems theory before the final section reviews Gunder Frank's later writings. It is in his later works that Gunder Frank's disenchantment with the 'Eurocentric' bias of imperialism theory, Marxism and Western social theory becomes manifest.

Dependency theory: theoretical and historical context

Those intellectuals and activists who shared concerns about the lack of social, political and economic development of the peripheral countries, due to the latter's integration into the global capitalist system, sought a theoretical framework that explained that lack of development. They also sought a political strategy for extricating Third World nations from this situation. Dependency theory challenged the modernisation model that suggested countries in the Third World should emulate the developed countries of the West in their 'take-off' to industrialisation. According to Bjorn Hettne, the dependency school:

> emerged from the convergence of two major intellectual trends: one with its background in the Marxist tradition, which in turn contained several theoretical orientations, i.e. classical Marxism, Marxism-Leninism, neo-Marxism; the other rooted in the Latin American structuralist discussion on development which ultimately formed the CEPAL tradition (Hettne 1995: 88).

The CEPAL tradition (the Economic Commission for Latin America – CEPAL in Spanish) was informed by the strategies adopted by various Latin American countries to deal with the consequences of depression during the 1930s. The two major intellectual figures associated with CEPAL were Raul Prebisch and Celso Furtado, whose works on Latin America linked structuralism and dependency theory (Hettne 1995: 91). CEPAL doctrine contradicted the notion that trade benefited both the advanced countries as well as those less advanced, and put forward the proposition, using the centre-periphery model, that trade favoured the centre at the expense of the peripheral countries. CEPAL promoted economic nationalism through import substitution as a step towards industrialisation, along with state intervention and planning (Hettne 1995: 92). During the 1950s and 1960s, the 'reformist structuralism' of CEPAL became the accepted development strategy of many Latin American countries. This development strategy was an attempt to realign the history of Latin America's distorted economic development 'with a standard model of capitalist development through Keynesian forms of intervention' (Henfrey 1982: 17).

The CEPAL strategy came up against obstructions to its implementation. Consequently it was found to be inadequate, prompting a number of 'elaborations on the dependency approach, which resulted in a variety of "dependency schools", some of them continuations of the old CEPAL strategy, others more oriented towards Marxism of some kind' (Hettne 1995: 93). Reaching its zenith during the 1970s, dependency theory was part of the stimulus for the New International Economic Order (NIEO) (Hettne 1995: 103). By the late 1970s, it was clear that a number of Third World countries definitely had taken the path to industrialisation, thereby 'contradicting a generally held view that their development was blocked'. The credibility of the dependency paradigm had evaporated (Hettne 1995: 99).

With the demise of the dependency paradigm, new approaches dealing with the problems of the Third World's underdevelopment came to the fore. World Systems theory grew out of the dependency paradigm, but differed from it in not offering up a programme for development at all. This can be attributed to its more holistic, structuralist approach whereby the 'system' makes it very difficult for Third World countries to break the bonds of dependency and embark on internally generated development. The capitalist world system is quite constraining: 'there are indeed "limited possibilities of transformation within the capitalist world economy"' (Wallerstein cited in Hettne 1995: 142). World Systems theory took off in the late 1970s with the publication of Wallerstein's book and attracted the interest of theorists such as Gunder Frank, who had seen the writing on the wall for dependency theory.

Gunder Frank's first phase of writing: imperialism as underdevelopment

Gunder Frank, born in Berlin in 1929, was a prominent academic whose life was marked by constant travel. He left Germany with his parents when Hitler came to power, and four decades later he fled Chile after Pinochet's coup in 1973. He died in 2005 at seventy-six years of age. In one of his early essays on underdevelopment written in 1963 (but not published until 1975), Gunder Frank provided a sketch of the development-underdevelopment nexus. He argued that underdevelopment should be understood as not just lack of development but as a form of negative development of the countries of the periphery. That is, industrialisation and the capitalist accumulation process of advanced nations in Western Europe were predicated on the extraction of surplus from regions such as Latin America. Europe could *not* have developed without surplus extraction from the satellites. This surplus extraction had been the pattern since the incorporation of Latin America into the Spanish and Portuguese empires. By denying satellite countries access to their own surpluses, metropolitan powers ensured the social, political and economic dependence of the Third World (Gunder Frank 1971: 33).

The essence of Gunder Frank's theoretical enterprise in the early phase of his writing is that underdevelopment of the peripheral countries was the necessary antithesis of the development of Europe and the US. There was a 'matrix of zero-sum relations, in which the wealth of the metropoles is a direct function of surplus extraction from the satellites' (Howard and King 1992: 177). This was the key to understanding capitalism, colonialism and imperialism for Gunder Frank. It was in this early essay that Gunder Frank first elaborated on the key theme of the development of underdevelopment, which was to be a staple of his writing through the 1960s and into the 1970s (Gunder Frank 2000a: 190).

What is clear from this essay (and applies to other works in this early phase of Gunder Frank's writing) is the minimal attention he gave to defining terms such as imperialism, colonialism, capitalism and mercantilism. For Gunder Frank, history showed that 'mercantilism, capitalism, colonialism, and imperialism are inextricably intertwined ... {with} capitalism/imperialism ... never ceas{ing} to exploit the underdeveloped periphery to the benefit of the developed metropole' (Gunder Frank 1975: 72). Regarding imperialism proper, Gunder Frank states that:

> 'imperialism' must be understood not as the empire of some particular country but essentially as a certain kind of relation between the metropole or its members and the periphery. That is the way Lenin understood the term and, that is the way Marx and Smith and probably Petty before him understood the analogous concept (Gunder Frank 1975: 56).

It also was claimed by Gunder Frank that the term 'imperialism' was of 'relatively recent currency', having first been made popular by Hobson, Lenin and Bukharin. Their understanding of the term, according to Gunder Frank, encompassed 'certain world-wide relations of the end of the 19th and the beginning of the 20th centuries, a time of colonial expansion by the industrialized or industrializing metropole' (Gunder Frank 1975: 56). Gunder Frank asserted that, after Hobson, Lenin and Bukharin, imperialism was deemed to include relations such as those between the US and Latin America and the Near East where a formal colonial relationship did not exist. Imperialism, in other words, had changed some of its political forms; neo-colonialism becoming a favoured political approach, especially with the US. Gunder Frank also claimed that imperialism was used as a form of shorthand for contemporary capitalism (Gunder Frank 1975: 56). Also evident here was the minimal analysis of the political elements of imperialism, a feature of much of Gunder Frank's work on imperialism.

Gunder Frank's disinclination to provide much in the way of definitions can be traced through his subsequent work on underdevelopment. The rationale was that, for the underdeveloped countries of the periphery, the phenomena of mercantilism, colonialism, capitalism and imperialism meant basically the same thing – exploitation, lack of development and backwardness despite the changes in form between mercantilism, colonialism, capitalism and imperialism (Gunder Frank 1975: 72). In the Cold War era, with the emergence of a new 'American-style' form of imperialism, he stated that:

> Though differing in technical detail from its forerunners, it remains, especially for the underdeveloped world, essentially the same as all previous forms of capitalism-colonialism-imperialism: the source and systemization of exploitation and underdevelopment (Gunder Frank 1975: 61).

In *Capitalism and Underdevelopment in Latin America* (1971), Gunder Frank describes the various eras of capital accumulation and underdevelopment through which Europe and Latin America had gone: 'The colonial era of capitalist development' was when Europe started the process of capital accumulation. Gunder Frank claimed that Europe did not have reserves of capital and labour to embark on the process of capital accumulation. The initial capital, therefore:

> had to come from the work and the foreign finance of the Indians of Latin America and the Negroes of Africa, which cost these regions first the decimation of up to eight ninths of the population (in Mexico), then the destruction of several civilizations, and finally resulted in permanent underdevelopment (Gunder Frank 1971: 310).

This Spanish–American bonanza was indirectly the basis of the financing of the colonial economies of the Portuguese in Brazil and the subsequent Dutch, English and French incursions into the Caribbean (Gunder Frank 1971: 310). The early colonial relationship that Europe had with the Americas set in place the usurpation of Latin America's surplus to the detriment of that part of the world and the benefit of the metropolitan countries. Trade and finance were the principal mechanisms by which this surplus was extracted and underdevelopment engendered. Another consequence of these trade and financial arrangements was the establishment of political, economic and social structures of underdevelopment in the colonies. This process channelled investment into mining, agricultural and commercial concerns aimed at exporting to the metropolis. Most of the balance of the investment went to luxury importation from the metropolitan centre. Minimal investment was directed to the production and consumption associated with the domestic markets (Gunder Frank 1971: 312).

The imperialist era followed the colonial era. Gunder Frank claimed that 'new imperialist investment finance' quickly interposed or insinuated itself into the Latin American milieu, supplanting or superseding the old modes of finance. The reasons for this change, and how this differed from the previous mode of finance coming from the metropolitan countries, were not teased out. Drawing on Luxemburg's example of European usurpation of Egypt, Gunder Frank stated that imperialism went further in Latin America: 'It not only availed itself of the state to invade agriculture; it took over nearly all economic and political institutions to incorporate the entire economy into the imperialist system' (Gunder Frank 1971: 323). Gunder Frank did not delineate the social, political and economic differences between the colonial and imperialist eras.

Qualitative changes to the world capitalist system had occurred during the years of World War II. There had been a change of the metropolitan centre from Europe to the US, and, moreover, there had been a transformation from 'what had been industrial and then financial capitalism into monopoly capitalism' (Gunder Frank 1971: 324). First appearing in the US but also eventually in Europe and Japan as well was the:

> nationally-based but world embracing and really international giant monopoly corporation, which is a multi-industry, mass assembly-line producer of standardized products – and now of new technology as well – [which was ...] its own worldwide purchasing agent, salesman, financier, and often de facto government in many satellite countries and increasingly in many metropolitan ones as well' (Gunder Frank 1971: 324).

During the 1930s, the corporate state was the logical extension of this form of corporation and in the 1960s what he called the 'warfare state' functioned in that role. New instruments of foreign investment and finance were summoned by the needs of monopoly corporations and the metropolitan state, which were more important than foreign trade in retarding Latin America's development. All of these changes in the world capitalist system could only mean that imperialism had been transformed into neo-imperialism (Gunder Frank 1971: 324–5).

Gunder Frank's inclination to be inconsistent in his use of terms complicated his analysis of the three eras – colonial, imperialist and neo-imperialist. In one instance, he uses the terms neo-imperialism and monopoly capitalist development as separate entities when describing the underdevelopment process in Latin America, whereas two pages beforehand he had unified them as neo-imperialist monopoly capitalism (Gunder Frank 1971: 341, 343). Having established that underdevelopment was the key to Gunder Frank's early phase writing and that there were problems regarding his lack of rigour in defining terms central to his analysis, the focus now shifts to Gunder Frank's engagement with economic surplus. His proposition that Latin America had been integrated into the capitalist world economy since the sixteenth century, and his use of economic surplus, were subjected to strong criticism.

Economic surplus, Latin America and the world capitalist system since the sixteenth century

Economic surplus, a formative element of both development and underdevelopment, concerns 'the actual or potential excess of a social unit's production over its necessary consumption which may or may not be exploited or invested' (Gunder Frank 1975: 11). Economic surplus formed the basis for one of the three contradictions that lay at the heart of capitalist development and underdevelopment. The first was 'the contradiction of expropriation/appropriation of economic surplus' (Gunder Frank 1971: 30). Marx, according to Gunder Frank, had 'identified and emphasized the expropriation of the surplus value created by producers and its appropriation by capitalists' (Gunder Frank 1971: 30). Gunder Frank discerned a direct connection between surplus value and Baran's economic surplus. The connection between the two concepts was established by positing the *actual* surplus (which was part of the current production that was saved and invested) as being a subset or component of surplus value (Gunder Frank 1971: 30). The *potential* surplus was what could have been available to a society for investment if it had not been stymied by the monopoly structure of advanced capitalist countries. Gunder Frank, then, seemingly contradicts himself by suggesting that, though the monopoly structure of capitalist society prevented the production of *potential* surplus, whatever was produced nonetheless was 'appropriated and wasted through luxury consumption' (Gunder Frank 1971: 30–1).

Even so, for Gunder Frank economic surplus was a crucial element in the production and maintenance of economic domination and subordination, and, by extension, a system of states arranged hierarchically with dominant states forming the metropolitan powers and subordinate states their satellites. This last issue – the system of states and its attendant relations – was the second of the contradictions Gunder Frank associated with the development-underdevelopment nexus, which he termed 'the contradiction of metropolis–satellite polarization' (Gunder Frank 1971: 32). Economic surplus was expropriated by the metropolis and used for its own economic development as the:

> satellites remain underdeveloped for lack of access to their own surplus and as a consequence of the same polarization and exploitative contradictions which the metropolis introduces and maintains in the satellite's domestic economic structure. The combination of these contradictions, once firmly implanted, reinforces the processes of development in the increasingly dominant metropolis and underdevelopment in the ever more dependent satellites until they are resolved through the abandonment of capitalism by one or both interdependent parts (Gunder Frank 1971: 33).

The process of surplus extraction had spanned centuries in the case of Latin America. By virtue of participation in the world capitalist system through the stages of mercantilism, free trade and imperialism, Latin American countries had been incorporated into the 'monopolistic metropolis-satellite structure' of world capitalism. From the sixteenth century onwards, this process served to 'suck capital or economic surplus out of ... satellites and to channel part of this surplus to the world metropolis of which all are satellites' (Gunder Frank 1969: 6–7). As has been established in the discussion of Baran's and Sweezy's use of surplus in the previous chapter, surpluses have been the by-product of all socio-economic formations. By using this economic concept, the specific features of the political economic relationships between the metropolises and satellites through the colonial, mercantile, capitalist and imperialist eras could not be clearly drawn in Gunder Frank's analyses.

Criticisms have been made by Laclau that Gunder Frank tended to blur or run together different historical epochs and thus economic, social and political conditions. Laclau argues that Gunder Frank's work is undermined by a fundamental misunderstanding of the specificity of the capitalist mode of production and its attendant relations of production. Gunder Frank associated capitalism with previous political economic formations in too sweeping a fashion. Whilst it can be argued from a Marxist perspective that, indeed, capitalism and previous social and political economic structures were class-based and predicated on exploitation of some sort, each epoch had its specific forms of exploitation. According to Laclau, Gunder Frank's statement that 'capitalism's essential internal contradiction between the exploiting and the exploited appears within nations no less than between them' can be taken as being the closest Gunder Frank came to defining capitalism (Gunder Frank cited in Laclau 1979: 22). Such imprecision, which is so symptomatic of Gunder Frank's work, was too broad a definition of capitalism. Laclau further states: 'This lack of rigour in determining the object of his analysis is, moreover, only one example of the conceptual imprecision from which all of Gunder Frank's work suffers' (Laclau 1979: 22). A corollary of this imprecision is the assumption that Gunder Frank appears to make that European expansion from the sixteenth century onwards was necessarily capitalist because merchant's capital (mercantilism) was involved.

Telling, for Laclau, is that Gunder Frank (and other neo-Marxists) privilege the distribution process (markets), or what Laclau calls the 'field of circulation', rather than the production process with its attendant production relations, which apparently is where the contradictions of capitalism begin (Laclau 1979: 34). The shifting of the principal contradictions of capitalism from the production process to the arena of distribution (or markets) was the focus for much criticism that came Gunder Frank's way.

Despite attracting quite a bit of criticism, for some time Gunder Frank continued to employ a neo-Marxist analysis of imperialism, centring his investigations firmly in the Third World and Latin America in particular. His writing during the 1960s and 1970s often was polemical yet empirically rich, concurrently shaping and reflecting the upsurge in revolutionary sentiment felt in many quarters. Gunder Frank's construction of his underdevelopment thesis, whilst subjected to much criticism, was a significant contribution to discourse on dependency. Gunder Frank became synonymous with dependency theory and he has been referred to as the 'historian of the stagnation model' (Henfrey 1982: 22, 33). He established a reputation for being critical of Marxist orthodoxy and mainstream economic thinking, and for putting himself at some risk by actually going to Latin America to work there (he fled Pinochet's Chile, for instance). There is no question that, during this early phase, Gunder Frank was an ardent supporter of Latin American attempts to seek alternate routes to development, preferably through socialism. By the late 1970s, Gunder Frank himself regarded dependency theory as discredited after the crisis that heralded the end of the Long Boom of post-war capitalism. Abandoning dependency theory, Gunder Frank gravitated towards a more global approach to analysing the world economy and its attendant social and political systems.

Gunder Frank's second phase of theoretical writing

According to Gunder Frank, his writing during the 1960s and 1970s tended to converge towards the concepts and themes that exercised the minds of Immanuel Wallerstein and others such as Terence Hopkins, Giovanni Arrighi and Samir Amin. The principal concern of these writers was the unravelling of the intricacies of global capitalism, not so much on the basis of individual capitalist nations but rather as a systemic whole, hence the label World Systems theory. Gunder Frank stated that he had started to push for investigation into the 'world system' in the mid 1960s and produced a paper in 1970 with the aim to develop a 'theory ... adequate to encompass the structure and development of the capitalist system on an integrated worlds [sic] scale' (Gunder Frank

2000b: 217). Prior to his exile from Chile, he received a copy of Wallerstein's *Modern World-System* (Wallerstein 1974) and he recognised the parallel concerns, concepts and themes that both he and Wallerstein were intent on pursuing (Gunder Frank 2000b: 217–18).

Both Wallerstein and Gunder Frank had been pre-occupied by the origins of the world capitalist system 'from its origins in Europe between 1450 and 1500 and its spread from its West European' centre and its incorporation of the rest of the world into its social, political and economic networks (Gunder Frank 2000b: 218). Although there were differences in their emphases, Gunder Frank felt that throughout the 1970s and 1980s his and Wallerstein's theorising was intertwined. Gunder Frank was influenced by Wallerstein's resurrection of a little known Soviet economist's hypothesis about large scale cycles in capitalism. The Kondratieff cycles – which purport to show the appearance of long waves or cycles in capitalism since its inception, with periods of growth, stagnation and decline – have been at the core of Wallerstein's World Systems theory and became part of Gunder Frank's work, too. Gunder Frank and Amin, jointly and individually in works undertaken through the 1970s and 1980s, were concerned with the political and other ramifications consequent upon the Kondratieff cycles (Gunder Frank 2000b: 219).

Other commonalities in Wallerstein's and Gunder Frank's work are the focus on centre-periphery relations plus a shared interest in East-West European relations. The major difference in Gunder Frank's mind, especially in the earlier stage of their intellectual coming together, concerned Wallerstein's:

> more detailed focus on the core/periphery/semi-periphery structure of the system as compared to my attempt to identify the cyclical dynamics of the system, especially how the recurrent long economic crises of capital accumulation modified the geographic and economic structure of the world capitalist system (Gunder Frank 2000b: 218).

By the late 1980s to early 1990s, Gunder Frank's position on the capitalist world system started to diverge from Wallerstein's. A fundamental characteristic of Wallerstein's theorising was that the capitalist world system was finite and would be replaced by some other 'system'. Gunder Frank took a more jaundiced view because he saw 'less evidence [of] any such ... "systemic" transformation'. Also, Gunder Frank questioned the defining features of capitalism that Wallerstein had identified (which firmly fixed its origins in Europe). Gunder Frank argued that the features Wallerstein had put forward not only could have been found elsewhere in the world but also prior to when Wallerstein suggested that they came into existence: 'Therefore it could not be true that the [modern World System] was born and bred in Europe, and there is nothing distinctive about "capitalism" and even less about "feudalism" and "socialism"' (Gunder Frank 2000b: 221).

Another problem for Gunder Frank was the 'Eurocentricity' of Wallerstein's position. Gunder Frank (and some of his colleagues) claimed no special place for the capitalist mode of production. Gunder Frank and Gills asserted that their world system which extended back five thousand years had existed independently of and prior to 'any mode of production or combination thereof, be they supposedly feudal or other tributary, capitalist or socialist' (Gunder Frank and Gills 1993a: xx–xxi). This was, indeed, a major theoretical claim by Gunder Frank and his new collaborator. To suggest that this world system existed independently of any mode of production, and that capitalism, feudalism and socialism were not distinctive, reveals how far he had departed from any semblance of a Marxist critique of social structures, societies and political economies by the 1990s. In addition, throughout this second phase of Gunder Frank's writing a concern that he had shown when investigating the consequences for Latin American development of the latter's involvement with mercantilism, colonialism and imperialism was of secondary importance. Analysis of the political and economic aspects of imperialism did not figure highly in this phase of Gunder Frank's writing.

Gunder Frank's later work: disenchantment with Marxism and Western social theory

Gunder Frank's third phase of work can be said to start with the publication of *The World System: Five Hundred Years or Five Thousand* (Gunder Frank and Gills 1993a). This book, which he co-edited with Barry Gills, contains a chapter of Gunder Frank's called 'Transitional ideological modes: feudalism, capitalism, socialism' (Gunder Frank

1993a). In it Gunder Frank detailed his newfound concerns about Wallerstein's World Systems theory and particularly the problems he believed were to be found throughout Wallerstein's work on world systems (Gunder Frank 1993a: 200–17). There is no explicit mention of imperialism in this chapter. In fact, chapters that Gunder Frank wrote in conjunction with Gills contain only brief mentions of imperialism and these refer specifically to ancient empires including Persia, Rome and Assyria, or in terms of how 'imperialism' was a more efficient method of what they termed state accumulation (Gills and Gunder Frank 1993: 89, 99). Gunder Frank and Gills ostensibly aimed to 'retain and seek to refine the basic perspective of *historical materialism*, which of course was neither original nor exclusive to Marx' (Gunder Frank and Gills 1993b: 301 emphasis in original). In the process of refining historical materialism, they obscured the important economic category of capital and its dominance of specific economies by suggesting that capital and capital accumulation took place in epochs prior to the rise of capitalism in Western Europe. Aspects of this proposition are in accord with orthodox Marxist political economy. Marx had identified the appearance of capital in the form of usurers' capital (interest bearing capital) as well as 'its twin brother, merchant's capital' long before the capitalist mode of production and 'in the most diverse socio-economic formations' (Marx 1981: 728).

What is not in accord with an orthodox Marxist viewpoint is Gunder Frank's and Gills's suggestion that, because capital had been identified in earlier socio-economic formations, it was impossible to speak about the rise of capitalism in Western Europe and its expansion throughout the rest of the world from the 1500s or the 1800s. Clearly this strikes at the heart of the assumptions made by Marx through to the classical Marxist theorists of imperialism, namely that capitalism (which, according to writers like Lenin, in its monopoly phase becomes imperialism) had its origins in Europe and then spread to the rest of the world. The problem with Gunder Frank's and Gills's proposition is that, whilst Marx had acknowledged that capital had appeared in places prior to the late eighteenth and early nineteenth centuries, Marx stated that capital did not dominate the mode of production in these previous eras. Capital, put another way, only becomes the dominant feature of a specific, and thus historical, mode of production, namely capitalism (for the treatment of the antediluvian forms of capital see Marx 1981: 728–48).

The Gunder Frank and Gills proposition, if correct, had important implications for the conceptualisation of capitalism and previous socio-economic formations and also for imperialism. If, as they suggest, capital is not unique to capitalism and capitalism thereby loses its distinctive character compared to previous socio-economic formations, then the link classical Marxist writers made between capitalism and imperialism in the twentieth century is rendered largely invalid. This would help explain the disappearance of imperialism from Gunder Frank's writing over time. As noted throughout this review of Gunder Frank's work, he exhibited a strong tendency not to clearly define some of the major concepts with which he worked, leading to difficulties in how he theorised capitalism, monopoly capitalism and imperialism. One way to resolve such difficulties is to abandon the concepts, deny their importance or modify them, a combination of which seems to have transpired in this later work of Gunder Frank.

Another contention by these two writers was that political economists and historians had placed too much emphasis on the distinction, or 'analytical separation', between agrarian and industrial modes of accumulation. At first glance, this admonition seems reasonable. Yet, as Eric Hobsbawm observes, the significance of the Industrial Revolution could not be diminished: 'some time in the 1780s, and for the first time in human history, the shackles were taken off the productive power of human societies, which henceforth became capable of the constant, rapid and . . . [seemingly] limitless multiplication of men, goods and services' (Hobsbawm 1977: 43). This was in no uncertain terms a remarkable breakthrough: 'No previous society had been able to break through the ceiling which a pre-industrial social structure, defective science and technology, and consequently periodic breakdown, famine and death, imposed on production' (Hobsbawm 1977: 43). A question that springs to mind is why would Gunder Frank (and Gills) feel the need to blur over the distinctive differences between the agrarian and industrial eras? The answer can be found in the interests that Gunder Frank pursued in this latter period of his writing and especially in his last major book published a few years before his death *ReORIENT Global Economy in the Asian Age* (Gunder Frank 1998).

In *ReORIENT* Gunder Frank seeks to address the 'Eurocentric' assumptions that bedevilled much Western social theory. He felt that so many scholars had succumbed to the notion of European exceptionalism – how Europe seemingly was the foundation of the world economy and around which the rest of the world orbited – resulting in profoundly flawed social theory. As a consequence, 'the architects of our social theory ... Marx, Weber, Werner Sombart, Karl Polanyi, and others, as well as Braudel and Wallerstein [and Gunder Frank included his own earlier work here] ... (mis)-attributed a central place in their theories to Europe, which it never had in the real world economy' (Gunder Frank 1998: xxv).

The Marxist fixation with modes of production not only was unilinear and too simplistic, but the notion 'mode of production' is deeply flawed. Marx's designation of pre-capitalist Asian economies as being of the despotic Asiatic mode of production drew Gunder Frank's ire (Gunder Frank 1998: 14–15). There were so many problems, not only with Marx but also with numbers of other theorists that writing on social theory, world history and the world economy had to be re-cast in the light of greater awareness of the role that Asia had played and would continue to play in the global economy.

Missing from the book was any attempt to theorise imperialism because, for Gunder Frank, this was part of the problem that too many social theorists had and still have with their non-holistic focus on Europe. Lenin, stated Gunder Frank, therefore was wrong regarding imperialism being a stage of capitalism because he assumed that it was an outgrowth, a development that had originated in Europe and had spread outwards from there (Gunder Frank 1998: 18). The obscuring of the distinction between the agrarian and industrial eras as well as the problematising of capitalism, imperialism, 'Eurocentric' social theory, and modes of production and so on can be attributed to Gunder Frank's disenchantment with Marxism, and much Western scholarship in general.

Further discussion of Gunder Frank's last major work need not be undertaken here. What we can see from the above analysis is a progressive moving away from any Marxist theorising on imperialism, and as is evident in his last book an almost total disenchantment with Marxist theorising at all. In the last years of his life Gunder Frank was immersed in what he called macro-history, what he thought was a more holistic approach to world economy and world systems that generated much in the way of sweeping claims about world history, trade, and connectedness between the world's regions but very little on the analysis of imperialism.

Conclusion: Gunder Frank's writing on imperialism

In Gunder Frank's first phase writing, colonialism, mercantilism, imperialism, monopoly capitalism and underdevelopment were prominent (albeit for the first four of these concepts rather poorly defined). He suggested that imperialism could be described as being specific relations between metropoles and satellites, with capitalism, colonialism and imperialism giving the same results for the satellites – exploitation, lack of development and backwardness. Hence Gunder Frank's somewhat casual approach to defining capitalism, colonialism and imperialism; no matter what the form, the result was the same. Additionally, the economic surplus, which was a key element in Baran's and Sweezy's theorising, featured prominently in Gunder Frank's first phase writing. The use of the economic surplus by Gunder Frank also contributed to the haziness of his understanding and depictions of capitalism and its relationship with imperialism. Ultimately, Gunder Frank did not provide a sophisticated analysis of the social, political and economic dynamics of capitalist imperialism.

Gunder Frank's second phase writing was deeply involved with World Systems theory. The examination of the complexities of the world capitalist system as *system* was the goal of much of the research that emanated from the group of writers working within this 'school'. Centre-periphery or metropolis-satellite relations were of particular concern for both Gunder Frank and Wallerstein, who relied on the long wave or cyclical theory of Kondratieff that purportedly identifies phases of capitalist growth, stagnation and decline over an extended time frame. By the late 1980s to early 1990s, Gunder Frank had diverged from Wallerstein on the grounds of scepticism about the defining features of capitalism and its origins in Europe, plus scepticism about the prospect of systemic change (that is, the transition from capitalism to a post-capitalist world).

Gunder Frank's concerns about aspects of Wallerstein's theorising was the harbinger of a wider disbelief in and disenchantment with Marxism, historical materialism and, by extension, Marxist theories of imperialism. This disenchantment culminates in his *ReORIENT* where Western social theory is deemed to be compromised, due to its 'Eurocentricity'. It is fair to conclude that, by this last phase of his writing, Gunder Frank had ceased to write about imperialism because he was disillusioned with Marxism and had decided that there was nothing distinctive about capitalism. He left these problems behind to pursue a more macro-historical approach to global economy. His specific interest being the role that Asia had played in the world economy in the past and how it would once again become an economic centre on the global stage.

In the next chapter, Wallerstein's approach to imperialism is subjected to critical review. Wallerstein, unlike Gunder Frank, continued to assert that capitalism was distinctive and that the appearance of capitalism on the world stage heralded a qualitatively new era in the world's political economic systems.

CHAPTER 5

IMMANUEL WALLERSTEIN AND THE MODERN WORLD SYSTEM

HEGEMONY AND THE LONG WAVE CYCLES OF CAPITALISM

Introduction

Wallerstein's prodigious writing on what he called the 'modern World System', unlike dependency theory, continues to arouse interest and feature in academic discourse. Compared with Gunder Frank, Wallerstein did not abandon the belief that capitalism was distinctly important and continued to play a key role in the shaping of the global economy and global politics. Wallerstein's theorising has been influential across the social sciences, though he tended to skirt the issue of imperialism. He preferred to view questions of political and economic preponderance through the prism of hegemony rather than imperialism. One reason for subjecting some of Wallerstein's writing on World Systems theory to scrutiny is that it grew out of the anti-systemic movements of the 1960s and 1970s, which were significantly informed by imperialism theory. Furthermore, although imperialism was not central to his theoretical concerns, Wallerstein conceded that it had been and was an inherent part of the modern World System. An aim of Wallerstein's remains the unravelling of core, periphery and semi-periphery relationships in order to inform the struggle for the building of a post-capitalist world system. The three-tiered structure of states, or 'tri-modal hierarchy of the world capitalist economy' (Howard and King

1992: 178), is Wallerstein's modification of the neo-Marxist standard bifurcation of states. Wallerstein is closely associated with neo-Marxist approaches to the theorising of imperialism.

Adopting a long-term approach in his theoretical work based on Fernand Braudel's *la longue durée* historiographical method (Howard and King 1992: 178), Wallerstein was especially interested in the rise and decline of hegemonic powers. Another important element in Wallerstein's World Systems theory – Kondratieff cycles – postulate alternating phases of expansion and contraction in capitalist economies over forty-five to sixty year time frames. The emphasis Wallerstein places on the long-term (*longue durée*) is matched by his emphasis on the global rather than on smaller units of analysis such as nation-states. Such emphases on the long-term and the global means that Wallerstein tended to overlook those qualitative changes to capitalism that occurred in the late nineteenth and early twentieth century identified by the 'pioneers of imperialism theory'.

This chapter argues that Wallerstein's macro-level analysis led him to minimise the role of imperialism in his theorising. In the grand sweep of world history and the world economy, imperialism, for Wallerstein, like globalisation, perhaps is merely a 'momentary expression of reality' reified into a fashionable theory (Wallerstein 2000: xviii–xix). According to Wallerstein, problems associated with 'stages' of development when not viewed from a broader World Systems perspective make certain analyses – modernisation theory and some Marxist theorising, for example – untenable. Wallerstein claims that this was a unit of analysis problem, with writers mistakenly focusing on parts of the totality (such as nation-states) and neglecting the wider systemic structure (Wallerstein 1980: 3–10). On this basis it would be reasonable to maintain that Lenin's observation of imperialism as the highest stage of capitalism did not interest Wallerstein, because such an assertion is a generalisation, abstracted from the changes to specific national economies. What is clear is that Wallerstein's minimal engagement with imperialism and imperialism theory is in keeping with the diffusion of interest in imperialism common to the neo-Marxists whose writing has been critically analysed thus far.

As Wallerstein has been so prolific, it is beyond the scope of this chapter to critically analyse all his works in depth. Choice selections, then, are taken from his work in order to illustrate the major elements of his meta-theory. These include volume one of *The Modern World-System* (Wallerstein 1974), a collection of essays titled *The Capitalist World-Economy* (1980a), another collection of his essays called *The Essential Wallerstein* (2000) and *The Decline of American Power* (2003). Prior to examining the relevant sections of Wallerstein's work, the first section of this chapter provides a brief summary of the historical and theoretical context out of which Wallerstein's World Systems theory emerged. The chapter then outlines the most salient aspects of Wallerstein's World Systems theory before presenting an overview of his three-tiered system of states. The next section examines how labour is divided between the core, semiperipheral and peripheral regions and the type of labour control that was typical of each region. World-empire, hegemony and hegemonic cycles are the subjects of the fifth section. Here it is discussed how Wallerstein recognised that imperialism has a role in the modern World System, yet he preferred to use hegemony to map out the dynamics of the geopolitics of the modern era. The sixth section considers the connections that Wallerstein made between his notion of hegemonic cycles and Kondratieff's long wave economic cycles. On the basis of the marriage between these long-term views, Wallerstein predicted that the US was in a period of hegemonic decline and the modern World System was in transition. Finally, it is argued that Wallerstein's macro-historical and large unit of analysis approach precludes him from substantive engagement with imperialism theory before some concluding remarks summarise what has been covered.

Historical and theoretical context of Wallerstein's work

World Systems theory grew out of the ferment of the 1960s and 1970s. Its genesis was so similar to dependency theory that Brewer positions Wallerstein within 'the dependency tradition' (Brewer 1990: 162). With the demise of dependency theory brought about by the ending of the Long Boom in the 1970s, some writers sought a theoretical framework that encompassed a more holistic approach. Gunder Frank, for instance, had been exploring a world systems approach of his own. What appealed to him and others was Wallerstein's elaboration of World Systems theory in his major work from 1974, *The Modern World-System Volume 1*. This book appeared when there was a 'peak of intellectual, political and academic interest in international power and exploitation' (Friedman

1996: 320). With the Vietnam War ending, and calls emanating from the Third World for the restructuring of the world's economic order (the New International Economic Order), there was a shift from military conflict between East and West to North-South economic confrontation (Friedman 1996: 320–1). In addition, as William Martin suggests, there was a flourishing of academic work on international issues:

> with one group of scholars seeking to advance 'political order in changing societies' from Vietnam to South Africa, while others attacked such programs through critiques of Euro-American modernization theory and inconclusive attempts to theorize post World [War] II imperialism (Martin 2000: 239).

Wallerstein has suggested that writers such as Raul Prebisch, Celso Furtado and Gunder Frank, who were opposed to the modernisation paradigm and also the rigid Marxist formulation of stages of political economic development (rendered usually as primitive communism-slavery-feudalism-capitalism), could be designated as having adopted a 'world-system perspective' (Wallerstein 1980a: 53). For Wallerstein, then, there is little substantial difference between those writers who wrote from a dependency or underdevelopment perspective and his own world-system perspective.

Wallerstein, the capitalist world economy and the World System

The publication of the first book in his highly influential trilogy *The Modern World-System 1: Capitalist Agriculture and the European World Economy in the Sixteenth Century* (1974), established Wallerstein's reputation as an important theorist operating in the Marxian tradition. Born in New York in 1930, he had first-hand experience of African politics as a Ford Foundation scholar in Africa in the 1950s. His experiences there convinced him that 'the most important thing happening in the twentieth century was the struggle to overcome the control by the West of the rest of the world' (Wallerstein 2000: xvi–xvii).

A central concept to Wallerstein's analysis is the world system. A world system fundamentally is a social system. In Wallerstein's purview, the set of social systems have been comprised of 'mini-systems' (local economies), 'world-empires' and 'world-economies' culminating in the era of the capitalist world economy in the capitalist world system or what he calls the 'modern World System'. One of the defining characteristics of a world system is the division of labour, whereby the provisioning of needs can be met through exchange. Whereas world systems can incorporate multiple cultural systems, they do not necessarily have to take in the whole globe (though, arguably, the capitalist world system must). The capitalist world system is a world economy 'without a single, central authority' (Wallerstein cited in Brewer 1990: 176).

Materialising in the late fifteenth and early sixteenth century, a cornerstone of the modern is 'a European world-economy' (Wallerstein 1974: 15). This world economy was not an empire as such, for empires are largely political units. Wallerstein claims that within its bounds the 'European world-economy' encompassed empires, city-states and nation-states. The world economy did not necessarily take in the entire globe, but nonetheless could be deemed to be a 'world' economy because it was 'larger than any juridically-defined political unit' (Wallerstein 1974: 15). Its main linkages were economic, hence world *economy*, with secondary linkages found in the realms of culture and political arrangements 'and even confederal structures' (Wallerstein 1974: 15).

Wallerstein utilises Shmuel Eisenstadt's definition of empire for purposes of clarification. In 1968, Eisenstadt claimed that empires are political systems that contain widespread albeit relatively highly centralised territories with an autonomous centre (in the sense of both the political institutions and in the person of the emperor), unified often by a universal political and cultural orientation (Eisenstadt cited in Wallerstein 1974: 15). Empires had been a common attribute of the world's history for 5,000 years. Part of the strength of an empire is its ability to guarantee economic flows from the periphery to the centre through such forceful mechanisms as tribute (Wallerstein 1974: 15). One common weakness is the siphoning of too much profit by the enlargement of bureaucracy, a consequence of empire maintenance and administration. In addition, empires by their very nature are repressive and exploitative, which in turn leads to increased military expenditure in order to ensure that power remains centralised.

A number of world economies that had existed subsequently transformed into empires in China, Persia and Rome. The capitalist world economy, then, was not a feature, though it differed from previous versions in that it had not given rise to a unified political structure, that is, an empire. Capitalism was more efficient in appropriating surpluses compared to previous forms of a world economy (Wallerstein 1974: 16). Integral to this efficiency was the ability of the capitalist world economy to use the political process to secure what Wallerstein termed monopoly rights. For Wallerstein this means that:

> The state becomes less the central economic enterprise than the means of assuring certain terms of trade in other economic transactions. In this way the operation of the market (not the *free* operation but nonetheless its operation) creates incentives to increased productivity and all the consequent accompaniment of modern economic development (Wallerstein 1974: 16 emphasis in original).

From its inception in the sixteenth century, the state played a vital role in the development and maintenance of the capitalist world economy. For Wallerstein, a bifurcation exists between the economic and the political in the capitalist world economy, with economic decisions 'oriented primarily to the arena of the world-economy, while political decisions are oriented primarily to the smaller structures that have legal control, the states... within the world-economy' (Wallerstein 1974: 67).

Wallerstein's claim for the sixteenth century being the dawn of the capitalist world economy is based on Marx. In *Capital Volume 1*, the capitalist system emerged with the birth of world-embracing commerce and a world-embracing market (Wallerstein 1974: 77). Elsewhere in *Capital Volume 1* Marx was more circumspect about the emergence of capitalism in the sixteenth century, claiming that it was in the 1500s that 'the modern history of capital starts to unfold' (Marx 1976: 247). He also noted that as early as the fourteenth or fifteenth centuries capitalist production had taken place in various Italian cities, but had not developed any further (Marx 1976: 876). With such apparent hedging by Marx, it is no surprise that claims made about the emergence of capitalism and the capitalist world economy in the sixteenth century have been disputed. Wallerstein himself makes the term 'sixteenth century' somewhat rubbery. On the basis of Braudel's work he argues that 'for the European world-economy as a whole... 1450–1640 [was] the meaningful time unit, during which was created a capitalist world-economy' (Wallerstein 1974: 68).

Here is just one of the challenges associated with taking such a long-term or macro-historical view of the development of global capitalism. The problem concerns the establishment of so-called turning points or transitions in historical structures. Another problem associated with the macro-historical approach is that the structures being analysed take on almost monolithic qualities, where the subjects of history seem to be merely passive observers of the rise and decline of world-economies, empires and hegemonic powers. This is especially true for Wallerstein's World Systems theory, leading Jan Nederveen Pieterse to remark that Wallerstein's 'reification of "the system"... [leads to the positioning of] only one historical subject in this world view: the world system' (Pieterse 1988: 260). Peter Worsley holds much the same view, suggesting that Wallerstein's model of the world capitalist economy:

> is a model which emphasises the capacity of the ruling classes to manipulate the system, and others in it, as they wish, whilst underplaying resistance to their domination. 'The system', at times, is as endowed with a logic, power and even quasi-personality as it is in that other major variant of Marxist system-theory, Althusserianism. But systems do not take decisions. Ruling classes do. They try to run the system in their own interests. In this, overall, they succeed – by definition, otherwise they wouldn't continue to rule. But those they rule also try to maximise their interests. Such models therefore underestimate agency, especially resistance to domination (Worsley 1980: 305).

As Brewer observes, Wallerstein's propensity to provide 'a mass of detailed historical material that often seems to have little connection with his overall generalizations' (Brewer 1990: 178) only serves to compound the overemphasis on structure or 'the system'. Nonetheless, although not problem-free Wallerstein's research on the modern World System has produced tangible insights into the totalising tendencies of global capitalism, the complexities of global politics, the role of the state and, the nature of US hegemony. The distinguishing feature of Wallerstein's impressive catalogue of work is his emphasis on scale: in covering empires, world economies and hegemonic powers, his time continuum spans several centuries. Wallerstein generally has eschewed smaller-scale analysis. Nation-states, for example, are subsumed in the three-tiered state system.

Core, periphery and semi-periphery: the three-tiered state system

There are, according to Wallerstein's conceptual framework, 'three zones of the world-economy ... the semiperiphery, the core, and the periphery' (Wallerstein 1974: 63). The formation of the world economy was predicated on three essential factors: first, the expansion of Europe, initiated by Portugal; second, advances in the methods and techniques of labour control both for the various zones of the world economy and for diverse products; and, finally, 'the creation of relatively strong state machineries in what would become the core-states of this capitalist world-economy' (Wallerstein 1974: 38).

Since the advent of the capitalist world economy in the sixteenth century, 'the core and the periphery [did not exist as] two separate "economies" with two separate "laws" but one capitalist economic system with different *sectors* performing different functions' (Wallerstein 1980a: 68 emphasis in original). Through a series of fortunate accidents during the 1500s, Wallerstein suggests, Northwest Europe became the core area of the world economy 'specializing in agricultural production of higher skill levels, which favoured ... tenancy and wage labor as the modes of labor control' (Wallerstein 1980a: 18). The peripheral areas at this time were Eastern Europe and the Western Hemisphere, whose specialisations were 'the export of grains, bullion, wood, cotton, sugar – all of which favored the use of slavery and coerced cash crop labor as the modes of labor control' (Wallerstein 1980a: 18).

Core areas had strong state mechanisms. One consequence of such state strength was that it gave rise to 'unequal exchange' where the strong core states were able to appropriate the surplus of the whole world economy, which helped to maintain their positions as core states relative to the peripheral zones (Wallerstein 1980a: 18–19). The relationship of superordination and subordination between the core and the periphery remained in place from the period of agricultural capitalism through to the stage of industrial capitalism (Wallerstein 1980a: 19).

The third zone – the semi-periphery – acted and continues to act as the stabiliser of the world economy. Discontent that potentially could emanate from unified peripheral states – aggrieved at the privileges and power enjoyed by core states – can be dissipated (Wallerstein 1980a: 23). Opportunities to move from the lowest of the three tiers to the semi-periphery, combined with the concentration of military power in the dominant states and the 'pervasiveness of an ideological commitment to the system as a whole', helped ensure the relative political stability of world systems (Wallerstein 1980a: 22).

Division of labour and modes of labour control

This three-tiered structure, for so long a part of world history, also had and continues to have 'an extensive division of labor' (Wallerstein 1974: 349). The division of labour was not only functional (occupational) but geographical, too, with economic tasks unevenly spread throughout the world system. Such an uneven spread of tasks can be attributed in part to ecological factors, but mainly can be explained by how work is organised, which 'magnifies and legitimizes the ability of some groups within the system to exploit the labor of others, that is to receive a larger share of the surplus' (Wallerstein 1974: 349).

The division of labour within the capitalist world system has not been static. During the epoch of industrial capitalism, for example, Britain changed its division of labour, from agricultural exporter to the role of 'workshop of the world'. Some of the then semi-peripheral countries – France, Germany (Prussia), Belgium and the US, with fledgling manufacturing bases of their own – sought to deprive Britain of outlets for its manufactured goods. The ensuing tension in the world system motivated, in part, the partitioning of Africa and a reallocation of the division of labour. For the core areas in this period, the new role in industrial manufacture became the provisioning of machines that made the manufactures and infrastructure such as railroads (Wallerstein 1980a: 29–30).

From the combination of productive activities and exchanges that have taken place within and between world systems over the epochs, Wallerstein identifies two main types of exchanges: essential exchanges; and luxury exchanges. Regarding luxury items or 'preciosities', Wallerstein makes it clear that in such exchanges importers reap not merely profits but windfalls (Wallerstein 1980a: 14). An important distinction for Wallerstein, due to his understanding of capitalism, has as one of its key premises the centrality of exchange: 'the essential feature of a capitalist world economy ... is production for sale in a market in which the object is to realize the maximum profit' (Wallerstein 1980a: 15).

Modes of labour control supplement the division of labour. Forms of labour control have varied, and some that Wallerstein identifies include slavery, serfdom, wage labour and self-employment. Differing types of labour control have featured in different zones of the world economy. Slavery and 'feudalism' were prominent in the periphery, with wage labour and self-employment concentrated in the core areas, whereas share-cropping was the favoured form of labour control in the semi-periphery. In turn, the predominant modes of labour control in the three zones of the world economy have 'greatly affect[ed] the political system [s] (in particular the strength of the state apparatus)' in the various zones throughout history (Wallerstein 1974: 87). Furthermore, the world economy was predicated on the core, periphery and semi-periphery having divergent *dominant* forms of labour control and, by extension, differing levels of productivity. Without the different types of labour control and differing levels of productivity, the flow of surplus would not have been sufficient to have established the capitalist system (Wallerstein 1974: 87).

For some critics like Worsley, Wallerstein's analysis of the division of labour and modes of labour control do not present a clearer understanding of exploitation. Wallerstein, whilst acknowledging the differences in the forms of labour and the forms of labour control over the long-term (as well as the different ideological devices used to legitimate said labour control), nonetheless flattened out the distinctions between these social relationships. There was a reduction to the level of exploitation-in-general discernible in Wallerstein's analysis, which, analogously at the 'system level, would be simply to treat capitalism, feudalism, slavery, etc. as variants of class society'. Worsley insists that these social forms are, indeed, class-based, 'but the analytical problems we face require going beyond this level of abstraction to the specific properties of each *type* of social relationship and institution' (Worsley 1980: 305 emphasis in original).

Worsley, moreover, considers Wallerstein's analysis of modes of labour control and the division of labour problematic not only because it reduces the differences between social relationships and modes of production (social epochs), but also due to the way it privileges the role of exchange (Worsley, 1980: 304). As discussed in the previous chapter, this echoes the emphasis Gunder Frank places on exchange (that is, market relations or trade).

Wallerstein's definition of capitalism as the production for sale in the market for maximum profit, privileging exchange or trade, coupled with his prioritising of the division of labour, precluded a deeper understanding of the historically specific form of capitalism. As Brenner notes, trade – or what he terms commercial relations – and the consequent divisions of labour had been a feature of history for millennia (Brenner 1977: 40). Like Gunder Frank, Wallerstein's perspective of what really drives capitalist expansion and the consequent social, political and economic relationships between the core and the periphery privileges the surface phenomenon of trade. The essence of capitalism – the dynamics of the production process – is not covered in their work.

World empire, hegemony and hegemonic cycles

Wallerstein uses the category of world empire within the political realm of World Systems theorising to denote the complete political dominance of one particular (usually centralised) regime over other regions or territories. World empires had existed prior to the appearance of the nation-state. In a 1980 essay on the rise and future demise of capitalism, Wallerstein stated that the nineteenth-century British and French empires were distinctly different empires from what had gone before; they were 'nation-states with colonial appendages' and not world empires (Wallerstein 1980a: 6). The distinction here is important because political entities such as empires, city-states and nation-states, for Wallerstein, are subsumed within a world economy, but the appearance of the nation-state was intimately bound up with the appearance of the capitalist world economy only. The development of the capitalist world economy during the long sixteenth century actually limited the potential for further world empires to materialise. Through techniques and technology the capitalist world economy has been able to 'thrive, produce and expand without the emergence of a unified political structure' and furthermore:

> What capitalism does is offer an alternative and more lucrative source of surplus appropriation (at least more lucrative over a long run). An empire is a mechanism for collecting tribute ... In a capitalist world-economy, political energy is used to secure monopoly rights (or as near to it as can be achieved). The state becomes less the central economic enterprise than the means of assuring certain terms of trade in other economic transactions. In this way the operation of the market (not the *free* operation but nonetheless its operation) creates incentives to increased productivity and all the consequent accompaniment of modern economic development (Wallerstein 1974: 16 emphasis in original).

The advent and expansion of the capitalist world economy meant that the social, political and, moreover, the economic conditions that formed the bases of world empires were supplanted. Taking the place of the old-style imperial power was the new hegemonic power. Imperialism, though, was and is a characteristic feature of the modern World System:

> The reality of the modern world-system, the capitalist world-economy, is that it is a hierarchical, unequal, polarizing system, whose political structure is that of an interstate system in which some states are manifestly stronger than others. In furtherance of the process of the endless accumulation of capital, stronger states are constantly imposing their will on weaker states, to the degree that they can. This is called imperialism, and is inherent in the structure of the world- system (Wallerstein 2003: 131).

Yet, even though Wallerstein acknowledged imperialism as a seemingly permanent feature of the modern World System with strong states imposing their will on weaker states due to the accumulation process of capital, he nonetheless did not theorise explicitly about imperialism, nor did he make much more than minimal use of the concept, preferring instead to use hegemony.

Hegemony exists at one end of a continuum 'which describes the rivalry relations of great powers to each other' (Wallerstein 2003: 255). The relationships are such that one of a great power has a preponderance of power and thus can set the rules in the political, economic, military, diplomatic and cultural arenas (Wallerstein, 2000: 255). A key difference between hegemony and world empire hinges on the extent of power, with a hegemon in the modern World System constrained by the interstate system. Sovereign states that form the network that is the interstate system, each pursuing their interests, act to constrain and curtail any one state from establishing total political sway (Wallerstein 2003: 254). The balance of power thus precludes the growth of world empire.

On the basis of a hegemonic cycle of ascendancy, consolidation and decline (a cycle which is of comparatively brief duration), Wallerstein confidently asserts that the US, having lost its productive edge but not its commercial and financial superiorities nor its political and military advantages, nonetheless is experiencing a period of hegemonic decline. He argues that this has been the case since the ending of the post-war Long Boom of capitalism since the late 1960s to the mid 1970s. Wallerstein maintains that, despite the collapse of the Soviet Union and the ending of the Cold War in favour of the West and especially the hegemonic US, the decline phase of the hegemonic cycle dictates that the modern World System is in a period of transition (Wallerstein 2003: 45–6).

Wallerstein's engagement with hegemony, hegemonic cycles and world empire covers the geopolitical and global economic terrain that classical Marxists took as the starting point for their investigations into imperialism. Wallerstein acknowledges that imperialism had a role in the world system. He saw imperialism as the imposition of the will of the stronger states on the weaker states, a process stemming from the capitalist accumulation process. Along with imperialism, another feature of the modern World System was the hegemonic power of the US. Unfortunately, the connections between imperialism and hegemonic power were not drawn out by Wallerstein. Imperialism, it would appear, was shelved by Wallerstein in favour of the grander concept of hegemony.

Kondratieff and Wallerstein: proponents of long-term patterns

According to Richard Day, in the English-speaking world Joseph Schumpeter's book *Business Cycles* first drew attention to the fifty-year cycles that a little known Soviet economist called Nikolai Kondratieff (or Kondratiev) had claimed were statistically verifiable. Day claims that Kondratieff first broached long cycles when his book (in Russian) called *The World Economy and its Conjunctures During and After the War* was published in 1922 (Day 1976: 67). The book was a tentative historical generalisation that sought to explain the crises and equilibriums that were characteristics of capitalism (Day 1976: 68). Kondratieff's initial findings based on his analysis of prices going back to the late 1780s contended that there had been two completed waves or cycles of approximately fifty years in duration. The third cycle started with the expanding phase taking in the period 1896 to 1920 (Day 1976: 68). The 1920s financial crises, then, were just the start of a declining wave during which a new equilibrium would be established.

Kondratieff modified aspects of his long wave cycles in response to criticism, but essentially they remained fixed at approximately fifty years with alternating phases of expansion and decline or stagnation. In Wallerstein's hands, the Kondratieff cycles have a duration of forty-five to sixty years. The phases of expansion are deemed to be A-phases, where there is innovation, investment and expansion, whereas the declining phases become B-phases, characterised by the purging of 'inefficient producers and lines of production' (Wallerstein 2000: 218).

Wallerstein makes a connection between Kondratieff cycles and hegemonic cycles, a connection mediated through longer term phases called 'logistics'. The details need not concern us; it suffices to say that for each period of hegemonic ascendancy and decline in the modern World System there has been a corresponding pattern played out in the world economy, observable in the Kondratieff A- and B-phases. For Wallerstein, then, patterns found in the political structure of the modern World System – hegemonic cycles of ascendancy and decline – are matched by the patterns of the Kondratieff A- and B-phases. Thus, the modern World System is an entity that displays autonomy from external forces, which is to say that 'its patterns are explicable largely in terms of its internal dynamics' (Wallerstein 2003: 253).

Kondratieff cycles were criticised by Trotsky in the 1920s. Trotsky asserted that Kondratieff assumed that it was an internal regulator that determined capitalist development. The contrary was the case, argued

Trotsky, with external conditions such as the incorporation of new countries and continents and wars and revolutions determining expansion or stagnation in capitalist development (Day 1976: 71). Patterns that Wallerstein detects in the modern World System are predicated on his privileging of structure at the expense of agency combined with a privileging of the internal dynamics of a system over and above external factors. Additionally, Wallerstein insists on viewing developments in the modern World System by using a long-term perspective, with the primary focus remaining fixed on the system as a whole rather than on individual units such as nation-states. Consequently, aspects of Marxist writing on global capitalism and geopolitics such as imperialism were not important to Wallerstein because they fell outside his unit of analysis – the system as a whole.

Wallerstein's missing element: imperialism theory

As has been made clear in the preceding engagement with the central components of Wallerstein's World Systems theory, there is very little in his work that can be said to explore in any depth the connections between global capitalism and imperialism. For Wallerstein, capitalism is best described as production for sale in the market for maximum profit, with a trade-based division of labour as a corollary. The emphasis on trade allied with the three-tiered structure that forms the basis of the inter-state system (core, periphery and semi-periphery) means that, for Wallerstein, surplus extraction by the core states from the periphery and the semi-periphery is the fundamental feature of the capitalist world economy. For critics such as Brenner and Worsley, Wallerstein's understanding of global capitalism has led him to gloss over the differences between social epochs and modes of production. The connection between monopoly capitalism and imperialism (drawn out, for example, in Sweezy's early work and a characteristic of much of the classical Marxist writers) is missing from Wallerstein's work. Wallerstein himself, perhaps, would view such criticism as being misguided for it would be too much of a short term view based on changes within national economies, which he sees as the wrong unit of analysis.

The unit of analysis Wallerstein employs – the system as a whole rather than individual national economies – subsequently has witnessed an eschewal of detailed analysis of those national economies. If compared with the work of Bukharin and Lenin, for example, Wallerstein's critique of capitalism was conducted at a very abstract level. The macro-historical sweep of Wallerstein's writing, and his focus on hegemony, hegemonic cycles and Kondratieff cycles, means that Wallerstein has not felt the need to immerse himself in imperialism theory. He had, after all, constructed a body of theoretical work encompassing impressive sweeps of history, situated the geopolitical within its purview and allowed for general predictions of how the world system would develop over the remaining years of the current Kondratieff B-phase. For Wallerstein, then, to become embroiled in arguments over whether imperialism was the highest stage of capitalism was a unit of analysis error. Imperialism theory, for Wallerstein, simply is a side issue that is not of fundamental importance in understanding the world system and the world economy.

Conclusion

There is no doubt that Wallerstein's broad analysis of the long-term political, social and economic structures of the world grew out of and extended the neo-Marxist involvement with the impact of global capitalism on the Third World. Wallerstein's understanding of what capitalism is and how it works follows on from the market- or trade-based view of global capitalism already seen in the works of the neo-Marxists Baran, Sweezy and Gunder Frank. Like the dependency theorists, Wallerstein sought to understand why the Third World or peripheral countries consistently had been in a position of dependence on or servitude to the core countries over centuries. Wallerstein constructed a comprehensive theoretical world view enabling him to make cogent analyses of the global capitalist economy and geopolitics. Imperialism theory is conspicuously absent from his work, replaced by a highly abstract World Systems theory. The neo-Marxist trend (identified in the later writing of Sweezy, Baran and Gunder Frank) of a decline in interest in theorising imperialism has to be modified when it comes to Wallerstein as he has consistently shown minimal interest in theorising imperialism.

In the next chapter, Samir Amin's interventions in the field of imperialism theory are the subject of analysis. Like Gunder Frank and

Wallerstein, Amin favoured the long-term view and a large-scale unit of analysis – centre and periphery as opposed to the national. There are further similarities in Amin's writing when compared with Gunder Frank and Wallerstein, yet there are important differences, too. Amin, for instance, preferred to use historical materialism as his philosophical framework and utilised classical Marxist themes such as imperialism and the capitalist accumulation process. Nonetheless, Amin's theorising of imperialism fits squarely within the neo-Marxist tradition.

CHAPTER 6

SAMIR AMIN
A BRIDGE FROM NEO-MARXISM TO 'GLOBALISATION-ERA' MARXIST THEORISING

Introduction

In the pantheon of neo-Marxist writers and theoreticians, Samir Amin occupies a distinct position. He has had strong connections with other neo-Marxists, collaborating with the likes of Wallerstein and Gunder Frank. Yet he has established a reputation for investigating and analysing more orthodox Marxist tropes such as the accumulation process, class forces and the capitalist mode of production. From his academic and other positions in Africa, he has been well placed to gauge at first hand the impact of imperialism, globalisation and global capitalism on the peripheral countries. As part of a prolific life, he has written extensively on imperialism and has been a strong critic of 'Eurocentrism' and the current incarnation of imperialism in the guise of globalisation. Amin, in fact, was among the first neo-Marxists to critically examine at some length globalisation and its relationship with global capitalism, capitalist expansion and imperialism. Although he is not opposed to globalisation *in toto*, Amin is opposed to the dominant ideological discourse on globalisation. As an alternative, he advocates a humanist project of globalisation, one with a socialist outlook (Amin 1997b: ix). Some of the results of his critiquing of globalisation anticipated the insights made by a number of the 'globalisation-era' Marxist thinkers. Over the course of five decades of research, analysis and publications, Amin has made important contributions to the body of literature on imperialism. For this reason alone, his writing on imperialism, Eurocentrism and globalisation is deserving of close analysis.

This chapter commences by outlining Amin's understanding of imperialism. In one of his early books he described Lenin's *Imperialism: the Highest Stage of Capitalism* (1973) as a work that defined 'the essentials of the contemporary system' (Amin 1977: 106). Following a similar pattern to Sweezy, Baran and Gunder Frank, Amin's conceptualising of imperialism changed over time. His early books used Lenin's definition of imperialism as a foundation, on top of which he added neo-Marxist concepts such as underdevelopment, the core-periphery stratification of nation-states (centre-periphery is how Amin terms it) and the identification of the working classes of the periphery as the leaders of resistance to imperialism. The left along with the working classes in the West were unable to offer such leadership as they had been compromised by revisionism and a Western-centric ideological outlook, known as 'Eurocentrism'. His later offerings have dropped the reliance on Lenin, with imperialism functioning as shorthand for the exploitation of the periphery by the advanced capitalist states of the centre. Over time, imperialism has become less rigorously defined by Amin. The argument about Amin's conceptualising of imperialism is that the evolution of his understanding of the subject mirrors that of the neo-Marxists Sweezy, Baran and Gunder Frank. Unlike them, though, he did not abandon the concept entirely, instead continuing to use it as part of his ongoing critical responses to contemporary capitalist development, geopolitics and globalisation.

Amin felt the need to take on the assumptions about European cultural, economic and political superiority that lay at the heart of 'Eurocentrism', a concept he identifies as being primarily a 'culturalist phenomenon' (Amin 1989: vii). He unravels the mythical nature of 'Eurocentrism' in order to inform 'correct positive responses', amongst which he suggests is a 'program for the future' addressing 'humanity as a whole' (Amin 1989: xi). This chapter argues that Amin's opposition to 'Eurocentrism' impels him to make a summary dismissal of any hope of leadership in the struggle against imperialism and for the building of future progressive programs from the working classes of the West. This, perhaps, is too jaundiced a view. Amin's engagement with 'Eurocentrism' is scrutinised in the second chapter section. The chapter then explores how Amin handles the complex and ambiguous notion of globalisation. He has risen to the challenge presented by globalisation seeing it not only as the intrinsic expansiveness of capitalism but also a wholly new period of capitalist development. This new period – the age of globalisation – has brought to light a new set of problems centred on the globalised nature of economic management and the continued existence of national political systems. Whilst there is some opacity about how Amin defines globalisation (he refers to it either as capitalist expansiveness or a qualitatively new phase of capitalist development, and even as a euphemism for imperialism), he does outline several of its essential features. His writing on globalisation grapples with some concerns shared by 'globalisation-era' Marxists; he pre-figured some of their claims about it. The argument here is that Amin's work on globalisation establishes him as a bridge between neo-Marxist and 'globalisation-era' Marxist theorising on globalisation and imperialism.

Throughout the 1960s and into the 1970s, many leftists considered the Third World to be the last bastion of revolutionary social transformation. The Western industrial working classes were deemed to be 'a favoured labour aristocracy' and thus 'an enemy of radicalism'. As the promise of 1968 went unfulfilled, the 'future of revolution lay in the... peasant hinterlands of the Third World' (Hobsbawm 1998a: 446–7). Although the Long Boom of capitalism had started to wane prior to the oil crisis of 1973, as eminent Cambridge historian David Reynolds explains this episode proved such a particular shock that 'the cumulative effect of rising inflation [and] falling share values' in combination with mounting oil prices damaged confidence, investment and profits heralding the end of the golden decades of post-war growth (Reynolds 2001: 407). Throughout the 1970s and into the 1980s, a key economic problem was inflation. Keynesianism (and its variants) was replaced by a new economic paradigm labelled neo-liberalism. Aspects of neo-liberalism were first trialled in the financial crisis that confronted New York in the 1970s, and received its big boost in the late 1970s to early 1980s courtesy of the Reagan and Thatcher stewardships in the US and Britain respectively (Henwood 2003: 204–6, 208–9, 219–21). The unrolling of neo-liberalism, the collapse of communism and the hegemony of one nation-state, the US, with a new seemingly irresistible phenomenon in prospect (globalisation) shaped the late 1980s and most of the 1990s. For Amin, who was born in Cairo in 1930 and worked in the country of his birth as well as Mali and Senegal as a committed Marxist intellectual, developments in the second half of the twentieth century provided the backdrop for his contributions on imperialism, the capitalist accumulation process, 'Eurocentrism' and globalisation.

Amin's early views on imperialism: a blend of Lenin and neo-Marxism

Amin's intention in *Accumulation on a World Scale* (1974) was to shed light on the accumulation process of the capitalist world system and to explore the 'relations between the formations of the "developed" or advanced world ... and those of the "underdeveloped" world (the periphery)' (Amin 1974: 3). The capitalist world system establishes and maintains the underdevelopment of peripheral countries for the benefit of the developed countries of the centre. Such a description of the world system is standard neo-Marxist dependency fare. Amin declares that the theory associated with accumulation and the connectedness of countries through networks of finance, commerce and 'other relations' had not been substantially improved 'since Lenin's *Imperialism*' (Amin 1974: 1). Amin's *Accumulation on a World Scale* contributes towards updating and advancing theories surrounding world capitalist accumulation, which had stagnated since Lenin.

Unequal Development (1976) sought to delineate the 'characteristics and dynamic properties of the social formations of peripheral capitalism' (Leaver 1983: 60). What there is of imperialism in the book can be summed up briefly. Imperialism came into being because the 'possibilities of capitalist development on the old basis had been exhausted, through the completion of the first Industrial Revolution in Europe and North America' (Amin 1976: 187). To continue functioning, capitalism needed to incorporate new territories, new markets – in short, it needed to expand. Amin applied Lenin's understanding of the term as his benchmark in this instance. He identifies three expansionist phases of global capitalism: commercial expansionism; imperialism 'in Lenin's sense of the term'; and post-imperialism (Amin, 1976: 191).

Imperialism rates much more highly in *Imperialism and Unequal Development* (1977), where it is elevated to the status of a fundamental question. Here we are told that '[i]mperialism's second crisis, begun a few years ago, is giving new relevance to Lenin's basic conclusions' (Amin 1977: 103). The key elements of Lenin's theorising that continued to have relevance were 'the close relationship between the new hegemony of monopolies, the worldwide expansion of capitalism and colonial oppression, the development of a labor aristocracy in the capitalist center, and the first social democratic revisionism' (Amin 1977: 103). Amin states that, for imperialism, there were two phases of crisis: the first lasted from 1914 to 1945 resulting in the Russian and Chinese revolutions; the second crisis phase presumably had occurred in the 1960s and 1970s.

Unequal development and differential rates of exploitation count amongst the consequences of imperialism. Monopoly capitalism had not only made the export of capital possible on a huge scale, but also it gave momentum to the 'unequal international division of labor', which had the special attribute of differential rates of exploitation of labour (Amin 1977: 107–8). The rates of exploitation differed in two ways: first, the way that workers employed to produce similar goods in the centre and periphery at similar levels of productivity were not paid matching rates (workers in the centre, of course, were paid higher wages); the second occurred in the sectors of production only formally dominated (compared with 'real' domination) by capital, where 'the surplus generated by formerly free producers was appropriated' (Amin 1977: 108).

Such differing rates of exploitation married to a privileged section of the working class in the centre, aided and abetted by revisionism, meant that shifting class alliances and new class struggles on a world scale were the key characteristics of imperialism (Amin 1977: 108). Having established the key characteristics, Amin offered up the principal contradiction of imperialism, which he described as the contradiction 'between monopoly capital and the over-exploited masses of the periphery' (Amin 1977: 108–9). A consequence of this contradiction was the shifting of the centre of gravity of class struggle against capital from the centre to the periphery (Amin 1977: 109). Thus, the agents for emancipation or liberation had become the oppressed peoples of the periphery, led by the working class of the periphery.

Amin defined imperialism as 'the highest phase of capitalism' (Amin 1977: 112). There were two ways that imperialism could be regarded as the ultimate capitalist phase:

> First, the centralization of capital has gone so far that its further development will mean a departure from the capitalist mode of production proper, because the latter implies the fragmentation of control of the means of production, the noncentralization of that control at the state level ... Second, the era of imperialism is already in effect the era of socialist revolutions, that is, the era of the decline of capitalism (Amin 1977: 112).

Such a definition is familiar, being a re-iteration of Lenin's principal argument about the relationship between capitalism and imperialism, with the latter being the necessary outcome of the moribund nature of monopoly capitalism. Amin later added some more phases to the two crisis phases of imperialism mentioned above, citing two expansionist phases of imperialism. The first expansionist phase lasted from 1880 until 1914, and the second phase started in 1945 and finished in 1970. Unequal exchange between metropolitan countries and the periphery counted among the characteristics of the first phase of expansion. Another characteristic, a 'substratum' of the first, was the division of labour between the industrial and agricultural countries. Following on from this division of labour, Amin identifies the peculiarities of agriculture in the periphery – *latifundia*, colonial trade system – as the third characteristic. Making up the fourth characteristic of the first expansionist phase of imperialism is the imperialist class alliances with imperialists and comprador bourgeoisie as well as 'feudalists' on one side and on the other the proletariat, exploited peasantry, petty bourgeoisie and the national bourgeoisie. Finally, the political forms in this phase tended to take the forms of 'direct colonisation, protectorates and semi-protectorates' (Amin 1977: 113–14). From the perspective of the countries of the centre, the first phase of expansion was marked by '(1) national monopolies; (2) "equilibrium" between the great imperialist powers; (3) the formation of a labor aristocracy and of the first revisionism' (Amin 1977: 114).

The primary factor in determining the phases of expansion of imperialism is the efficacy of anti-imperialist struggles. It is a mistake to look for the determining factor(s) in the evolution of capitalism in the centre, because to do so renders one's position as either economistic and/or West-centric (Amin 1977: 113). Class struggle, which at the global level plays out as anti-imperialist struggle, is the key to understanding both the expansion and crisis phases of imperialism. A prime example of this is the anti-imperialist struggles in Vietnam and the Middle East, which played a decisive part in bringing the contradictions of imperialism to a head in the 1960s and 1970s. The first expansion phase of imperialism ended, ushering in the second crisis phase of imperialism. Changes ensued:

> The evolutions in the economy of the center – so-called multinational firms, generalization of the new forms of the absorption of surplus – are responses to these developments of the class struggle throughout the world and not 'autonomous causes' which determine their framework (Amin 1977: 116).

Summing up, there is no doubt that Amin acknowledged Lenin's theory as the foundation for his early forays on imperialism. Also apparent is the core-periphery binary – a familiar neo-Marxist trope – modified slightly by Amin as centre-periphery. There is mention of an 'unequal international division of labour', which has as its basis two different rates of exploitation. Ultimately, the different rates of exploitation helped to establish privileged working classes in the centre through payment of higher wages. When married to the revisionism of the social democratic parties of the advanced capitalist countries, Amin asserts that the challenge to imperialism could only come from the marginalised people in the periphery led by the working class of the periphery.

According to Amin, debate between Marxists about the nature of capitalism and its need for external markets in what he called the first crisis phase of imperialism (1914–45) took place among two groups of economists. These were the right-wing evolutionist revisionist group comprised of Pannekoek, Tugan-Baranovsky, Hilferding and Kautsky, opposed by the left-wing crisis or catastrophe group whose main proponent was Luxemburg. Configuring the debate in these terms allows Amin to make the claim that Lenin's theses on imperialism not only had transcended the pitfalls of 'Eurocentric' economism, but also had prefigured the concerns and concepts of neo-Marxist theories of imperialism (Amin 1977: 110–12). Noteworthy, too, is Amin's reliance on phases or stages of capitalist expansion and imperialism. There are expansionist and crisis phases of imperialism in *Imperialism and Unequal Development*, while three phases of capitalist expansion are identified in

Unequal Development: the commercial expansionism phase; the imperialist phase; and the post-imperialist. Amin has a penchant for incorporating phases in his writing, which, rather than clarifying things, often leads to confusion.

Critical responses to Amin's early theorising of imperialism

Charles Barone acknowledges Amin's ambitious attempt to theorise underdevelopment and imperialism within the 'context of the process of capital accumulation and social/productive relations' (Barone 1982: 18). One of Barone's major criticisms, however, is the eclecticism of Amin's theoretical approach where use is made of Marxist, Keynesian, neo-Ricardian and neo-classical methodologies, making 'it impossible to come up with any internally consistent theory of expansion and imperialism' (Barone 1982: 18). The lack of a consistent theoretical approach, according to Barone, hampers Amin's exposition of capitalist expansion and leads to a composite theory of imperialism. This composite theory is comprised of 'the falling rate of profit, underconsumption, economic crises, unequal exchange, surplus absorption, and the organic composition of labor' (Barone 1982: 16).

Brewer summarises Amin's accounting of the centre-periphery relationship as a 'plausible account of the evolution of a periphery which is integrated, by stages, into a world market, while retaining a distinct wage level, a distinct social structure (persistence of pre-capitalist modes) and a lagging productivity level, at least in some sectors' (Brewer 1990: 195). Brewer categorises Amin's writing as a variant of the dependency approach, which adds sophisticated insights into how the capitalist development of the peripheral countries had been blocked by the capitalist countries of the centre (Brewer 1990: 199). Polychroniou applauds Amin's use of Lenin's analysis of imperialism, his periodisation of imperialism and the influence of classical Marxist imperialism theory, but is more reserved about the neo-Marxist's misplaced emphasis on exchange (Polychroniou 1991: 128, 130).

The periodisation employed by Amin suggests that the capitalist world system is subject to change, and that the peripheral countries performed divergent functions in the system over time. Neo-Marxists, claims Richard Leaver, 'tended to see the world capitalist system in a highly aggregative manner; Frank, for instance ... stress[ed] the continuities of the system as a whole over the particularities of any given situation' (Leaver 1983: 62). Systemic change is a difficulty with which structural approaches such as dependency theory must contend. Amin's use of periodisation, Leaver asserts, makes for a more sophisticated analysis of imperialism when compared with Gunder Frank. Such a positive view of Amin's use of periodisation may have been warranted at the time that Leaver wrote, but Amin has tended to overuse this device with confusing results.

Barone's criticism of the composite nature of Amin's understanding of imperialism highlights the eclecticism of Amin's approach to imperialism theory. Amin's use of Lenin's definition of imperialism as a foundation for his work, upon which other neo-Marxist elements were added such as the centre-periphery relationship, shifting of revolutionary potential to the periphery and surplus extraction, indicate that Amin is not averse to blending elements garnered from different 'schools'. Despite the use of Lenin to provide a shorthand definition, Amin does not really appear to have worked out a clear and coherent definition of imperialism, and nor has he consistently defined its relationship with global capitalism. Over time, imperialism in Amin's hands has shifted from being the highest stage of capitalism to the inherent expansiveness of capitalism (Amin 2001: 6). It is apposite to review a sample of Amin's more recent offerings to follow the trajectory of his views on imperialism.

What changed in Amin's view of imperialism? Some later works

Amin's three books published in the 1970s contain a combination of neo-Marxist and classical Marxist approaches to theorising imperialism. In some of his more current books, he has continued to use imperialism as a conceptual tool. The close reliance on aspects of Lenin's theorising, however, faded away.

In *Eurocentrism* (1989), a book whose primary purpose was to critique the Western-centric ideology of capitalism, Amin gave a warning. By ignoring the centrality of the centre-periphery contradiction, 'the forces of the left and of socialism in the West have finally given up on giving the imperialist dimension of capitalist expansion the central place it must occupy' in critical analysis and strategising (Amin 1989: 141).

Therefore, the left forces in the West have succumbed to two of the essential elements of bourgeois ideology: economism; and 'Eurocentrism'. A further consequence of the embracing of bourgeois ideology by the forces of the left in the West was the disappearance of imperialism from their lexicon:

> The very term imperialism has been placed under prohibition, has been judged to be 'unscientific.' Considerable contortions are required to replace it with a more 'objective' term like 'international capital' or 'transnational capital.' As if the world were fashioned purely by economic laws, expressions of the technical demands of the reproduction of capital. As if the state and politics, diplomacy and armies had disappeared from the scene! Imperialism is precisely an amalgamation of the requirements and laws for the reproduction of capital; the social, national and international alliances that underlie them; and the political strategies employed by these alliances (Amin 1989: 141).

Here in the last sentence is a succinct description of the 'ingredients' of imperialism. That is, imperialism combines geopolitics, diplomacy, military affairs and the laws associated with the reproduction of capital. Such is the extent of the engagement with imperialism in this volume.

The centre-periphery contradiction was central to Amin's interpretation of imperialism and this was the case in *Spectres of Capitalism: A Critique of Current Intellectual Fashions* (1998). After summarising Lenin's theory of imperialism and the generalisations and assumptions that led Lenin to posit the spreading of revolutions from the weakest links to the advanced capitalist countries, Amin argued that the revolutions Lenin had hoped for had started in the East not the West. The spreading of revolution eastwards rather than westwards revealed 'the decisive nature of the polarization between central and peripheral countries produced by the capitalist system' (Amin 1998: 25). Periodisation also is evident in *Spectres of Capitalism*, though the names given to the periods differ in this offering. For instance, the period from 1880 to 1945 is termed the 'monopolistic nationalist liberal phase', whereas the period starting in 1945 and culminating in 1980 is described as the 'social and national post war phase' (Amin 1998: 45). Not only have the names of the periods changed but there is some confusion about what constitutes an important date, given the number of phases of capitalist expansion (three), the number of phases of imperialist expansion and crises (two of each) seen in earlier books. Notwithstanding Leaver's comments about Amin's use of periodisation representing a step-forward from the structuralism of neo-Marxists like Gunder Frank, the lack of consistency in how Amin frames and names the periods or phases confuses matters.

Leaving this problem to one side, during the 'monopolistic nationalist liberal phase' (1880 to 1945) 'imperialism was ... synonymous with conflict among imperialist powers, in the Leninist sense' (Amin 1998: 45). In the following 'social and national post war phase' (1945 to 1980), there was a 'strategic convergence of national imperialisms' over which loomed the hegemonic US. A constraint was placed on imperialism in this post-war phase courtesy of the removal of various nation-states from the imperialist domain, these being the Soviet Union, Eastern Europe and China (Amin 1998: 45). It was during this period that imperialism had to negotiate with the countries of 'real socialism' and the national liberation movements, over the terms that would enable the continued dominance of the centres over the African, Asian and Latin American peripheries (Amin 1998: 45). With the demise of 'really existing socialism' and the collapse of radical populism in the Third World, imperialism once again was on the offensive. In this post-Cold War phase imperialism takes on a new mask: 'the "globalization" thesis proclaimed so arrogantly by the current ideology is nothing but a new way in which the inherently imperialist nature of the system asserts itself' (Amin 1998: 45).

In his examination of US hegemony, the polarisation that was the necessary product of centre-periphery relationships had become synonymous with imperialism (Amin 2006b: 3). More interesting from the viewpoint of the development of Amin's conceptualising are his remarks:

> I am not among those who reserve the term 'imperialist' for types of political behaviour designed to subjugate one nation to another – behaviour that can be found through the successive ages of the human story, associated with various modes of production and social organization. My analytic interest is anyway geared only to the imperialism of modern times, the product of the immanent

> logic of capitalist expansion ... In this sense, imperialism is not a stage of capitalism but the permanent feature of its global expansion (Amin 2006b: 3).

Here Amin is making a definite break with the 'stagist' view of imperialism. The break is further compounded when he suggests that the origins of imperialism date from the sixteenth century (Amin 2006b: 4). To recall, for Lenin imperialism was the highest stage of capitalism and thus historically specific. The years of the late nineteenth and early twentieth century marked the transition to imperialism. The conclusion that can be drawn from following Amin's writing through all the books reviewed is that the dependence he once had on a particular classical Marxist position (Lenin's) to anchor his definition of imperialism, is not observable in his later offerings. Also missing from his recent theorising of imperialism is not only the 'highest stage' proposition but also the insistence that he once had about the centrality of class struggle in the shaping of the expansion and crises phases of imperialism (Amin 1977: 113).

A new configuration of imperialism observable after 1945 was the 'collective imperialism of the "triad" (USA, Europe, Japan) [... which] replaced the multiplicity of imperialisms' (Amin 2006b: 4). The advent of the collective imperialism of the triad was partially determined by the transformation of the competitive conditions of capitalism. Large corporations now regard the global market as their 'first patch' and, if successful, they can go on to assert themselves in their 'home' market. Global presence both conditions and reinforces strength in the national market (Amin 2006b: 4). The dominant segments of transnational capital possess a solidarity based on the acceptance of neo-liberalism, or what Amin calls 'globalized neoliberalism'. The solidarity of the transnational corporations based on neo-liberalism is underpinned by the power of the US state (Amin 2006b: 4). Competition has not been eliminated; for the dominant transnationals the primary site of competitive struggle is the global marketplace. Nor is the triad necessarily a collective of equals. The US does not share its power, rather, according to Amin, it 'seeks to reduce its allies ... to the status of vassals, and is unwilling to allow them minor concessions' (Amin 2006b: 5). Rounding out this conspectus of the collective imperialism of the triad is the positing of four phases of globalisation. Amin's penchant for periodisation and the confusion that arises thereby needs no further comment.

Summarising these relatively recent excursions of Amin's into the field of imperialism theory we find that he provides the 'ingredients' for a definition of imperialism in passing in *Eurocentrism* (though he did not expand upon the characteristics he identified). He adds depth to his analysis in his description of the post-World War II forms of national imperialism and the collective imperialism of the triad. The dominance of the US, the spread of neo-liberalism and its impact and the disappearance of imperialism from the lexicon of the left in the West are noteworthy, too. Amin moved away from his hybrid blend of classical Marxist and neo-Marxist perspectives that featured in his early books, to a position that is best described as distinctly neo-Marxist. That his theoretical position changed over time is understandable and shows that the shifting geopolitical and global economic conditions were reflected in his writing. As Lenin's definition faded from his more recent interpretations, however, the problem of what constitutes imperialism for Amin becomes increasingly apparent. Was it only capitalist expansiveness like globalisation (itself a euphemism for imperialism)? In not having a consistent and comprehensive definition of imperialism, Amin's analysis was confused and confusing.

The trajectory of Amin's thinking on imperialism does not quite fit the pattern of Sweezy's, Baran's, Gunder Frank's or Wallerstein's declining or little interest in the subject. He continued to employ imperialism as part of his critical arsenal, though his later version of imperialism was not well defined, having become synonymous with polarisation, capitalist expansiveness and even globalisation. The blend of Lenin and neo-Marxist tropes that characterised his earlier writing was replaced by a rather opaque neo-Marxist position.

'Eurocentrism' and the corruption of the left in the West

One of the continuities evident in neo-Marxist writing canvassed in this book is the critique of the privileging of European development as harbinger or model for developing countries. From Sweezy and Baran, through to Gunder Frank, Wallerstein and Amin, all these writers sought to correct what they perceived as the fixation on and privileging of European political, economic and cultural development. They showed, *inter alia*, that Europe not only had traded and interacted with other parts of the world for hundreds of years prior to the advent of capitalism, Europe itself had been peripheral to some of the largest empires. Furthermore, they stress that the wealth and resources coming from and connected with the New World and Asia (gold, slavery, sugar, spices) had underpinned much of European development. For these theorists, it also was very important to expose and analyse the negative impacts that the capitalist world system and imperialism had on the underdeveloped countries of the periphery. Gunder Frank directed a considerable amount of his theoretical endeavours towards arguing against 'Eurocentrism'. Gunder Frank, Wallerstein and Amin, when making their respective contributions to world-systems analysis, put the expansion of the capitalist world economy in perspective by insisting on a long-term and global view of political and economic development. At its best, such a long-term view has been able to challenge the issue of European exceptionalism and its potential as developmental model for the rest of the world. The systematic critique and correction of 'Eurocentric' biases and assumptions is one of the undoubted positives to have come out of the neo-Marxist canon.

The cultural basis of 'Eurocentrism'

A determining feature of 'Eurocentrism' is the mythological reconstruction of European history, which addresses, albeit distortedly, real problems and questions that accompanied the advent and expansion of capitalism (Amin 1989: ix). Prior to the Renaissance, Europe was part of a 'regional tributary system' whose members included Arabs, Christians and Muslims. The centre of this regional tributary system was at the Eastern end of the Mediterranean, thus making the rest of Europe at the time the periphery:

> From the Renaissance on, the capitalist world system shifts its center towards the shores of the Atlantic, while the Mediterranean region becomes, in turn, the periphery. The new European culture reconstructs itself around a myth that creates an opposition between an alleged European continuity and the world to the South of the Mediterranean, which forms the new center/periphery boundary. The whole of Eurocentrism lies in this mythic construct (Amin 1989: 10–11).

Having established this mythical historical construct, Amin outlines the consensus of ideas and opinions held by those in the West that rationalised the belief in the innate superiority of Europe and the Europeans. Not only was the West the site of material wealth and power (military might included) it also was the source of rationality, practical efficiency and diversity of opinions as well as being a centre of tolerance, human rights and democracy. Such an amalgam, asserts Amin, added up to Europe being the beacon of hope for the rest of the world. Therefore, 'it becomes impossible to contemplate any other future for the world than its progressive Europeanization' (Amin 1989: 107).

Whilst this picture of 'Eurocentrism' is simplistic, it nonetheless captures the ideological essence of the paradigm. Such is the influence of this paradigm that both the political left and right in the West, even though they hold divergent views on democracy, social justice and economic efficiency and the means necessary to accomplish those ends, wittingly or unwittingly are possessed of 'Eurocentric' assumptions (Amin 1989: 107–8). Such a pessimistic view, especially of the left, unable to rid itself completely of economism and 'Eurocentrism', meant for Amin that Western left and socialist forces were unable to lead the anti-imperialist struggle.

Amin makes strong claims about the corruption of the working classes of the West courtesy of 'Eurocentrism', economism and revisionism. On the face of it, there does not seem to be much potential for a revolutionary upsurge issuing from the working classes in the advanced capitalist countries of the centre. Even so, his jaundiced view led him to dismiss out of hand the working classes of the West. In short, Amin goes too far in his opposition to 'Eurocentrism', succumbing to a 'Periphero-centrism'. A more balanced perspective would have led him to acknowledge that there still existed pockets of resistance to imperialism in the working classes of the centre, or, at least, a dormant potential for fighting for socialism.

Globalisation as capitalist expansion, or imperialism by another name

Globalisation and the strong claims made about its inevitability drew Amin's ire. He wrote *Capitalism in the Age of Globalization* (1997b) as 'a systematic critique of the ruling discourse about the ineluctability of globalization' (Amin 1997b: xii). The central problem of globalisation is polarisation, which concerns the unequal development of peripheral countries compared with the countries of the centre. Globalisation was the expansion of capitalist relations of production and the globalising of these production relations was predicated on and reinforced unequal development. The core nations have greater productive capacity than those of the periphery and are able to invest more and get more in the way of return on their investments compared to peripheral countries. Also, countries should be classified 'according to the relative weight of the "active army" and the "reserve army" of labour within their society' (Amin 1997b: ix). Such claims are consistent with Amin's long-held position on unequal development stemming from the centre-periphery bifurcation of the world's countries.

Exponential increases in worldwide financial linkages that followed the ending of the Bretton Woods financial framework, and the de-regulation of finance that progressively unfolded through the 1980s and 1990s, showed that finance capital is now 'the most globalized component' of capitalism. Amin describes the financial changes that have occurred as the 'globalization of finance' (Amin 1997b: 4). Globalisation in this context means globalism or the broadening and deepening of not only financial but also economic connections. Such an understanding of globalisation as the expansiveness, the drive of capitalism to penetrate every market, to broaden and deepen its connections, is a feature of Amin's later writing. Globalisation, though, is not only current capitalist expansiveness; it has been a permanent trait of capitalism throughout its history. After the Cold War, globalisation has been used as a euphemism for imperialism (Amin 1998: 45).

Amin contends that globalisation is a combination of recent qualitative changes to global capitalism, a euphemism for imperialism, historical capitalist expansiveness and it is implicated in polarisation (unequal development). Globalisation also is regarded as capitalist expansiveness by 'globalisation-era' Marxists. Regarding the euphemism claim, James Petras and Henry Veltmeyer argue that globalisation is considerably more than just a euphemism; it is the ideological masking of imperialism. Independently of Amin, another 'globalisation-era' Marxist, Humphrey McQueen, conflates historical expansiveness with recent changes to capitalism and comes up with stages of globalisation.

What he arrives at, *inter alia*, is the periodisation of globalisation, with imperialism as a stage of the latter. A more detailed analysis of how globalisation is viewed by 'globalisation-era' Marxists is a significant part of Chapter Eight. Here it suffices to say that Amin's critique of globalisation pre-figured some of the 'globalisation-era' Marxists' views, effectively making a bridge between his neo-Marxist position and the new 'globalisation-era' phase of Marxist imperialism theory.

Globalisation and the nation-state

A major claim made about globalisation is its ineluctability, a claim that Amin sought to counter. Part of the ineluctability argument is the proposition that nation-states have little capacity to avoid globalisation and, moreover, globalisation erodes whatever power is held by nation-states. Intriguingly, Amin agrees that the power of the nation-state has been undermined. He suggests that the corrosive influence of globalisation on state power creates another set of problems:

> By definition, the new globalization erodes the efficiency of economic management by national states. However, it does not abolish their existence. Thus it produces a new contradiction which . . . is insurmountable under capitalism. The reason for this is that capitalism is more than just an economic system; its economy is inconceivable without a social and political dimension which implies a state (Amin 1997b: 32).

Not only a state, but because the management demands of economic, financial and monetary systems are now so great, the logical requirement is for 'the construction of a world political system able to respond to the challenge' of globalisation (Amin 1997b: 22). The insurmountable problem in this age of globalisation is the 'separation between the globalized space of capitalism's economic management and the national spaces of its political and social management' (Amin 1997b: 32).

The current phase of globalisation (a qualitatively different phase starting in 1990), does not allow for de-linking by states and nor does it allow opting out on the grounds of ethnicity or religious fundamentalism. These last themes are not adequate responses to globalisation, which has its progressive aspects. Amin argues that modification, not opposition, is the right approach to the contradictions of globalisation. Only through the ultimate modification can globalisation's promise be fulfilled; that is, through the advent of socialism (Amin 1997b: 75). There is an implicit acceptance here of the inevitability of globalisation. Another point that he makes about this current era, and which is taken up by the 'globalisation-era' Marxists, is that the only state capable of acting as the guarantor of order is the US, the sole military power (Amin 1997b: 120).

A problem with Amin's writing on globalisation is that it remains rather nebulous (a workable definition of globalisation is deferred for the next chapter as globalisation is an essential part of Hardt's and Negri's 'Empire' concept). With a small effort though, it is possible to discern what Amin thinks are globalisation's main characteristics. Since 1990, the qualitative changes to global capitalism were such that the world has entered the age of globalisation. Amin identifies two constants in globalisation: first is that at one level it is just the ceaseless drive of capitalism to expand; second is that globalisation perpetuates polarisation, the enrichment of the core at the expanse of the periphery. Regarding states and globalisation, no state can opt out of it and the ability of states to manage their economies has been curtailed. Amin asserts that there is scope for modifying the effects of globalisation (also known as imperialism) but the ultimate way to maximise its progressive side only can come through the attainment of global socialism. Despite some concerns with Amin's analysis of globalisation, his book *Capitalism in the Age of Globalization* was a timely intervention by an established Marxist thinker into the complex relationships between globalisation, capitalism and imperialism.

Summarising Amin's writing on imperialism

The critical analysis of imperialism, 'Eurocentrism' and globalisation that Samir Amin has undertaken over the course of five decades has produced insightful additions to Marxist imperialism theory. He has consistently argued that the central problem with imperialism and globalisation originates from the centre-periphery relationship. The product of this relationship is the unequal and uneven development of the countries of the periphery compared to the continued enrichment of the advanced capitalist countries of the centre. The polarisation that always is the result of the centre-periphery relationship has influenced the ideological outlook of the left (and others) in the West, such that many cannot perceive anything other than a Western-based model of development for the rest of the world. Culturally and ideologically, 'Eurocentrism' is the implicit and sometimes explicit belief in the superiority of European norms, beliefs and outlooks. 'Eurocentrism', combined with revisionism and the benefits of the centre's development, completely eroded the capacity of the working classes of the West to fight against imperialism and for socialism.

Having written extensively on imperialism since the 1950s, Amin's view of it has evolved. In his early books there was a reliance on Lenin's theory as the definitional fall-back position. He combined this minimalist classical Marxist version of imperialism, with class analysis and neo-Marxist tropes such as underdevelopment, centre (core)-periphery bifurcation and the promotion of the working class in the Third World to the leaders of resistance to imperialism. In his later works, references to Lenin's insights into imperialism were dropped as was class analysis. The hallmark of neo-Marxist thought on imperialism, the unequal and uneven development of the peripheral countries and the consequent enrichment of the core or centre countries remained. Despite the problem of confusion stemming from the lack of a well thought out and consistent definition of imperialism, Amin has made and continues to make useful additions to the corpus of Marxist imperialism theory. Regarding globalisation, Amin's understanding of it as a euphemism for imperialism, as capitalist expansiveness and also as a qualitatively new phase of global capitalism, are taken up by 'globalisation-era' Marxists. He has helped set some of the parameters for subsequent Marxist interrogation of globalisation discourse, and in doing so he has acted as a bridge between neo-Marxist and 'globalisation-era' Marxist imperialism theory.

The neo-Marxists and imperialism theory: a case of declining interest

Looking back over the collective contributions to the theorising of imperialism by the neo-Marxists a pattern emerges. Sweezy's first book endorsed Lenin's theory of imperialism, reworking it to account for developments that had occurred after Lenin's death. With the passage of time, Sweezy and his collaborator Baran, moved away from imperialism theory and the term is superseded by Monopoly Capital in their co-authored book (Baran and Sweezy 1968). For Gunder Frank, imperialism and imperialism theory disappeared from his later work, because of his disenchantment with Western social theory. Wallerstein has only been marginally interested in imperialism, preferring to focus on the macro-historical and larger social structures such as the modern World System and the capitalist world economy. Amin has consistently used imperialism theory as a resource to unpack the complexities of global politics and the skewed development of the periphery. Nonetheless, his understanding of imperialism has suffered from inconsistencies in how he has defined imperialism. Aside from Amin, the neo-Marxists showed a demonstrable decline in interest in defining and engaging with the concept of imperialism.

One of the problems of the work of Gunder Frank, Wallerstein and, to a lesser extent Amin, is their promotion of exchange relations as the determining feature of capitalism. The determining feature of capitalism according to classical Marxist doctrine is found in the production process with its attendant production relations. Consequently there has been an issue with Gunder Frank's, Wallerstein's and Amin's understanding of the political economy of capitalism, and their portrayal of the history and spread of the capitalist world economy. This issue taken together with the noticeable decline in interest in imperialism and its theorising by most of the neo-Marxists can only lead to the conclusion that under their stewardship the conceptualising of imperialism atrophied.

A positive aspect of neo-Marxist engagement with imperialism theory is Amin's critical examination of globalisation. His conclusion that globalisation was the form that imperialism took in the current period of US hegemony foreshadowed similar arguments made by the 'globalisation-era' Marxists Petras and Veltmeyer. In so doing, Amin acts as a bridge between the second phase and third phase 'globalisation-era' Marxist theorising on imperialism.

Having concluded the examination of the second phase of Marxist imperialism theory attention turns to the next generation of theories, the third phase 'globalisation-era' Marxist offerings. It starts with Hardt's and Negri's powerful challenge to classical Marxist and neo-Marxist perspectives on imperialism.

CHAPTER 7

EMPIRE ACCORDING TO HARDT AND NEGRI

Introduction

The appearance of Michael Hardt's and Antonio Negri's *Empire* (2000), with its promotion of a de-centred and de-territorialised vision of stateless sovereignty, or 'Empire', shook the foundations of Marxist thinking. They claim that 'Empire' not only is distinct from imperialism (Hardt and Negri 2000: xii), but that with the coming into being of the former, imperialism had been consigned to history. Hardt, an American academic born in 1960, and Negri, a political activist and intellectual born in Padua in 1931, argue that, although World Systems theorists were right to emphasise that capitalism has functioned since its inception as a world economy, and therefore that capitalist development always has had a universalising dimension, nonetheless there has been a 'significant historical shift' (Hardt and Negri 2000: 8). The shift to which they refer is the globalisation of capitalist production, and the change in global relations of power where economic power and political power are brought together to make what they call 'a properly capitalist order' (Hardt and Negri 2000: 8–9).

At the heart of 'Empire' sits a complex mixture of both system and hierarchy. In order to function, 'Empire' needs an established power to anchor it; somewhat paradoxical given that 'Empire' supposedly also is a de-centred, de-territorialised entity. The complexity of *Empire* is underpinned by many things. One is the by now familiar claim that globalisation has brought in its train the undermining of the sovereignty of the state. Another is the proposition that, because of changes in global capitalism and the system of states, especially after the Vietnam War and the crises of the 1970s, all the old certainties of the left such as imperialism, classes and class struggle no longer apply.

The claims Hardt and Negri make about globalisation effecting changes to the production process ('informatization' leading to a new category of labour, namely 'immaterial labor'), to the capitalist accumulation process and global politics, are cathartic. The questions that Hardt's and Negri's tome engendered are many: does the US act as an imperialist state or is it just a great power that has possessed the necessary muscle to maintain order in a de-centred network of capitalist powers? Has globalisation changed the system of states and eroded the nation-state to such an extent that these political forms are redundant? What has changed in capitalism? Is imperialism a thing of the past?

What emerged from the jolt that Hardt and Negri gave to Marxist thinking was not only a number of journal articles and books written in response to *Empire*, but also a number of common concerns or themes have been discerned. It will be argued that three particular themes connect Hardt's and Negri's work with the studies of other 'globalisation-era' Marxists whose writing is analysed in the next chapter. These three themes are: globalisation; 'Empire' or empire/imperialism; and the state and the system of states. Regarding Hardt's and Negri's understanding and use of globalisation, the argument is that their understanding of globalisation has similarities to what has been termed the hyper-globalist wave of globalisation scholarship and the deconstructionist wave that Holton (Holton 2005) and Held and McGrew (Held and McGrew 2007) respectively identify. A further argument made is that there are problems in the way Hardt and Negri theorise globalisation. There is too little in the way of explication of globalisation and too much emphasis placed on its transformative capacity. That there have been changes in capitalism and world politics since the end of the Cold War is beyond dispute. What is debatable, though, is whether globalisation is the cause of those changes or whether they are due to other factors such as the innate propensity of capitalism to revolutionise the production and labour processes.

In the second of the three themes, 'Empire' or empire/imperialism, Hardt and Negri make big claims. With the transition from modernity to postmodernity and the advent of 'Empire', the previous manifestations of empire (Roman, Spanish, and British, for example) have been transcended. The new form is not limited by national boundaries nor does it require a 'centre'. Not only are old forms of empire rendered obsolete but so is imperialism. At issue here is whether the concept of 'Empire' has supplanted imperialism and empires, or if, like the transformations associated with globalisation, Hardt and Negri overstate the case about epoch-making developments having occurred. This chapter argues that, indeed, the 'Empire' concept is based on an overzealous reading of the changes that supposedly follow on from globalisation. Whilst Hardt and Negri assign imperialism and imperialism theory to the 'dustbin of history', they acknowledge that prior to the epochal transformations Lenin's theory was not only very insightful but there were indications in his work that 'Empire' was a possibility. Hardt and Negri invoke Lenin to validate their claims about the new de-centred, de-territorialised entity. In so doing it becomes apparent that the understanding that the two writers have of imperialism is too narrow. They see imperialism almost solely as a political phenomenon, failing to draw out its connections with the capitalist accumulation process. The conclusion drawn about 'Empire' is that the concept does not explain the complexities of contemporary imperialism, rather it avoids those complexities through the assertion that the era of imperialism and empires has passed.

On the subject of the third theme – the state and the system of states – here it is argued that in promoting 'Empire' as a smooth space with a subordinate role for the nation-state and the system of states, Hardt and Negri take too simplistic an approach to state theory and geopolitics.

Criticisms of Hardt's and Negri's ambitious and challenging book should not be taken as outright dismissal. The book was quite popular, selling well enough to make the Amazon bestseller list (Panitch and Gindin 2002: 17). This is somewhat surprising given that it addresses issues of imperialism, empire, globalisation and the transformation of capitalism, culminating with the authors proclaiming that the prospects for revolutionary militancy are high and therefore there is an 'irrepressible lightness and joy [associated with] being communist' (Hardt and Negri 2000: 413). Drawing popular attention to these issues is commendable enough, but to be a pivotal part in the revival of interest in imperialism and imperialism theory deserves respect.

This chapter commences with a summary of the waves of globalisation theory, then it provides a definition of globalisation so as to properly situate and contextualise the work of Hardt and Negri and other 'globalisation-era' Marxists. Critical analysis of Hardt's and Negri's treatment of globalisation comes next, followed by their engagement with empire and imperialism. The chapter concludes by scrutinising how the two conceive of the state and the states system.

Globalisation: waves of theory and a definition

Globalisation as a term only came into use in the last ten or fifteen years of the twentieth century. As Doug Henwood has suggested, like many words that are ideologically loaded it is 'rarely defined explicitly; everyone is expected to know what it means' (Henwood 2003: 145). Whilst opinions vary as to when the term first came to notice, for the purposes of the ensuing discussion it is sufficient to bookend the globalisation era from the late 1980s to the present. David Held and Anthony McGrew have surveyed the scholarship on globalisation and, basing themselves on the work of Robert Holton they modify the three waves of globalisation scholarship: the hyper-globalist; sceptical; and post-sceptical waves (Holton 2005: 5). Held and McGrew claim that there are four distinct waves discernible, which they call: the theoretical; the historical; the institutional; and the deconstructive. They elaborate:

> The initial theoretical wave was generally concerned with debates about the conceptualization of globalization, its principal dynamics and its systemic and structural consequences as a secular process of worldwide social change ... By contrast the historical wave, drawing upon the historical sociology of global development, was principally concerned with exploring in what ways, if any, contemporary globalization could be considered novel or unique – whether it defined a new epoch, or transformation, in the socio-economic and political organization of human affairs (Held and McGrew 2007: 5).

The third or institutional wave of globalisation theorising is characterised as being sceptical towards the large claims made about globalisation and structural transformation. Scholars involved in this wave concentrated on 'questions of institutional change and resilience, whether in national models of capitalism, state restructuring or cultural life' (Held and McGrew 2007: 6). The third wave of scholarship takes in the influence of constructivism and post-structuralism, hence the deconstructive tag that Held and McGrew give it. The critical analysis of globalisation that emanates from the deconstructionist wave highlights 'ideas, agency, communication, contingency and normative change' as central concerns of an analysis of globalisation. Furthermore, there is considerable debate about whether the present is best seen as 'competing and alternative globalizations' (Held and McGrew 2007: 6).

Aside from the four waves of scholarship that Held and McGrew claim are discernible in globalisation theorising, there are normative and ethical aspects that are integral to the debates. The important issue of whether globalisation is benign or malign, or both, cannot be avoided. Held and McGrew also claim that there is no easy correspondence between particular normative positions on globalisation and one's position on the political spectrum (Held and McGrew 2007: 6). As we shall see, there are those on the left such as Hardt and Negri who see the opening up of new possibilities for transformation that largely have been brought about by the changes linked with globalisation. Others on the left and on the right, however, view globalisation as primarily a malign influence. Leaving normative and ethical concerns and the four waves of theoretical approaches to one side, it is opportune to pass on to the more complex task of defining globalisation.

Holton asserts that definitions of globalisation have served differing purposes at different times. Existing alongside analytical functions there are moral, political and commercial interests and or influences that have coloured how globalisation is defined. Nonetheless, drawing on what he calls 'third wave agent-centered' approaches, which emphasise 'themes of interconnection, inter-dependence and global consciousness', Holton offers a definition of globalisation that incorporates:

(a) The intensified movement of goods, money, technology, information, people, ideas and cultural practices across political and cultural boundaries. Such movements combine cause and effect. They implicate the interests and activities of merchants and bankers, migrants and religious leaders, media representatives and activists.

(b) The inter-dependence of social processes across the globe, such that all social activity is profoundly interconnected rather than separated off into different national and cultural spaces. Once again inter-dependence arises out of human activity and involves particular agents, whether global entrepreneurs or regulators, medical professionals or lawyers, social movement activists or world musicians. It involves formally organized undertakings as well as those embodied in networks and looser forms of co-operation and conflict.
(c) Consciousness of and identification with the world as a single place, as in forms [of] cosmopolitanism, religion or earth-focused environmentalism (Holton 2005: 15).

The three definitional elements are part of what Holton terms the ongoing process of globalisation. He does not privilege any of the three elements and points out that they are all shaped by human agency. The definition offered by Holton is not exhaustive. Ray Kiely (2005) uses a combination of definitional tropes sourced from the work of Anthony Giddens, especially his *The Consequences of Modernity* (1990), and Held, McGrew, Jonathan Perraton and David Goldblatt's *Global Transformations* (1999) amongst others. From Giddens comes the 'intensification of worldwide social relations which link distant localities in such a way that local happenings are shaped by events occurring many miles away and vice versa' (Giddens cited in Kiely 2005: 8). This is matched with the definition that Held *et al.* proffer, which is that globalisation is a:

> process (or set of processes) which embodies a transformation in the spatial organization of social relations and transactions – assessed in terms of their extensivity, velocity and impact – generating transcontinental or interregional flows and networks of activity, interaction, and the exercise of power' (Held *et al.* cited in Kiely 2005: 8).

A problem associated with defining globalisation is the sheer volume of writing on the subject. The common element amongst the definitions, however, is the increased interconnectedness across national borders and the 'increase in speed and intensity of these connections' (Kiely 2005: 8). A combination of Holton's three elements and Kiely's insightful additions garnered from Giddens and Held *et al.* give a sufficient working definition of globalisation; sufficient for the purposes of the following analysis of Hardt's and Negri's *Empire* and also for the discussion of the work of the 'globalisation-era' Marxists in the next chapter.

Interconnectedness is a vital element of globalisation, yet, as sceptics point out, interconnectedness is not necessarily unique to globalisation. Claims of a new era of heightened interconnections, of time-space compression courtesy of globalisation, have been sharply criticised by sceptics such as Paul Hirst and Grahame Thomson (1999), Justin Rosenberg (2000), Robert Gilpin (2002) and Colin Hay (2004). As Rosenberg states:

> The recognition that temporality and spatiality have varied across periods and cultures, that they have been socially constructed and mentally experienced in different ways and that those different ways have themselves been highly consequential for the constitution of social orders – all this has been long and well established (Rosenberg 2000: 4).

From this we can conclude that globalisation is a contested concept with a number of analytical 'positions' readily identifiable.

Notwithstanding the complex and contested nature of globalisation, a time frame for the globalisation era has been established and a workable definition proposed that meets the requirements for this and the following chapter on the remainder of the 'globalisation-era' Marxists. The term 'globalisation-era' Marxists has been chosen because not only does their work fall within the era of globalisation, but also globalisation and its impact on imperialism theory forms a critical part of their analyses.

Globalisation from above: capitalism and geopolitics fundamentally change

According to Hardt and Negri, globalisation occurs either from the top down or from the bottom up. Central to the two writers' argument about the changes that they perceive to have occurred in global power relations and the capitalist world economy is the transformative nature of globalisation (Hardt and Negri 2000: 8). In this last instance, the globalisation that is referred to is of the top down variety, or globalisation from above. The processes of globalisation are not unified nor are they univocal: the top down version of globalisation can be resisted, re-organised and re-directed to serve other ends. Hence globalisation from below, where the 'creative forces of the multitude that sustain Empire are also capable of autonomously constructing a counter-Empire, an alternative political organization of global flows and exchanges' (Hardt and Negri 2000: xv). It is globalisation from above, however, that has helped bring about the historical shift Hardt and Negri focus on throughout the book.

There had been vital developments in capitalism and geopolitics that saw the coming together of economic power with political power such that in the last years of the twentieth century there was now a 'properly capitalist order' (Hardt and Negri 2000: 9). This shift to a genuine capitalist order has as its crowning achievement a 'single supranational figure of political power' or 'Empire', which supplants the conflictual nature of relationships between rival imperialist powers. Such a supranational political power is in Hardt and Negri's terms 'a new notion of right . . . a new inscription of authority and a new design of the production of norms and legal instruments of coercion that guarantee contracts and resolve conflicts' (Hardt and Negri 2000: 9). 'Empire' is not only post-colonial but also post-imperialist, too.

Globalisation has played a powerful role in the birth of such a transcendent phenomenon as 'Empire'. Referring back to the waves of globalisation scholarship that have been canvassed above and especially the three waves that Holton identified, Hardt's and Negri's understanding of globalisation would align them with the hyper-globalist group. A difficulty with such categorisation is that Hardt and Negri do not suggest that globalisation is solely responsible for bringing about 'Empire'. The transformation to a 'properly capitalist order' also has its roots in the political and economic crises of the 1970s. The two writers go back further, positioning the Vietnam War as:

> a real turning point in the history of contemporary capitalism insofar as the Vietnamese resistance is conceived as the symbolic center of a whole series of struggles around the world that had up

until that point remained separate and distant from one another (Hardt and Negri 2000: 260).

Globalisation, then, when allied with the challenges to the capitalist system that started with the Vietnam War and continued with the turmoil of the 1970s, has been the catalyst for a real historical shift.

Another difficulty connected with Hardt's and Negri's work – a problem Henwood has outlined – is that they do not explicitly define what they mean by the term 'globalisation'. One of its key components is communication, which 'not only expresses but also organizes the movement' of globalisation by 'multiplying and structuring interconnections through networks' (Hardt and Negri 2000: 32). Communication is not only a vital element in globalisation, it is what the two writers call a 'hegemonic sector of production' (Hardt and Negri 2000: 33). Such an emphasis on communication is redolent of the fourth or deconstructionist wave of globalisation scholarship that Held and McGrew identified above.

Communication also shapes the production process in an elemental way. Since the early 1970s, the capitalist production process has been in the process of being transformed into an 'information economy'. Starting in the US and spreading to the other advanced capitalist nations, the information revolution or what the writers call 'informatization' has heralded the eclipse of modernisation. In this instance, modernisation is equated with industrial production and its dominance of not only other economic forms but also social phenomena (Hardt and Negri 2000: 285). A characteristic of modernisation has been the migration of jobs from agriculture to industry (from the primary sector to the secondary), whereas with informatisation, or postmodernisation, labour has been migrating from industry to the service sector (tertiary sector). The latter sector takes in health care, finance, transport, entertainment, education and advertising. Those employed in these areas are required to have flexible skills and be mobile. Crucial to such employment is the part played by 'knowledge, information, affect, and communication' (Hardt and Negri 2000: 285).

Whilst the postmodernisation of capitalism does not mean that industrialisation is completely redundant, the significant shift that Hardt and Negri attest to here nonetheless relegates industrialisation/ modernisation to a secondary role. The service sectors in the advanced capitalist countries are now the dominant sectors of those economies. A consequence of this shift from industrialisation as the dominant aspect of capitalist economies has been the appearance of immaterial labour, so called because the end product of such labour is not a material good. Rather, the end product is a service, a cultural product, communication or knowledge (Hardt and Negri 2000: 290).

An important outcome of the informatisation of production is the increased homogenisation of labour practices. That is, the skills associated with specific concrete tasks, tailoring or weaving for example, are minimised with the advent of computerised production. The denuding of concrete, specific skills associated with the production of use-values is directly related to the increased employment of the 'universal tool', the computer. The impact of the computer on this type of immaterial labour is profound, yet in the area of affective labour, or the immaterial labour concerned with human contact and interaction, the impact is not as dramatic. It is from the labour practices associated with affective labour – health services and caring, for example – that Hardt and Negri suggest that forms of community, social networks and biopower springs from (Hardt and Negri 2000: 292–3).

In summarising their analysis of the informatisation or postmodernisation of the global capitalist economy, Hardt and Negri identify three forms of immaterial labour that 'drive the service sector at the top of the informational economy'. They encapsulate these forms as:

> The first [form] is involved in an industrial production that has been informationalized and has incorporated communication technologies in a way that transforms the production process itself. Manufacturing is regarded as a service, and the material labor of the production of durable goods mixes with and tends towards immaterial labor. Second is the immaterial labor of analytical and symbolic tasks, which itself breaks down into creative and intelligent manipulation on the one hand and routine symbolic tasks on the other. Finally, a third type of immaterial labor involves the production and manipulation of affect and requires (virtual or actual) human contact, labor in the bodily mode (Hardt and Negri 2000: 293).

Taken overall, immaterial labour is inherently cooperative and involves social interaction. It is argued that, because productivity and wealth creation is now so largely dependent on and influenced by 'cooperative interactivity through linguistic, communicational, and affective networks', the notion of capital as the activating force of the production process is redundant now (Hardt and Negri 2000: 294). The capacity to organise the production process is no longer a preserve of capital and capitalists, rather, the information economy and its attendant networks ensure that production is de-centralised and dependent on highly cooperative labour. It is asserted that the capacity to organise the production process has now passed from capital and it is now the 'multitude' that influences decisions about investment and production. In addition, the dominant service sectors of the information economy have become de-territorialised. This de-territorialisation is due to the ongoing reduction of distance and the compression of time, courtesy of highly efficient communication networks. Geographical location is thus rendered irrelevant (Hardt and Negri 2000: 296).

The transformations noted here – the postmodernisation of the capitalist production process, the information economy, the centrality of communication, immaterial labour and the de-territorialisation of production – stem in large part from globalisation. This is not to forget that acting in concert with (but pre-dating) globalisation was a series of political, social and cultural challenges which had their genesis in the Vietnam War and continued on through the 1970s, which also played an influential part in bringing about the above transformations. In their critical analysis of *Empire*, Panitch and Gindin point out that what sets the book apart from others concerned with globalisation is the hybrid theoretical approach the authors adopt: Marxist and postmodernist. Panitch and Gindin add:

> They employ this theoretical hybrid to identify globalisation with a new type of capitalist political regime, drawing a distinction between the imperialisms of the past (territorial sovereignty being extended through colonies) and what they call the new 'empire' (the supranational 'penetration of boundaries') (Panitch and Gindin 2002: 18).

The supranational penetration of boundaries is markedly different to the concept of the borderless world that Kenichi Ohmae argued would result from globalisation (1996). Unlike Ohmae, Hardt and Negri derive from the transformations outlined above not just the erosion of nation-state borders but a new, diffuse (because it is de-centred and de-territorialised) geopolitical entity. Such an entity has within it the potential for qualitative change. Immanent within 'Empire' is a perceived higher social order, that of communism. Here Hardt and Negri follow in the footsteps of Hegel and Marx, that is, all four of them share 'a teleological theory of historical development, in which each new stage of evolution creates the potential for a fuller expression of human potential' (Rustin 2002: 451).

The hybrid approach of Hardt and Negri to globalisation: just how transformative has globalisation been?

It is clear that globalisation for the authors of *Empire* marks a watershed in the development of global capitalism *and* in global politics. By highlighting the advances in communication as a constitutive element of globalisation, Hardt and Negri seemingly fall within the scope of the deconstructionist wave identified by Held and McGrew. Complicating matters in seeking to categorise Hardt's and Negri's interpretation of globalisation is their avowed Marxist approach to two issues: first, the potential for transcendence of global capitalism inherent in the changes that globalisation has sparked; and, second, their concern with changes to the production process, long a staple of Marxian analysis. There is too much Marxism in the two writer's work for them to be easily pigeon-holed as unreservedly belonging to a deconstructionist wave of globalisation analysis. Additionally, we have seen how positive their view is of the developments associated with globalisation, culminating in their projection of 'Empire' as a potential stepping stone to communist societies. Hyper-globalists (Holton 2005: 5) also see globalisation as a foundation-shaking phenomenon. There are aspects of Hardt's and Negri's depiction of the consequences of globalisation that mirror some of the hyper-globalists' assertions. In the realm of global politics and specifically national borders, the notion of a borderless world finds reflection in *Empire*, where Hardt and Negri claim that with the further realisation of the world market the boundaries of the nation-state are deconstructed (Hardt and Negri 2000: 150). Hardt's and Negri's conceptualising of globalisation does not fit wholly in the deconstructionist or hyper-globalist waves. It is a hybrid approach that sees globalisation as a powerful vehicle for transformation.

Critics have acknowledged the importance of globalisation for Hardt and Negri (Amin 2005: 2; Arrighi 2002: 3–5; Callinicos 2002: 319; Panitch and Gindin 2002: 18; Rustin 2002: 451). Yet, what has been overlooked by many critics is how Hardt and Negri fail to define the term. Also problematic, as Panitch and Gindin observe, is the lack of empirical evidence to support many of the claims made in their book (Panitch and Gindin 2002: 19). This criticism can be extended to include Hardt's and Negri's analysis of globalisation. They assume that globalisation is something relatively new, which has had powerful transformative effects in politics, societies and economies. Amin suggests that what Hardt and Negri offer regarding globalisation is a 'naïve vision' that merely reflects the 'dominant discourse'. In such a vision, 'transnationalization has already abolished imperialism (and imperialism in conflict), replacing it with a system in which the center is both nowhere and everywhere' (Amin 2005: 2). What follows from these critiques are a number of questions. Is Hardt's and Negri's version of globalisation strong enough to account for the changes that they detail? How much of what they claim has happened as a result of globalisation is attributable to the capitalist production process itself, which is:

> a gigantic process of value production, of surplus-value extraction, out of living labour ... a gigantic movement constantly revolutionizing the means of production, the organization of production, the labour process and the producers themselves (Mandel 1976a: 36).

This gives rise to the major question concerning globalisation and global capitalism: what is the relationship between these two phenomena? For Hardt and Negri, the answer appears to be that globalisation is superordinate to global capitalism. Globalisation has determined qualitative changes to the production processes in advanced capitalist countries, and it also has brought political, social and cultural changes in its train. The problem with Hardt's and Negri's position on globalisation is that they have not defined what they mean by it, nor have they provided sufficient evidence to back up the large claims they make about it. This is not to suggest that the changes that they describe have not happened. Rather, it could be that certain transformations such as improvements in communication – the prominence of the service sector in the advanced capitalist countries, for example – are the consequences of the revolutionising of the production and labour processes that are an inherent feature of capitalism. Other changes that they mention such as the erosion of national borders and the coming into being of a supranational entity that supersedes the nation-state, 'Empire', are disputed by critics as discussed already. Amongst the latter are some other 'globalisation-era' Marxists, whose work is reviewed in the next chapter. In conclusion, how Hardt and Negri view globalisation and what they claim that it has done and is doing is debatable at best. At worst, the transformations that they claim stem from globalisation may well be the result of the normal unfolding of capitalism. The relationship between globalisation and global capitalism is inadequately explored in their book. Consequently, Hardt's and Negri's version of globalisation does not appear strong enough to account for the changes that they detail.

The importance of the issue of what is globalisation and what is its relationship with global capitalism cannot be overstated. This holds not only for the work of Hardt and Negri but also for other 'globalisation-era' Marxists. The struggles to analyse globalisation, to find out what it has meant for social, political, economic and cultural development as well as the struggles to analyse the globalisation-global capitalism nexus is a thread that connects the work of Hardt and Negri with some of their strongest Marxist critics. Changes have occurred in global capitalism and geopolitics since the end of the Cold War. How to analyse these changes and what role globalisation may play in them are central concerns for those attempting to critically analyse the state of the post-Cold War world. Having now completed the investigation of Hardt's and Negri's version of globalisation, it is time to scrutinise their next theme: 'Empire' and imperialism.

The ascension of 'Empire'

The Gulf War of 1991 marked the appearance of a new entity in the guise of an old term: 'Empire'. This was in the process of being created during the political, social and cultural challenges of the 1960s and 1970s, though not until the bipolarity of the Cold War was sundered could this new form of sovereignty take its place on the world stage. Hardt's and Negri's hypothesis is that:

> sovereignty has taken a new form, composed of a series of national and supranational organisms united under a single logic of rule ... The new form of sovereignty is the result of the decline of the nation-state, where the inability of nation-states to effectively regulate both economic and cultural exchanges is symptomatic 'of the coming of Empire' (Hardt and Negri 2000: xii).

The old term empire takes on new meaning for the two writers, changing from a metaphor that 'would require demonstration of the resemblances between today's world order and the Empires of Rome, China, the Americas, and so forth ... [to] a *concept*, which calls primarily for a theoretical approach' (Hardt and Negri 2000: xiv emphasis in original). This new form of 'Empire' is not limited by national boundaries, nor do the authors see any limitation to its rule:

> First and foremost, then, the concept of Empire posits a regime that effectively encompasses the spatial totality, or really that rules over the entire 'civilized' world. No territorial boundaries limit its reign. Second, the concept of Empire presents itself not as a historical regime originating in conquest, but rather as an order that effectively suspends history and thereby fixes the existing state of affairs for eternity (Hardt and Negri 2000: xiv).

'Empire' works through all levels of the social order and tries to rule over human nature itself. By trying to impose its rule over social life *in toto*, 'Empire' becomes the 'paradigmatic form of biopower' (Hardt and Negri 2000: xv). Biopower is a Foucaldian conception that has its genesis in his influential work on social forms and especially his exposition of the shift from disciplinary society to a society of control. A society of control is one where 'mechanisms of command become ever more "democratic", ever more immanent to the social field, distributed throughout the brains and bodies of the citizens' (Hardt and Negri 2000: 23). The citizenry in a society of control becomes imbued with certain behaviours, certain mechanisms of command that are interiorised. Because of this interiorising of values, commands and so on, societies and more importantly, life itself, its production and reproduction, becomes the object of power. And, thus, we have biopower, which is 'a control that extends throughout the depths of the consciousness and bodies of the population – and at the same time across the entirety of social relations'. Both the society of control and biopower are constituent elements of 'Empire' (Hardt and Negri 2000: 24–5).

The concept of biopower – a power that is not centralised but nevertheless reaches to every level of society and makes life itself its object – shares important characteristics with 'Empire'. Apparent in both concepts is the diffusion of power, the lack of a centre, yet this does not limit the powerful capacities of both to control and impose order.

In summary, 'Empire' has grown out of and in turn reinforces the erosion of the power of the nation-state. The relegation of the nation-state and the system of states (the international order, also known as the 'international community') to the margins comes courtesy of the new smooth space of 'Empire' uncovered by Hardt and Negri. It is 'smooth' because the territorial foundations of the nation-state – so much a part of modernisation – have been rendered largely irrelevant by the de-centred, de-territorialised brave new world. What this means for imperialism and theories of imperialism is succinctly summed up by Hardt and Negri: 'Many of these arguments [critiques of imperialism] are today certainly outdated and the situation they refer to is utterly transformed' (Hardt and Negri 2000: 221). Whilst Hardt and Negri claim that imperialism has been superseded, they nonetheless devote space to analysing it because they see it as a precursor to 'Empire'.

Imperialism as territorialising political entity

According to Hardt and Negri, there is an intrinsic connection between capitalist expansiveness and imperialism, with the pressure to extend and deepen the world market in the modern era invariably taking 'the political form of imperialism' (Hardt and Negri 2000: 221). Marx had shown that the dynamic of capitalism was such that it could not be confined to a fixed territory and that it had to reconfigure the boundaries of both the inside and the outside (Hardt and Negri 2000: 221). Following the development of imperialism theory from Luxemburg through to Lenin (and tracing the influences of Hilferding, Hobson and Kautsky on the latter's work along the way) Hardt and Negri conclude that Lenin saw imperialism as a hindrance to capitalist expansion because of the imposition of tariffs, trade exclusivities, the imperialist practices of colonial administrations and the suppression of competition courtesy of the growth of monopolies (Hardt and Negri 2000: 233). Imperialism had been the political handmaiden to the extension of the capitalist world market, but as Lenin had shown it had become a limiting factor. Therefore, Hardt and Negri argue, to continue to expand capital had to destroy the barriers to inside and outside that imperialism had erected. They elaborate further on this problem by stating:

> Imperialism is a machine of global striation, channelling, coding, and territorializing the flows of capital, blocking certain flows and facilitating others. The world market, in contrast, requires a smooth space of uncoded and deterritorialised flows (Hardt and Negri 2000: 333).

The key ingredients of Hardt's and Negri's account of imperialism are its territorialising nature – the creation and dissemination of national boundaries throughout the world – as well as its political nature. The latter theme takes in colonialism, the spread of the nation-state and the solving of political contradictions in the metropolitan countries by exporting class struggle and civil war overseas (Hardt and Negri 2000: 232). By their account, imperialism is historically specific and the old analyses of imperialism cannot be recycled as they only focus on 'the contradictions of capital's own development' (Hardt and Negri 2000: 235).

The summary of imperialism theory by Hardt and Negri pins down some of the important points in the work of Luxemburg and Lenin. Certain problems nonetheless exist in their interpretation of Lenin's work on imperialism. Notably, they suggest that Lenin had 'glimpsed beyond modernity' and had foreseen an 'emerging imperial sovereignty' that somehow accompanied 'a new phase of capital beyond imperialism' (Hardt and Negri 2000: 232). The new phase of capitalism beyond imperialism, according to Hardt's and Negri's interpretation of Lenin, will be necessarily attended by a new form of state and a new form of sovereignty. Apparently 'Lenin saw imperialism as a structural stage in the evolution of the modern state' (Hardt and Negri 2000: 232). Finally, the alternatives allegedly implicit in Lenin's writing on imperialism are those of world communist revolution or 'Empire' (Hardt and Negri 2000: 234).

What Hardt and Negri are attempting here is to position Lenin's theorising of imperialism as a precursor to their theory of 'Empire'. It is a difficult proposition as they are aware that there is no smooth transition from Lenin's theses to their observations because of the 'epochal shift in contemporary history', which is to say the transition from modernity to postmodernity (Hardt and Negri 2000: 237). This 'epochal shift' negates any smooth transition. Another sticking point is the claim that Lenin had implicitly projected 'Empire' as an alternative to world communist revolution. In Lenin's writing on imperialism one would be hard pressed to impute the concept of 'Empire' as expounded by the two writers. Also at issue is the claim that Hardt and Negri make about Lenin foreseeing new forms of sovereignty – imperial sovereignty – and new phases of post-imperialist capitalism. Finally, there is doubt about Lenin having had insight into a new form of state that must follow from post-imperialist capitalism. The reason why these claims are doubtful is that, as Chapter Two has addressed earlier, Lenin's *Imperialism* (1973) is concerned with summing up what he thought were the consequences of the monopoly phase of capitalism, a phase or stage of capitalism that he termed imperialism. There are no musings in *Imperialism* on the possibilities of new phases of capitalism after imperialism, or on new forms of the state and sovereignty as suggested by Hardt and Negri. It seems that what they are doing in their recruitment of aspects of classical Marxist theories of imperialism (however problematic because of the major changes associated with globalisation/postmodernity) is an attempt to legitimise their analysis of 'Empire'.

The understanding of Marxist imperialism theory displayed by Hardt and Negri identifies some important aspects of the classical theories, such as the intrinsic connection between imperialism and the expansiveness of capitalism and the contradictions deriving from this relationship. Unfortunately there are a number of interpolations to Lenin's work on imperialism in particular that raise concerns about their use and understanding of imperialism and imperialism theory. In their attempt to bestow legitimacy on their 'Empire' concept, Hardt and Negri have misinterpreted or misused Lenin's theory of imperialism. Moreover, imperialism as they interpret it is primarily a political phenomenon: imperialism as the political form of capitalist expansiveness.

Things of the past: the state and the system of states

The distinctive analysis of 'Empire' that posits an amalgam of the national and the supranational resulting in a smooth space is predicated on a particular view of the state and sovereignty. Hardt and Negri map the development of sovereignty over centuries in Europe, interpreting it as a response to specific problems that modernity brings in its train. In tracing the development of the concept, Hardt and Negri come to the conclusion that sovereignty was specifically European and evolved to 'guarantee survival against the mortal dangers of war'. Part of the process of avoiding such dangers was a pact between leader(s), which assigned absolute power to the leader(s), with the exception of the means of reproduction and survival. Such an implicit contract transferred the 'autonomous power of the multitude to a sovereign power that stands above and rules it' (Hardt and Negri 2000: 84).

At the juncture of the eighteenth and nineteenth centuries, 'the concept of national sovereignty finally emerged in European thought in its completed form' (Hardt and Negri 2000: 101). This melding of sovereignty with the concept of nation was the direct result of the trauma associated with the French Revolution and the counter-revolutionary aftermath. For Hardt and Negri, it was the spiritual body of the nation that supplanted the divine body of the monarch as the 'physical territory and population were conceived as the extension of the transcendent essence of the nation' (Hardt and Negri 2000: 95). The notion of a counter-revolutionary aftermath is important because it was during the reaction to the French Revolution that the spontaneous violence and power of the populace (the multitude) were constrained. This was achieved by reconstructing the 'people' as an integral part of the nation-state. The transcendent apparatus that is the nation-state, as the sovereign body, was thus able to 'impose order on the multitude and prevent it from organizing itself spontaneously and expressing its creativity autonomously' (Hardt and Negri 2000: 83). Detailed analysis Hardt and Negri provide of the historical and philosophical development of the concepts of nation-state and sovereignty need not detain us. Their elaboration of the concept of sovereignty as it evolved through the centuries sees sovereignty as eventually vesting in the nation-state in the modern era, and from there they go on to identify other variants such as imperial sovereignty (which covers the expansion of Europe throughout much of the rest of the world via the colonial process).

With the coming of postmodernity, colonial boundaries were basically torn down (Hardt and Negri 2000: 136). It is only with the erosion of national boundaries (which also are boundaries to the full realisation of a proper capitalist order) that 'the state and capital [can] effectively coincide', and when a Marxist theory of the state can be successfully undertaken (Hardt and Negri 2000: 236). The characterisation of the state as an executive board managing the interests of capitalists has been transformed in the era of postmodernity by the transferring of some of the state's functions to the transnational level of power. What this means is that some of the command functions of states have been usurped by transnational bodies such as banks, transnational corporations and international planning bodies. With postmodernity comes not the complete undermining of the nation-state and conversely the complete empowerment of transnational corporations, but rather it heralds a decline of the traditional national constitutional system and its replacement by a supranational constitutional power or Empire (Hardt and Negri 2000: 308–9).

The supranational constitutional framework that Hardt and Negri posit is pyramidal. The pyramid of global constitution is a new model of international order that replaces the international system of states. Mirroring the decline of the power of the nation-state, there has been a corresponding dissolution of the international order based on a society of states. The new pyramidal structure, according to Hardt and Negri, has three tiers with several levels on each tier. At the top of the pyramid, on the first tier, resides the sole superpower the US, who enjoys this position due to its possession of an unprecedented quantity of the means of violence. On this first tier, but on another level, sit nation-states that 'have the ability to regulate international exchanges' through the control of global monetary instruments. What binds these nation-states together are 'organisms' like Davos, the G7 and the London and Paris Clubs. On the third level of the first tier reside 'a heterogeneous set of associations' that include to a greater or lesser extent the nation-states that have hegemony over the military and monetary aspects of global political economy and who also organise biopolitical and cultural power globally (Hardt and Negri 2000: 309–10).

In the second tier of this pyramid the structure is based on the networks that transnational corporations have brought to the world market. Examples of such networks are capital, population and technology flows. These transnational networks are able to operate freely under the aegis of the 'central power' that resides in the first tier of global power. It is the world market, however, which has the capacity to homogenise and differentiate territories, re-drawing global geography (Hardt and Negri 2000: 310). Still on this second tier yet subordinated to the power of the transnational corporations are to be found the 'general set' of sovereign nation-states. These nation-states have some political functions such as 'political mediation with respect to the global hegemonic powers, bargaining with respect to the transnational corporations, and redistribution of income according to biopolitical needs within their own limited territories'. In addition, the nation-states act as a conduit, capturing and distributing wealth from the global power and channelling wealth back to that entity. The disciplining of the populace still is part of the remit of nation-states on this tier of the pyramid (Hardt and Negri 2000: 310).

The third and last tier in this schema consists of the representative bodies of popular interests and the multitude. For the multitude to have input into the global constitution it is necessary for a modification to occur; the undifferentiated mass must become the 'people'. The representatives of the 'people' can range from NGOs to nation-states (Hardt and Negri 2000: 311–14). Also functioning as representative bodies of popular interests in particular circumstances are the media and religious organisations. What we have in this last tier perhaps is better known as global civil society – a term that Hardt and Negri employ as an alternative (Hardt and Negri 2000: 311).

The three tiers of the global constitution, with their accompanying levels, are the essential components of 'Empire'. What is noticeable is that nation-states lurk at every tier. At the top of the pyramid is the hegemonic state the US, whose role as guarantor of order (acting also in conjunction with the nation-states in the second level of the first tier), provides the security framework without which the productive organisations could not operate (Hardt and Negri 2000: 310). Nation-states and in particular one nation-state remain indispensable elements of 'Empire'. The problem with this is that 'Empire' purportedly has no boundaries (Hardt and Negri 2000: xiv) and the nation-state and the system of states have lost their status. Yet, as can be seen, the quintessential territorial entity – the nation-state – features in all three tiers of Hardt's and Negri's pyramidal structure. They appear, then, to overstate the case about the decline in status of the nation-state and the system of states.

The theorisation of the state and the system of states in Empire

A feature of the analysis of sovereignty and the nation-state throughout the book is the influence of Foucauldian concepts, evident, for example, in the authors' detailed treatment of the genealogy of sovereignty. Additionally, there is the tracking of the development of social forms starting with disciplinary society and culminating in the society of control, concepts that have been mentioned already in the analysis of 'Empire'. Such reliance on these concepts diverts attention away from the 'structured sites of social institutions' and into the realm of biopower (Hardt and Negri 2000: 23). What this means is that the state is not given a comprehensive analysis, as it is one of the social institutions that have been superseded by the society of control. What analysis of the state there is has been described as recognisably anarchist because most 'forms of state power, in their view, alienate the autonomy of subjects and crush their creative power' (Rustin 2002: 452).

Consequently, Hardt and Negri devote minimal attention to theorising about the state and the system of states. This flows logically from their 'Empire' concept, which is purportedly a single supranational power that over-determines individual states and the system of states. That there is any single supranational power over-determining states and the state system is difficult to accept because of the lack of empirical evidence that Hardt and Negri offer in support of their claim.

Summarising the treatment of the state and the system of states in *Empire*, for Hardt and Negri the state is a social institution that operates to impose order on the multitude and keep the latter's creative power in check. The state is a specific response to problems that have arisen out of modernity. A key issue for Hardt and Negri is the incorporation of the multitude as the 'people' in the nation-state, which enabled the latter to become a sovereign power. The advent of 'Empire' ensured that the old political forms have been surpassed. In this formulation, state theory and geopolitics necessarily is under-theorised and over-simplified. The continued dependence of capital on many states is ignored and the central role of the US state in the construction of global capitalism is obscured. Among other 'globalisation-era' Marxist writers, no one takes up the 'Empire' concept and the power of the state and the system of states remain considered by many Marxist writers to be powerful factors in the creation and maintenance of imperialism.

Critical responses to Empire

In the critical literature that the book stimulated, the supersession of imperialism by 'Empire' has been the subject of close critical analysis. So, too, has Hardt's and Negri's interpretation of imperialism. Amin argues that, in *Empire*, imperialism means the 'extension of the formal power of the state beyond its own borders, thereby confusing imperialism with colonialism' (Amin 2005: 1). For Amin, this opens the way to reaching the conclusion that with the ending of colonialism in the 1970s, imperialism must have disappeared, too (Amin 2005: 1). Simon Bromley also remarks on how the two authors view imperialism as mainly a political process, as an extension of sovereignty of the metropolitan nation-states throughout the rest of the world. Compared with imperialism, 'Empire' is not concerned with 'direct imperial control of some political-territorial units over others', but rather 'Empire' is an 'essentially deterritorialised field of economic and cultural relationships' (Bromley 2003: 18). The novelty of 'Empire' is its universality and the unhitching of its power from a territorial centre. Its power is anchored in a global constitution, which, in turn, means that the nature of power in this configuration is mainly cultural, not political (Bromley 2003: 18). The economic aspects of imperialism are noted by the two writers, but as Panitch and Gindin point out their rendition of the impulses that drove pre-World War I capitalism relies on underconsumption and, taking their cue from Luxemburg, the need for exports to non-capitalist countries (Panitch and Gindin

2002: 21–2). Additionally, Hardt and Negri bypass the crucial role of finance in the current form of global capitalism and they do not explore the uneven development of capitalism within social formations as well as between them (Panitch and Gindin 2002: 24).

Two other claims made in *Empire* have attracted substantial critical comment. First is the contention that, with the de-territorialising and de-centring that is the hallmark of the smooth space of 'Empire', borders and the system of states have been rendered redundant. Second is the claim that imperialism is now outmoded, attributable in large part to the 'unique character of the US' (Barkawi and Laffey 2002: 123).

Regarding the overcoming of borders and the system of states – an assumption mainly based on the transformative effects of globalisation bringing about the 'smooth space' of 'Empire' – Tarak Barkawi and Mark Laffey point out the deficiencies of such a claim. In emphasising the increasing flows of information, money and goods, what Hardt and Negri and hyper-globalists overlook is the obverse of this coin. In other words, there has been a 'massive effort to make it harder for undesirable flows – be they illegal economic immigrants, asylum seekers, illegal drugs, crime, or contraband – to cross borders' (Barkawi and Laffey 2002: 123). A clear example of the continuing existence of the system of states and the leading role of the US state within that system is the arc of military bases across central Asia established by the US and various governments in those regions in the early 2000s. Such patron-client relations are redolent of 'not only . . . past US engagements in the Third World but also with older histories of imperialism' (Barkawi and Laffey 2002: 124).

The centrality of the US in the system of states runs counter to the proposal that 'Empire' is a smooth space with no real centre. This is a point that Panitch and Gindin make, too. Whilst the latter two agree with Hardt and Negri about Madisonian 'network power' as a distinctive element in the American constitution (and therefore something that distinguishes the US state as perhaps unique), they disagree that such network power prefigured 'Empire'. Panitch and Gindin exclaim:

> far from anticipating the sort of decentred and amorphous power that Hardt and Negri imagine characterized the US historically

> (and characterizes 'Empire' today), the constitutional framework of the new American state gave great powers to the central government to expand trade and make war (Panitch and Gindin 2002: 10).

The de-centred, borderless world thesis of Hardt and Negri not only obscures the continuing dependence of capital on many states, but also 'the pre-eminent role of the American state in the making of global capitalism is marginalized' (Panitch and Gindin 2005: 101).

The amorphous power of 'Empire', then, has not been especially well received by critics. What also has attracted criticism is the lack of development of the empirical claim that inter-state conflicts have been overcome by 'Empire' (Callinicos 2002: 320). Post-Cold War geopolitics has shown that interstate conflicts have continued with the Balkan wars of the 1990s (with NATO intervention), followed by Afghanistan and Iraq in the new millennium. Interstate conflicts have continued but the inter-imperialist rivalry leading to conflict (central to Lenin's theory of imperialism) seems to have dissipated. On the evidence of current inter-state conflicts, it would be difficult to argue that 'Empire' has supplanted imperialism. Nonetheless, the precise nature of post-Cold War geopolitics remains contested. Barkawi, Laffey, Callinicos and Shaw all have debated about how to conceptualise the current era, an exchange prompted by their analyses of *Empire* (Barkawi and Laffey 2002; Callinicos 2002; Shaw 2002).

In their promotion of 'Empire', Hardt and Negri have been criticised for minimising the central role of the US in the global order and for minimising the ongoing role of the system of states in the maintenance of US hegemony in that global order. Such criticism stems from their assertions about the de-centred, de-territorialised nature of 'Empire'. Furthermore, their understanding of imperialism has been called into question because of its narrow political and territorial focus, which sees them consequently passing over much of the economic side of imperialism. Another concern is their use of Lenin's theory of imperialism as a partial precursor to 'Empire', which casts doubt on the two writers' understanding and application of imperialism theory. Such comprehensive criticism leads to the conclusion that the world has not witnessed the supplanting of imperialism by 'Empire'.

Conclusion

This chapter has scrutinised Hardt's and Negri's treatment of the three themes of globalisation, empire/imperialism and the state and the system of states in their provocative study titled *Empire*. It has argued that the concept of 'Empire' is predicated on a strong version of globalisation, which, acting in conjunction with social, political and cultural changes that pre-date the globalisation era (early 1970s onwards), dramatically transformed political economy and geopolitics. Hardt's and Negri's version of globalisation, however, does not explore the connections between the former and global capitalism to any real extent. Thus, the changes that they outline such as immaterial labour, the prominence of informatisation and so on may be just the typical revolutionising of the production process that is an essential feature of capitalism. Furthermore, the transformations that Hardt and Negri suggest have come with globalisation heralding a shift from modernity to postmodernity are not supported by enough evidence, a problem commented upon by critics such as Panitch and Gindin. Nevertheless, Hardt and Negri are right to claim that there have been changes in the global capitalist economy and in geopolitics in the globalisation era. Their hypothesis that, in the post-Cold War era a proper capitalist order has now been realised, challenges many assumptions of those on the left and right of the political spectrum. Another serious challenge, this time mainly to the left, is Hardt's and Negri's contention that imperialism has been made redundant by 'Empire'.

The challenges of *Empire* have motivated a 'renaissance' in imperialism theory. The smooth, de-centred nature of Empire, which demoted the state and the system of states from their positions as major actors in global politics, certainly generated a lot of critical commentary. After close examination of key elements in the book (and the critical literature it spawned), it was concluded that Hardt's and Negri's postmodern version of empire has not rendered imperialism irrelevant. The state and the system of states still are crucial elements of global politics and Hardt and Negri, in their enthusiasm for 'Empire', oversimplify the role of the state and the system of states in geopolitics.

There are a number of problems evident in Hardt's and Negri's treatment of the three themes of globalisation, empire/imperialism and the state and the system of states. Most of the problems can be traced back to the ambitious assertion that there have been major transformations throughout the global capitalist economy and global politics in the globalisation era. That these transformations appear to have been overstated should not detract from the real legacy of *Empire*, which is its galvanising of a renewed interest in imperialism theory, especially amongst the writers whose work is the subject of the next – and final – chapter.

CHAPTER 8

THE BIG THREE

GLOBALISATION, EMPIRE, STATE AND THE THIRD PHASE OF MARXIST IMPERIALISM THEORY

Introduction

All the signs pointed to dramatic transformations. The 1990s started with the end to the bipolarity that had been such a feature of international politics for virtually a half-century. Freed from the constraints imposed on it by rivalry with the 'evil empire', the US felt more able to resort to force projection. The start of the decade saw a major military build-up in Saudi Arabia and the launching of Operation Desert Storm, with the US as leader of coalition forces, successfully driving out the Iraqi occupiers of Kuwait in 1991. Then, under the rubric of humanitarian intervention (and at the request of the UN), US troops were deployed to Somalia in 1992–3, and later in the decade, under the auspices of NATO, the US was the major supplier of air power in the bombing of the Serbian remnant of the Federal Republic of Yugoslavia. The trend towards a greater willingness to call on the services of the military reached its apogee after September 2001, with the occupation of Afghanistan and then Iraq in 2003. These instances, as well as others, served to put the world on notice: a resurgent US was now the global hegemon and the military option would be exercised. Apart from mass popular opposition to the Iraq invasion (which largely dissolved after the event), and German and French refusal to back the US attempt to get international approval for the military occupation of Iraq at the UN, the US seemingly faced no real challenge to its power. The twentieth century had not witnessed such unrivalled state power.

In the geopolitical arena a major transformation had taken place. Did the same hold true for the world economy? For Hardt and Negri, as we have seen in the last chapter, globalisation had utterly transformed global capitalism. Also, a new form of de-centred and de-territorialised entity called 'Empire' had arisen, supplanting imperialism and rendering obsolete much of Marxist state theory, imperialism theory and political economic analysis.

Such a powerful challenge to Marxist orthodoxy sparked a strong reaction. The arguments in *Empire* (Hardt and Negri 2000) and the response to them from Marxist critics coalesced around three problem areas: globalisation; 'Empire' or empire/imperialism; and the role of the state and the system of states. This chapter critically examines the responses of a number of Marxist writers to each of the problem areas starting with globalisation, moving on to the issues associated with empire and imperialism theory and concluding with the problems connected with the state and the international system of states. The responses demonstrate the rejuvenation of Marxist imperialism theory, given impetus by changes in the capitalist world economy and the international political scene plus Hardt's and Negri's book. Furthermore, it is argued that the critical responses possess a sophistication and calibre that does more than merely update Marxist imperialism theory. The collective output of the 'globalisation-era' Marxist theorists challenges some long-held theoretical positions not only preparing the ground for richer, more insightful theorising, but also taking the theorising to a higher level of abstraction. The work of the full complement of this cohort of writers has ushered in a new phase of Marxist imperialism theory, the phase of the 'globalisation-era' Marxists. Their writing deserves close scrutiny.

The spectre of globalisation: old or new ghost?

Prior to the publication of *Empire*, the neo-Marxist Samir Amin examined globalisation (see Chapter Six) and concluded that it was just capitalist expansion or imperialism by another name. Hardt and Negri have taken a hybrid position, one that has similarities to de-constructionist and hyper-globalist approaches (Held and McGrew 2007: 6; Holton 2005: 5). It also stresses globalisation's transformative capacity. Their view is at the opposite end of the spectrum to Amin's sceptical one. What did other Marxists make of globalisation and its relationship with capitalism and imperialism after the interventions of Amin and Hardt and Negri? As this chapter reveals, the responses vary. A selection of writing by four Marxist writers (two of whom acted as co-authors) on the problem of globalisation and its relationship with global capitalism and imperialism is critically analysed. Despite not representing an exhaustive survey of the existing literature, their analyses are broadly emblematic of contemporary Marxist scholarship (post-*Empire*) on the topic. For our first writer, Humphrey McQueen, globalisation is capitalist expansiveness, developmental stages and possibly part of an amalgam that includes capitalism and imperialism. James Petras and Henry Veltmeyer are much more straightforward in their view of globalisation, seeing it as a mask behind which lurks imperialism, a political project of a transnational ruling class. Ellen Meiksins Wood, the fourth and final writer in this section, sees globalisation as being a set of policies pursued by the US since the 1990s. The purpose of the policies was to stave off crises of overproduction, transferring the burden to other economies.

Stages of globalisation

In an interesting twist on the theme of stages, McQueen, an Australian Marxist historian (born in Brisbane in 1942), has taken the 'stagist' model of capitalist development, combined it with a long-term view (this last much favoured by World Systems analysts) and added globalisation. His summary of capitalist development depicts it as successive stages of globalisation or as he terms it globalisation Marks I through IV, and possibly Mark V for the current era (McQueen 2003: 104–7). McQueen claims that 'capitalism, imperialism and globalization are three of a kind', and then posits imperialism as monopolising capitals whose current incarnation might still be in the process of moving to 'a newer phase' (McQueen 2003: 103). Globalisation, then, is intimately bound up with imperialism and capitalism, with the key element connecting them for the past 600 years being the inexorable drive of capitalist expansion or what McQueen terms the 'world system for accumulation' (McQueen 2003: 104).

A summary of McQueen's stages of globalisation reveals some important points. The first phase of globalisation – what he terms 'globalization Mark I' – was the era of plunder of resources at home (Europe) and in the new world. This phase of globalisation received its impetus from the commercial and money dealing aspects of merchant's capital. The next phase – 'globalization Mark II' – was the age of mercantilism. 'Globalization Mark III', or 'the free trade interlude in the nineteenth century', was the period in which Britain industrialised, with its domination of global manufacturing established and consolidated. McQueen's 'globalization Mark IV' coincides with what he suggests is the era of Lenin's imperialism, or the era of 'monopolizing capitals', with the 'dominance of free-trading Britain driv[ing] its rivals towards protectionism' (McQueen 2003: 104–5).

Globalisation in its most recent form – 'Mark V' – has an uncertain status for as McQueen claims 'a question mark hangs over the recent past' (McQueen 2003: 106). Having highlighted the uncertainty of making claims about the recent past, McQueen pinpoints some substantial changes in the field of production-capital during the 1970s, which signalled the beginning of Mark V globalisation. Facing stiff competition from Japanese car manufacturers, American and European manufacturers, in an effort to cut production costs, dispersed production to locales where labour costs were lower. The scattering of production throughout the world gave rise to the 'world car'. The dispersal of production stages also became popular in computer production. This process of global integration 'encouraged financial deregulation to facilitate the transfer of investment funds and a reflux of profits' (McQueen 2003: 107). Globalisation's recent incarnation had its genesis in 'meeting the needs of rust-bucket industries' with flow-on effects not only in production but in the financial sphere as well (McQueen 2003: 107). Financial deregulation has enhanced the power of finance capital compared to production-capital. Also apparent is the increase in the monopolisation process, with mergers and acquisitions in automobile manufacturing, oil, pharmaceuticals, communications and finance (McQueen 2003: 108). Regarding technology, whilst this has brought about numerous changes to labour saving, control and discipline, the 'era of the most advanced technologies has been accompanied by [the] pushing up [of] the rate of exploitation through the crudest devices of exacting unpaid labour-time in the service sector, and by intensification everywhere' (McQueen 2003: 110).

McQueen's interesting and informative essay on globalisation is a thought-provoking modification of the concept of stages in the development of capitalism. By highlighting the globalising tendency of capitalism, and by calling the developmental stages of capitalism stages of globalisation, McQueen calls into question the proposition that globalisation is only a recent phenomenon. He suggests that 'capitalism, imperialism and globalization are three of a kind' and, furthermore, there might have been developments in monopolising capitals relatively recently that herald a new phase of imperialism/globalisation (McQueen 2003: 103). What globalisation really is and its connection with imperialism (monopolising capitals) is not completely clarified in this article. It is in his book on the history of the Coca-Cola Corporation (McQueen 2001) that the connections between capitalism, imperialism and globalisation are explored in greater depth. This book has the merit of being an empirical and historical study of a major corporation and its social, political and economic milieu. The bones of theoretical abstraction are fleshed out with empirical detail. A brief excursion into *The Essence of Capitalism the Origins of Our Future* (McQueen 2001) therefore is warranted.

Globalisation and imperialism: the Coca-Cola connections

An understanding of the globalising tendencies of capitalism is an integral element of McQueen's analysis of the growth of the Coca-Cola Corporation. Acknowledging that the 'McDonaldisation of the world' and the consequent 'erasure of regional tastes encouraged belief in the actuality of globalisation', McQueen nevertheless evinces a pessimism about the strong case for globalisation (McQueen 2001: 196). The term itself only came into widespread use from 1987 and initially referred to communications, high-tech industries and finance (McQueen 2001: 196–7). The strong case for globalisation – that is, its inevitability – is countered here by reference to its public relations role. Globalisation is used to give 'imperialism a public relations gloss'. The impression is disseminated in the public sphere that 'monopolising capitals [are] the outcome of ineluctable forces of nature, rather than of contestable social practices, {which} helps corporations to elude the hostility sparked by the word imperialism' (McQueen 2001: 197). The no-alternative-to-globalisation rhetoric masks the imperialist nature of monopolising capitals.

What, then, is globalisation and what is new about it? In the economic realm, McQueen claims that the new economy touted so fervently in the late 1990s and early 2000s has little to show, with the proponents for such a new economy not able to agree on a single model (McQueen 2001: 197). The popular belief in the new economy and globalisation stemmed from the internet with copious amounts of capital squandered on internet start-ups, which eventually led to the Dot.Com bubble. The computer screen has been a boon for transmittable services such as pornography and money and helps explain why 'financial trading is the ideal type of globalised commerce' (McQueen 2001: 197). The claim that globalisation has led to the sidelining of what McQueen terms 'nation-market-states' is dismissed. The imbalances between governments continue to exist with some modifying their position in the pecking order (China and India) but with the US still pre-eminent (McQueen 2001: 197). Thus, the conclusion must be that globalisation has not fundamentally influenced geopolitics. What is noticeable is that the richest third of the world since the 1970s has become more interlocked, with the US, the European Union and Japan through their economic interchanges accounting for 84 per cent of foreign direct investment (McQueen 2001: 198). The net result is that 'more domestic economies are being steered by their international connections' (McQueen 2001: 198).

Globalisation is mainly the further unfolding of the global capitalist economy. McQueen also contends that the novelty of globalisation is exaggerated. A comparison of recent changes to capitalism, with the central features of imperialism identified by Lenin, supports his contention. The dominance of monopolies and finance capital, the export of capital, the importance of international trusts and the division of the world amongst the capitalist powers remain evident, though with the latter there has been a qualitative change. The export of capital is as important now as when Lenin wrote about it, though with four additional objectives: 'stock market speculation'; the securing of 'raw materials and labour'; aiding the production and sale of commodities in overseas markets; and overseas production with the view to selling in the home market or third markets (McQueen 2001: 199). During the 1990s, the US economy relied on massive imports of capital that fuelled the record levels of the New York Stock Exchange and helped fund US current account deficits (McQueen, 2001: 199). The international trusts that had divided up the world in Lenin's time were now more extensive 'though they can never take a final form because mergers – and company failures – persist' (McQueen 2001: 199). Regarding the division of the globe by the capitalist powers, another of Lenin's core elements, McQueen identifies a change that has happened since the 1960s. With the demise of colonialism and colonisation, it is the provision of cheap labour in the former colonies that has attracted capital. The political and economic forms that support the structure of global capitalism have been modified, though not so much as to fundamentally change the subordinate status of much of the Third World (McQueen 2001: 200).

Rather than suggesting that an updated version of Lenin's theory of imperialism was robust enough to account for globalisation, McQueen concludes on the basis of his analysis of imperialism and globalisation that the latter is a higher stage of the former (McQueen 2001: 198). There is a problem with this proposition. If globalisation is not new and has been an integral part of capitalism since its inception, then to suggest that globalisation is 'a higher stage of imperialism' – that the world possibly has entered a new phase of globalisation – conflates the expansive drive of capitalism with developmental stages. The qualitative differences, the connections between globalisation and imperialism/monopoly capitals, are not really clarified in these two pieces of writing. Despite these problems, McQueen finds something unique about contemporary globalisation: 'it is most often Americanisation' (McQueen 2001: 210).

There is a real sense in McQueen's work that he remains open-minded about the ultimate significance of globalisation. In trying to explain what globalisation is the problematic suggestion was made that globalisation is a higher stage of imperialism. Globalisation is not a new phenomenon; in part, it is the usual expansiveness of capitalism and contemporaneously it often is Americanisation. But this not all; there is something to it that may only become apparent in due course. For McQueen, then, globalisation is an enigmatic phenomenon; a mixture of old and new that masks imperialism yet transcends the latter. We must await further developments. The next two writers, Petras and Veltmeyer, take a more jaundiced view of globalisation, viewing it (and much of the hypothesising about it) as an ideological smoke-and-mirrors trick that hides the imperialist nature of monopoly capitalism.

Globalisation as ideology: Petras and Veltmeyer

Petras and Veltmeyer, two academics from the US and Canada respectively, have written extensively on the impact of imperialism on Latin America. They have no doubts about what globalisation means. In *Globalization Unmasked Imperialism in the 21st Century* (2001), they posit two possible positions on globalisation. The first, favoured by 'most scholars', is that globalisation is a set of interrelated processes found in the structures stemming from 'capitalist modes of global production'. The second conceives globalisation not in structural terms but prefers to see it 'as the outcome of a consciously pursued strategy, the political project of a transnational capitalist class and formed on the basis of an institutional structure set up to serve and advance the interests of this class' (Petras and Veltmeyer 2001: 11). The two approaches to globalisation are poles apart, with those favouring the first position tending to see globalisation as an inevitability, necessitating structural adjustments. Countries are compelled to gain whatever advantage they can from globalisation (Petras and Veltmeyer 2001: 12). Those theorists who see the class project that lies behind globalisation adopt the second approach. For these writers globalisation is not inescapable and the term globalisation itself is suspect, seeing it 'as an ideological tool used for prescription rather than accurate description' (Petras and Veltmeyer 2001: 12).

The intentional and contingent aspects of globalisation are revealed when the second approach is adopted, with the controlling role of individuals and institutions coming in to focus. The interests of a 'new international capitalist class' are served by these individuals and institutions. The institutions mentioned here, which help form the basis of the international capitalist class, consist of 37,000 transnational corporations (TNCs). In addition, the class includes 'the bearers of capital and technology' and 'major agents of the new imperial order' (Petras and Veltmeyer 2001: 12).

Helping to organise this international capitalist class are the major institutions of global capitalism: the World Bank and the International Monetary Fund and other financial institutions which are designated as the international financial community (Petras and Veltmeyer 2001: 12). The other key elements making up this complex are planning and policy forums such as the Group of Seven (G7 – since expanded), the Trilateral Commission and the World Economic Forum. The role of the state has been restructured, in the core nations of global capitalism, to more effectively promote and expand global capitalism.

For Petras and Veltmeyer, globalisation is quite similar to previous projects of capitalist development such as modernisation, industrialisation and colonialism. Each project generated resistance and, like new imperialism, were 'fraught with contradictions' (Petras and Veltmeyer 2001: 12). They claim that the inevitability proposition is one of the main problems associated with the discourse about globalisation. An even greater problem is the way that the discourse obfuscates 'the form taken by imperialism in the current, increasingly worldwide capitalist system for organizing economic production and society' (Petras and Veltmeyer 2001: 13).

Nothing new under the sun of capitalism

Critical of much of the globalisation discourse, Petras and Veltmeyer present some historical analysis in order to contextualise globalisation. They conclude that it has been part of capitalism since its inception:

> The historical fact is that the US, Africa, Asia and Latin America have a history of several centuries of ties to overseas markets, exchanges and investments. Moreover, in the cases of North and Latin America, capitalism was born 'globalized,' in the sense that most of their early growth was based on overseas exchanges and investments. From the 15th to the 19th century Latin America's external trade and investment had greater significance than during the 20th century (Petras and Veltmeyer 2001: 28).

Like McQueen, for these two writers globalisation is just the expansive nature of capitalism, its tendency to find markets throughout the globe, its globalist push. They assert that the principal difference between earlier incarnations of globalisation and the twentieth-century version is that the current version is a 'deepening and extension of exploitative class relations into areas previously outside of capitalist production' (Petras and Veltmeyer 2001: 29). Also, they point out that, from the former colonial countries, a new breed of transnational capitalists has arisen whose expertise is centred in capital export, which both writers claim is a crucial difference compared to earlier times (Petras and Veltmeyer 2001: 29).

Causes of globalisation rhetoric

There are a number of reasons that Petras and Veltmeyer identify as helping to explain the rise of globalisation rhetoric. The major drivers were political, social and economic:

> Politically the 'big push' was a result of a dramatic change in political power away from leftist, populist and nationalist regimes towards globalist governments. In social terms, the 'big push' resulted from the defeat and retreat of trade unions, and the declining influence of the working class, lower middle class and the peasantry. The ascendancy of the social classes engaged in international networks of capital and trade, and particularly the financial sector, set the stage for the globalist counter-revolution. What began in certain Third World (Chile, Mexico) and imperial centres (the US and the UK) spread throughout the world in an uneven fashion (Petras and Veltmeyer 2001: 47).

The political and social push was balanced on the economic side by four economic developments: first, a crisis of over-accumulation; second, a profit-squeeze brought about by tensions in capital/labour relations; third, the heightening of capitalist competition on the international stage; and, finally, deregulation of financial markets leading to the marked growth in those markets (Petras and Veltmeyer 2001: 48). Contrary to the opinions of globalisation promoters, the nation-state played a pivotal role in the acceptance of globalisation. Far from being minimised or weakened by globalisation, imperial states were active in promoting and pushing for other states to accede to globalisation through incorporation into free trade zones and through IMF and World Bank 'reforms' (Petras and Veltmeyer 2001: 47–8).

Globalisation and its associated discourse also have been useful in covering up an ideological 'hole'. The rise of globalisation as an ideology is predicated in part on the decline of the left and the concerted attack on organised labour, waged by the ruling classes in the advanced capitalist countries (the US and Britain especially) throughout the 1980s and 1990s. The attack on wages and conditions in the First World had in certain cases a more dramatic counterpart in the Third World. In Chile, for example, Pinochet's dictatorship set about imposing a free market economic model based on advice received from 'Chicago school' luminaries such as Milton Friedman. Implementing such advice during the 1980s led to an unemployment rate of 26 per cent and a depression (Petras and Veltmeyer 2001: 112–13). The conjuncture of the 1980s and 1990s, with the US as the sole superpower after the winding up of the Soviet Union and its Eastern European satellite states, has brought into being the ideological masking of imperial relations. Globalisation rhetoric, claim Petras and Veltmeyer, is a product of specific global political, economic and social circumstances. It persists because it disguises US imperial power, economic and military dominance (Petras and Veltmeyer 2001: 62–3).

To sum up their views on globalisation, Petras and Veltmeyer in *Globalization Unmasked Imperialism in the 21st Century* (2001) counteracted what they perceived was the ideological masking of imperialism by globalisation rhetoric. They not only wanted to counter globalisation as an ideological device, but sought to recover or rehabilitate imperialism as an accepted discourse for the left. (Imperialism here is defined as the economic, political and in cases, military dominance of the Third World by the metropolitan nations of the First World.) The US is the imperialist state *par excellence* and it is in the interests of this state to have the ideology of globalisation advanced. The two authors acknowledge that globalisation is not rhetoric alone. It describes a complex of changes associated with the 'dynamics of capitalist development as well as the diffusion of values and cultural practices associated with this development'. They emphasise in particular the market side of globalisation, claiming that it refers to the 'widening and deepening of the international flows of trade, capital, technology and information within a single integrated global market'

(Petras and Veltmeyer 2001: 11). Ultimately, globalisation glosses over the problems of free market capitalism, and ultimately functions best as an ideological mask. Imperialism thus remains as the best analytical and descriptive tool for informing political practice.

Something new in the empire of capital?

Ellen Meiksins Wood, a renowned Marxist academic (born Ellen Meiksins in 1942 in the US to parents who had fled from war-ravaged Europe) has written a number of books and articles on political economy, historical materialism and the state amongst other things. In a volume published in 2003, *Empire of Capital*, she devotes some space to critically reflecting on globalisation.

For Wood, globalisation stems from a very real set of contradictions that arose in global capitalism and geopolitics in the 1990s. A combination of capitalist crisis of overproduction and overcapacity and the revival of Germany and Japan to the status of economic competitors to the US during this period proved to be critical (Wood 2003: 133). Facing pressure from the competitive challenge issuing from Germany and Japan and the downturn in its own economy the US sought to displace the crisis in space and time:

> What followed was the period we call globalization, the internationalization of capital, its free and rapid movements and the most predatory financial speculation around the globe. This was, as much as anything else, a response not to the successes but to the failures of capitalism. The US used its control of financial and commercial networks to postpone the day of reckoning for its own domestic capital, enabling it to shift the burden elsewhere, easing the movement of excess capital to seek profits wherever they were to be found, in an orgy of financial speculation (Wood 2003: 133).

When some of the developing economies were in crisis and seeking help, the US used its financial and commercial networks to good effect and was able to get some of them to sign up to the 'Washington consensus'. The 'consensus' – a set of policy prescriptions administered in the main by Washington based institutions such as the IMF, the World Bank and the

US Treasury – opened up various economies to structural adjustment. The target economy or economies were made more amenable to US-led global capital (Wood 2003: 133). Chief among the Washington consensus policies are trade liberalisation, production for export, privatisation of public services and financial deregulation. Through such mechanisms as the Washington consensus, and by 'manipulating debt, the rules of trade, foreign aid and the whole financial system', the US is able to transfer or displace the crisis of overproduction and overcapacity onto the developing economies (Wood 2003: 134).

Wood views the subordination or opening up of developing economies to the dictates of imperial capital as the essence of globalisation. Though economies may be opened up, this does not necessarily lead to a fully integrated world economy. There remain instances where integration or interdependence is not encouraged under globalisation. An example of this is that, whilst capital movement across borders is unhindered, the market imperative that would operate to bring about a worldwide common social average of labour costs and productivity is blocked (Wood 2003: 136). A fully integrated world economy would be a hindrance to globalisation as it relies on the fragmentation of the world into separate economies at the political apex of which stand sovereign nation-states. It is an important part of the role of those nation-sates to 'enforce the principle of nationality that makes it possible to manage the movements of labour by means of strict border controls and stringent immigration policies' (Wood 2003: 137). Nation-states make sure that labour markets are reasonably quiescent and not subject to the volatilities that mass immigration may cause.

In summary, for Wood globalisation is a set of policy prescriptions or choices that arose in the 1990s. From its inception, capitalism has been expansive with a universalising drive. The universalisation of what Wood calls 'capitalist imperatives' (Wood 2003: 20), however, was not fully achieved until the early 1990s (Wood 2003: 133). Responding to crises of overproduction and overcapacity and the rise of serious economic competitors, the US sought to maintain its imperial position in part by policy initiatives such as the Washington consensus. Acceptance of the consensus by other nation-states allowed the US to shift its economic problems offshore and thus put off the day of reckoning. Globalisation, for Wood, is not inevitable but rather just the latest set of imperialist policies, 'just as old-style imperialism represented policy choices in the interests of capital in a largely non-capitalist world' (Sivanandan and Wood 1997: 19–33).

Globalisation and its meaning for these 'globalisation-era' Marxists

The identification of globalisation as part of the hegemonic project of the US (also known as Americanisation) is a common feature of the analyses of all four writers. Another common element is the recognition of globalisation as either being another term for the expansive drive of capitalism, or the broadening and deepening of markets in the ceaseless striving for an integrated world economy. All four stress the primacy of the political economic in their viewpoints. Of interest is that none of them subscribe to the hyper-globalist view of Hardt and Negri. Whilst in Wood's work examined above there is no mention of an ideological aspect to globalisation, in an earlier article she had described globalisation 'as it is commonly understood [as] the heaviest ideological albatross around the neck of the left today' (Sivanandan and Wood 1997: 19–33). By this she meant the defeatism engendered by the idea that globalisation was somehow unstoppable or irresistible, an idea that had seized wide sections of the left prior to the upsurge in anti-corporate globalisation that occurred in the late 1990s. Thus, it can be said that all these writers acknowledge the existence of an ideological component in globalisation.

Differences contained in their accounts give a broad indication of the parameters of contemporary Marxist thinking about the globalisation-capitalism-imperialism nexus after the publication of *Empire* (2000). McQueen sees globalisation as both an incipient part of capitalist development over centuries and a new phase of that development process. In attempting to account for this ambiguity, McQueen had recourse to the analytical tool of periodisation. Whilst the periodisation of globalisation device is a twist on the stagist one employed by Lenin and others more recently,[1] McQueen does not clarify the nature of the relationship between globalisation, capitalism and imperialism. The lack of clarity is due to McQueen's belief that there is still some question about the nature of globalisation in its current incarnation. There may be something new and transforming about it but he is unsure of the extent, hence the lack of clarity about the tripartite relationship. Wood, too, perceives some substance in the claims made about globalisation. Where she differs from McQueen is in her insistence that it is a set of policies undertaken by the global hegemon to offset economic difficulties and to reinforce its geopolitical status. The relationship between globalisation, capitalism and imperialism is certain. Capitalism is the economic basis, with imperialism a set of policies utilised by capitalist states and globalisation a new subset of imperialist policies. Petras and Veltmeyer are more hostile to globalisation seeing it as mainly ideological. To the extent that globalisation does have substance, they see it as the extension and deepening of exploitation into areas previously outside of capitalist production processes. In short, it is the usual unfolding of capitalism. For them the relationship between globalisation, capitalism and imperialism is more properly understood as the relationship between capitalism and imperialism,[2] with the latter being the First World's political and economic (and sometimes military) dominance of the Third World.

So, then, there are three poles around which recent Marxist analysis of the tripartite relationship (globalisation, capitalism, and imperialism) hover. The first is uncertainty about the relationship between the three due to the possibility that there may be substance to some of the large claims made about the transformative power of globalisation as made by Hardt and Negri plus Robinson (see above). More studies into the nature and extent of globalisation, as well as the passing of time, are needed before any definitive insight can be given about the connections between the three. The second line of thinking sees some substance in globalisation but definitely not of the same order of magnitude typical of hyper-globalists. Consequently, globalisation is accorded the status of a minor in the relationship. Wood, as established already, slots globalisation into imperialism as a policy subset. At the third pole there is denial of a three-part relationship due to the rhetoric associated with globalisation. Globalisation has little substance other than that of ideology and so the focus must remain on the symbiotic relationship between capitalism and imperialism.

What can be said about the foregoing is that it is an indication of the depth and quality of the theoretical writing of Marxists who have been galvanised by the challenges of globalisation and by Hardt's and Negri's cathartic intervention. The grappling with the problem of globalisation is just one part of a more general enthusiasm for imperialism theory. Further evidence of that enthusiasm and the calibre of contemporary theorising about the matters of empire and new imperialism is found in the work of the next two writers.

Empire and imperialism redux: Wood and Harvey clarify

Ellen Meiksins Wood and David Harvey have produced two books that clarify and explicate issues about empire and imperialism. Wood, in particular, wrote in response to the challenge that Hardt's and Negri's *Empire* posed for imperialism theory and for the understanding of modes of empire. In *Empire of Capital*, which we have had occasion to explore already, she sought to clarify the structural differences between forms of empire. She asserts that there are three forms of empire, which are built on: property; commerce; and capital. The distinguishing feature of the empire of capital compared to the other two is the separation of economic power from what she calls the extra-economic. The latter encompasses the state and the forces needed to maintain order and/or control. The bifurcation of economic power from extra-economic power is a hallmark of the empire of capital. Each mode of empire has historically specific features and to propound a transcendent, decentred mode of empire – Hardt's and Negri's 'Empire' – only makes opaque the current state of capitalist imperialism. Harvey, on the other hand, focusses on new imperialism. His book arrives at a sophisticated definition of imperialism in the era of US hegemony. What he has done is address the need for clarity about the forces that combine to drive new imperialism. In addition, he has provided novel insights into the capitalist accumulation process and suggested two new variants of imperialism in the globalisation era. Such has been the quality of his work that an edition of the Marxist journal *Historical Materialism* (2006) devoted the major part of an issue to critical responses to *The New Imperialism* (2005). Taken together these two writers have done valuable work in 'theoretical underlabouring', or the process of clearing up matters associated with empire and imperialism. Our attention first turns to the different forms of empire as expounded by Wood.

Imperialism and empires, not 'Empire'

Wood situates the *Empire of Capital* (2003) as 'a political response to the current situation and an analytic/historical exploration of capitalist imperialism in general, of what drives it and has distinguished it from other imperial forms since its inception' (Wood 2003: x). According to Wood, the crucial defining quality of capitalist imperialism is the unique capacity that capitalism has in being able to divorce economic force from extra-economic force: 'amongst other things . . . the economic power of capital can reach far beyond the grasp of any existing, or conceivable, political and military power' (Wood 2003: 5). But the separation of the economic from the extra-economic in capitalism and, by extension, capitalist imperialism is not total. The economic power of capitalism relies on – 'cannot exist' – without the support of the military and political power that is concentrated in the state (Wood 2003: 5).

The separation of economic power from political coercion and military power in the empire of capital is possible because:

> Capitalists – unlike, say, feudal lords – generally need no direct control of coercive military or political force to exploit their workers, because being propertyless, workers must sell their labour power in exchange for a wage in order to work and live (Wood 2003: 10).

The market becomes a force of its own and thus compels everyone – 'capitalists as well as workers' – to adhere to 'impersonal systemic requirements of competition, accumulation and profit-maximization' (Wood 2003: 11).

Having established the defining features of the empire of capital, Wood turns her attention to how power was manifested in earlier forms of empire. Starting with the empire of property and moving on to the empire of commerce, the essential political and economic characteristics of these imperial forms will be briefly detailed. Her analysis serves to illustrate the historical, political and economic specificity of each form of empire.

Empire of property

The first example of this mode of empire is the Roman Empire. Replicating its own social property relations that prevailed at home throughout its imperial domains, what resulted was an empire based on a self-governing aristocracy of landowners. The state that controlled such a far-flung enterprise actually was not huge: 'Romans administered their empire with a relatively small central state, through what amounted to a wide-ranging coalition of local landed aristocracies, with the help of Roman colonists and colonial administrators' (Wood 2003: 28). The provisioning of garrisons to maintain order and control the subject populace was indispensible for these colonial outposts.

Centuries later, another variant of the empire of property came into being: the Spanish Empire. During the reign of Ferdinand and Isabella – a period famous for the 'discovery' of the Americas by Christopher Columbus – the monarchs sought to maintain their power and minimise or control the development of a feudal aristocracy in the colonies. This was accomplished during the time of Spain's epochal expansion into the New World 'by farming out the tasks of empire to private conquerors in pursuit of private wealth' (Wood 2003: 38). Here, too, military force was an absolute pre-requisite.

Empires of property were marked by the dependence of the imperial state – whether republican or monarchical – on a class of private property owners. These could be landowners or, as in the case of the Spanish Empire, conquerors whose motivation was the pursuit of gold and silver. The economic power of this form of empire was not sufficient on its own to maintain the far-flung colonies of the Roman and Spanish imperial states. Thus, extra-economic power was an indispensable prop. Economic power and extra-economic power were two parts of a whole.

Empire of commerce

The period after the decline of the Spanish Empire and before the advent of the late nineteenth- and early twentieth-century version of imperialism (the empire of capital) witnessed empires built on trade. The Arab Muslim Empire was dedicated to the control of trade more so than the control of territory. Like empires of property, empires of commerce could not function without a resort to or the threat of extra-economic power (Wood 2003: 45):

> The Arab Muslim empire and late medieval or early modern European commercial empires like the Venetian or the Dutch diverged in many ways, but they had one fundamental thing in

> common. However much their respective states differed, they all sustained their domination over a wide geographic expanse not simply by means of extending the reach of single powerful state but by perfecting their role as vital economic links among separate markets in dispersed communities and regions (Wood 2003: 47).

The cohesion of the Arab Muslim Empire was based on an elaborate trading network spread out over dispersed regions, underpinned by 'a structure of laws and offices' attributable to the state itself and more importantly, to the 'unique religious formulation associated with Muhammad and his followers'. Islam and its spread were both a cause and a consequence of the Arab trade networks (Wood 2003: 49).

Two other examples of commercial empires are the Venetian Empire – with its Italian city-states such as Florence and Venice – and the Dutch Republic. For the Italian city-states, their wealth was generated first and foremost by commerce with financial services a notable addition (Wood 2003: 55). Similarly with the Dutch Republic, commerce was its key element, having extensive commercial links 'from the Baltic to North America, and the East Indies to southern Africa' (Wood 2003: 61). The commercial dominance of the Dutch Republic, however, was not achieved by capitalist means. The dominance of the Dutch in their trading relations was due in large part to extra-economic superiority. The advantages that the Dutch were able to exploit in the field of extra-economic power were primarily shipping and military technology.

A feature of the Dutch empire and other empires established by the major European powers were settler colonies. It was in the next form of empire – the empire of capital, under the auspices of the British – that settler colonies acquired real significance. The nineteenth-century British Empire and its colonisation process was a response to the imperatives of capitalism, thus heralding a distinctly modern version of empire.

Empire of capital

Due to its late start in the European-led race for commercial supremacy, Britain was decidedly disadvantaged when it set out to expand overseas. Consequently, it turned to its own border regions 'and above all ... Ireland' in its efforts to establish its own colonial experiment (Wood 2003: 78). The colonisation of Ireland was a discrete process, with periods of intensive intervention by the English state. An important point in this subjugation process occurred in the sixteenth century when the Tudor monarchy sought not only to impose 'their government and law' on the Irish, but also to re-make Irish society itself. This re-making of Irish society was undertaken by means of the settlement of English and Scottish settlers in plantations (Wood 2003: 79). Military conquest, too, was a key ingredient in this early form of British imperialism, with Cromwell's military conquest of Ireland during the period 1649–52 being the prime example (Wood 2003: 83). What we see in this early period of colonisation and later British colonial rule in America and in India is a combination of commercial and territorial imperialism, based on extra-economic power.

It was only with the advent of capitalism in Britain in the nineteenth century that capitalist imperatives started to become the driving force behind imperialism. The advantages accruing to Britain from the rise of capitalism and the industrialisation that this spawned were crucial. These advantages eventually generated industrialisation in Britain's European rivals, but this did not mean that military and geopolitical concerns were immediately supplanted by economic competition. The nineteenth century was replete with 'ferocious campaigns of colonial expansion and conflicts over the division of the colonial world' (Wood 2003: 124). During this 'classic age of imperialism', capitalism remained at an advanced level in Europe and spread unevenly throughout the rest of the world. Hence, it was not economic imperatives that dominated in the colonial world but rather coercive force – otherwise known as extra-economic power (Wood 2003: 125).

The classical age of imperialism that Lenin and Luxemburg analysed ended after the catastrophe that was World War I.[3] Colonisation, so important in this age, continued in the world wars interregnum. The end of World War II marked not only the rise of the 'world's first truly economic empire', but also the start of a change in the form of empire: from the classical age of imperialism to something 'new' (Wood 2003: 128). The arrival on the world stage of the US after World War II and the onset of the Cold War did not herald the beginning of the dominance of economic power. What it did herald was a period when the objective of military might – specifically US military power – was concentrated away 'from the relatively well defined goals of imperial expansion and inter-imperialist rivalry to the open-ended objective of policing the world in the interests of (US) capital' (Wood 2003: 129). The US did not seek territorial expansion and generally opposed the moves of the European nations to restore their colonies after the war. Decolonisation after World War II took two or three decades to play out, which resulted in a change in interstate relationships from one dominated by imperial masters and colonial subjects to a more complex interaction between a world of nation states (Wood 2003: 129). The result of these changes was new imperialism, with the US as the 'strongest economic and military power' in the capitalist West. Opposed to the capitalist West were the Soviet Union and its bloc of states. The Cold War ended with the collapse of communism and the US transformed into the global hegemon. It is in this post-Cold War period of new imperialism and US dominance that economic imperatives rather than extra-economic power truly can be said to be *the* determining factor in the empire of capital (Wood 2003: 130).

Despite this claim, the role of the US and other states in the international system of states remains important. The ending of the Long Boom and the declining profitability and stagnation of the US and other economies meant that new policies had to be implemented to maintain US hegemony and ultimately the empire of capital. This is where globalisation comes in, which, according to Wood, is a set of policies like the Washington consensus. Only states can implement these policies and enforce them. Extra-economic power still has a role to play in the empire of capital.

The most positive attribute of this book (and, as we will see directly with Harvey's) is that it constitutes a valuable part of what can be called theoretical underlabouring. Theoretical underlabouring is a modification of philosophical underlabouring, a term used by Roy Bhaskar to describe his efforts at building a 'more adequate philosophy of science and society for socialism' (Bhaskar 1989: 2). His project in *Reclaiming Reality* (1989) was motivated in part by the desire first expressed by John Locke to clear the ground of the detritus that impeded the path to knowledge (Bhaskar 1989: vii). The claim being made here about Wood's book is that she has helped clear the path for studies of empire and imperialism by way of theoretical underlabouring. Her analysis of the three forms of empire gives a clearer understanding of the similarities and differences between them and shows why capitalist imperialism – the 'empire of capital' – is a historically specific form of imperialism. The bifurcation of economic power from extra-economic power also is an important and interesting addition to imperialism theory.

By focussing on the historical forms of empire Wood avoids thorny problems such as the role of stages in capitalist development. That being said, she identifies a qualitative change occurring in capitalist imperialism after World War II and especially in the post-Cold War globalisation era. Unlike Hardt and Negri, Wood does not subscribe to the supplanting of imperialism due to major transformation thesis. For her globalisation has not rendered the state increasingly irrelevant. The role of the state and the system of states in the present globalisation/new imperialism era remains important. This is in direct contrast to the type of stateless 'sovereignty' position that she suggests lies at the heart of Hardt's and Negri's opus. Her writing on modes of empire is a corrective to what she perceives is the confusion surrounding the 'Empire' concept, which has no centre, no territory and promises to be eternal. A consequence of Hardt's and Negri's theorising is that it renders us 'powerless to resist' capitalist imperialism (Wood 2003: 6).

Wood does not think that classical Marxist theories can form the basis for a radical critique of the contemporary world. She flags her concerns that the classical Marxist imperialism theories of Lenin and Luxemburg are not adequate to account for US hegemony, the disappearance of colonialism and the universalisation of capitalism. Despite not presenting her own theory, Wood's contribution is significant. It is part of the 'search for a systematic theory' and, along with Harvey, Wood has made a 'serious contribution to the renewal of theoretical debate about imperialism' (Sutcliffe 2006: 62).

David Harvey's imperialism: logics, fixes and dispossession

David Harvey, born in 1935 in Gillingham in Britain, has carved out an academic career on both sides of the Atlantic. Specialising in geography, he has described the philosophy underpinning his analytical writing as a variant of historical materialism: historical geographical materialism (Harvey 2005: 1). Two important components of Harvey's account of imperialism are the territorial and capitalist logics of power, concepts inspired by the work of Giovanni Arrighi. Capitalist imperialism, then, relies on and is produced by these distinctly different yet intertwined logics, which at times can operate seemingly at cross-purposes. Harvey's analysis of new imperialism extends further. He has finessed the overaccumulation-leading to crises-leading to export of capital argument. The result is what he calls the spatio-temporal fix. Also, he has refined the concept of primitive accumulation that Marx suggested was the starting point of the capitalist accumulation process. Using Hannah Arendt's observation that the robbery that characterised primitive accumulation had to be repeated lest the accumulation process wind down, Harvey asserts that primitive accumulation had evolved into accumulation by dispossession. The latter is a process that became especially relevant after the Long Boom of capitalism ended in the 1970s, which ushered in the start of new imperialism. The concepts of the territorial and capitalist logics of power, allied with the spatio-temporal fix and accumulation by dispossession, collectively represent the three key elements of Harvey's *The New Imperialism* (2005). Using these analytical tools Harvey claims that two new forms of imperialism have appeared in the globalisation era and his findings regarding these two new forms are summarised in the penultimate subsection.

The two logics of power in imperialism

According to Arendt, the perpetual accumulation of property has a corollary in the perpetual accumulation of power (Arendt cited in Harvey 2005: 34). The ever-expanding process of capital accumulation therefore has as a necessary requirement: the expansion and intensification of hegemonic power. There are differing priorities facing those involved in capitalist accumulation compared with those concerned with the accumulation of power:

> The capitalist holding money capital will wish to put it wherever profits can be had, and typically seeks to accumulate more capital. Politicians and statesmen typically seek outcomes that sustain or augment the power of their own state vis-à-vis other states. The capitalist seeks individual advantage and (though usually constrained by law) is responsible to no one other than his or her immediate social circle, while the statesman seeks a collective advantage and is constrained by the political and military

> situation of the state and is in some sense or other responsible to a citizenry or, more often, to an elite group, a class, a kinship structure, or some other social group. The capitalist operates in continuous space and time, whereas the politician operates in a territorialized space and, at least in democracies, in a temporality dictated by an electoral cycle. On the other hand, capitalist firms come and go, shift locations, merge, or go out of business, but states are long lived entities, cannot migrate, and are, except under exceptional circumstances of geographical conquest, confined within fixed territorial boundaries (Harvey 2005: 27).

The distinction between the territorial and capitalist logics of power often has been glossed over in the literature on imperialism and empire. Harvey claims that it is too readily accepted by writers that there is a fundamental unity between the territorial and capitalist logics of power, with the capitalist logic always the dominant factor. Put another way, the dictates of capital always are behind the decisions of a state at both the domestic and geopolitical levels. Not so: 'In practice the two logics frequently tug against each other, sometimes to the point of outright antagonism' (Harvey 2005: 29). Citing the Vietnam War and the invasion of Iraq as examples, Harvey argues that they could not be seen as being exclusively undertaken for purposes of capital accumulation (Harvey, 2005: 30). There is, then, a dialectical relationship that exists between the territorial and capitalist logics of power. Unravelling the complexities involved in actual situations requires the ability 'to keep the two sides of this dialectic simultaneously in motion and not to lapse into either a solely political or predominantly economic mode of argumentation' (Harvey 2005: 30).[4]

Imperialism, according to Harvey's interpretation, is the direct result of the symbiotic relationship between 'inter-state relations and flows of power [operating . . .] within a global system of capital accumulation' (Harvey 2005: 33). From the perspective of capital accumulation, imperialism is the sustaining and exploiting of advantages such as uneven geographical development, natural and other resources and what Harvey terms asymmetrical advantages that 'can be assembled by way of state power' (Harvey, 2005: 33). Like Wood, Harvey claims that what sets capitalist imperialism apart from previous forms of imperialism is that in the capitalist logic-territorial logic relationship it is the capitalist logic that tends to dominate, though there are times when the reverse is true.

The spatio-temporal fix

For over two decades, Harvey has grappled with the chronic tendency found in capitalism of overaccumulation. Acknowledging Lenin's and Luxemburg's attempts at casting imperialism as the answer to overaccumulation crises, Harvey attempts to tease out the strands further. He states that the surpluses of capital in commodity, money or productive capacity forms, and surpluses in labour power often exist side-by-side in overaccumulation crises. The problem was and is how to bring both types of surpluses together to re-commence profitable tasks (Harvey 2005: 88). What has been the usual way out of this impasse (which may last for a substantial period with capital becoming increasingly devalued and people immiserated) was 'geographical expansion and spatial reorganization' (Harvey 2005: 88). The crucial problem here is that of the capital surplus, argues Harvey, and it is the way that capital circulates in space and time creating its own historical geography that overaccumulation crises are temporarily overcome. The focus on the capitalist logic evident here has to be balanced by an understanding of the dialectical relationship between the former (molecular movements of capital accumulation) and the politics of empire and states (territorial logics of power). This balance is achieved by exploring how states provide the framework in which accumulation takes place.

What has emerged in the US since its malaise in mid 1970s is an institutional structure that Harvey calls the 'Wall Street-Treasury' complex. This draws on the conception put forward by Peter Gowan of a 'Dollar-Wall Street Regime' (1999) with some modifications and reservations. Such a financial sector, state conglomerate possesses 'vast financial power' and has the ability to control the IMF and thus, by extension, global capitalism.

The 'Wall Street-Treasury' complex not only represents the coming together of the state (in this instance the US) and finance capital, but also it is pivotal in maintaining the prominence of key nodal points, such New York, London and Tokyo (Harvey 2005: 134). Furthermore, the finance capital/state power matrix evident in the 'Wall Street-Treasury' complex contrives to bring about 'vulture capitalism' where accumulation by dispossession almost is the norm.

The spatio-temporal fix of crises of overaccumulation is a sophisticated addition to the understanding of one of the fundamental causes of imperialism, namely overaccumulation (also known as overproduction). There is no permanent solution to the problem of overaccumulation – only temporary measures – which usually involve a combination of spatial and temporal displacements. By bringing to light the dynamics of what he calls the molecular process of capital accumulation, Harvey has made an impressive contribution to enhancing previous work on the problem of accumulation. Next is the third key element of *The New Imperialism*, accumulation by dispossession.

Primitive accumulation revisited: accumulation by dispossession

The processes of expropriation by which the accumulation process of capitalism came into being were varied. Marx identified the 'commodification and privatization of land and the forceful expulsion of peasant populations; the conversion of various forms of property rights; the suppression of rights to commons' as being amongst the main methods of expropriation (Harvey 2005: 145). The expropriation techniques first witnessed in the pre-dawn of the Industrial Revolution still are part of the arsenal of capitalism.

With the advent of neo-liberalism, new techniques of expropriation have come to the fore. Two examples are the privatisation of nationalised industries and the usurping of family farms by agribusiness. There is a combination of old and new techniques and some fine-tuning of the old methods. One form of expropriation that has been fine-tuned is the financial system. Recognised by Lenin, Luxemburg and Hilferding as being one of the 'major levers of predation, fraud and thievery' in the early decades of the twentieth century, the financial system has enhanced its speculative and predatory nature in the last decades of that century and into the next (Harvey 2005: 147). Features of contemporary finance capitalism include: asset stripping through mergers and acquisitions; asset destruction via inflation; corporate fraud (Enron); and credit and stock manipulations amongst other financial manoeuvring. Not least prominent amongst these methods, suggests Harvey, is the 'speculative raiding carried out by hedge funds and other major institutions of finance capital {qualifying} as the cutting edge of accumulation by dispossession in recent times' (Harvey 2005: 147). The combination of old and new methods of expropriation observable in the accumulation process make the old terms of primitive or original accumulation redundant. Hence, the new term accumulation by dispossession.

The ongoing process of accumulation by dispossession acts as another outlet for over-accumulated capital. This opening up of another outlet is achieved by releasing a set of assets – including labour power – that can be turned to profitable use by surplus capital. During the time of the enclosures with the forcible expulsion of the English peasants from the land, the land so released found its way into the mainstream of accumulation. In addition, the landless peasants were absorbed into the production process as proletarians. Similarly, the Soviet Union's disintegration, and the opening up of China to market forces, have meant that an immense amount of formerly locked up assets became available to the capitalist accumulation process (Harvey 2005: 149).

Privatisation, asset devaluation, intellectual property rights, financial manipulation in the form of extension or denial of credit, capital flight, structural adjustment programmes, backed up by the power of the hegemonic state and international financial institutions such as the IMF and the World Bank affirm that the predatory nature of capitalism has not changed since its inception. The predation remains but the predatory methods have changed markedly. The ending of the Long Boom and the casting about for new policies that would arrest and reverse declining profitability and low growth rates saw the advent of neo-liberalism in the US and Britain. The triumph of neo-liberalism and the attendant fetishising of privatisation, amongst other policies, marks the transition from expanded reproduction to accumulation by dispossession, the latter becoming the preferred method of capitalist accumulation. Accumulation by dispossession is Harvey's attempt to refine understanding of the capitalist logic side of the territorial/capitalist logic dialectic.[5]

Different forms of imperialism in the globalisation era

In combination with the territorial and capitalist logics of power one also should look to the inner and outer relations of the capitalist state as a basis for interpreting contemporary imperialism. With such an interpretative framework it is possible to detect two new forms of imperialism. From 1973–5 until the election of George W. Bush in 2000, there existed a form of neo-liberal imperialism, which started in the US and Britain and spread through the international community of states. Neo-liberal policies of privatisation, structural adjustment programmes policed by the IMF, and others make up a large part of the policy armoury of neo-liberal imperialism. One structure that supports the neo-liberal form of imperialism is the Wall Street-Treasury-IMF complex, which acts in concert with European and Japanese authorities. Also implicated is a 'transnational capitalist class' (Harvey 2005: 185–7). This latter class comprises financiers, multinational CEOs and rentiers. These principal beneficiaries of the inner and outer relations between states (US, Europe and Japan) have pushed the costs of over-accumulation onto the weakest states and peoples.

With the ascension of Bush to the US presidency, the neo-liberal form of imperialism has been superseded by neo-conservative imperialism. The US has changed its political complexion and this is reflected in its internal and external policies. The neo-conservatives' primary objective 'is the establishment of and respect for order, both internally and upon the world stage' (Harvey 2005: 190). Internally, the curtailment of certain civil liberties came into effect through the passing of the Patriot and Homeland Security Acts, amongst others. Externally, the invasions of Afghanistan and Iraq, the 'War on Terrorism' and the promulgation of Iran, Iraq and North Korea as 'rogue states' by Bush, highlight the shift from the neo-liberal emphasis on hegemony through consent to that of hegemony through coercion (Harvey 2005: 201). A more overt use of military force is a defining characteristic of neo-conservative imperialism.

The common assumption of the neo-liberal and neo-conservative forms of imperialism is that free markets will deliver freedom and prosperity to all, that the capitalist accumulation process ultimately is beneficial for the majority of people. Under the neo-conservative variant, a disjuncture has occurred between the capitalist logic and the territorial logic. The expansion of military spending consequent upon the invasion and continued military presence in Afghanistan and Iraq (spending to support the territorial logic of power) has caused problems for the accumulation process in the US. With soaring budget deficits and the apparent switching to a permanent war economy, the US economy becomes more vulnerable to possible capital flight:

> much depends upon confidence in the US government, and the more it is recognized that it is currently dominated by a coalition of the military-industrial complex, neo-conservatives, and, even more worryingly, fundamentalist Christians, the more the logic of capital will look to regime change in Washington as necessary to its own survival. This would have the effect of bringing the neo-conservative version of imperialism to a crashing halt (Harvey 2005: 206–7).

Harvey's *The New Imperialism* (2005) makes a telling contribution to Marxist thought on imperialism. Similar to Wood's book, Harvey has confined himself to the abstract, concentrating on improving, expanding and elucidating on theoretical aspects of new imperialism. New imperialism started with the overaccumulation crisis of the 1970s, initiating qualitative changes in the accumulation process and prompting the casting about for new economic paradigms and policies. One of the remarkable developments of the globalisation/new imperialism era has been the unrivalled power of the US. To account for this and the last three decades of change, a re-configuration of Marxist imperialism theory was necessary, not its wholesale abandonment. A systematic attempt at both clearing the way for and contributing to the re-configuration process has been Harvey's goal. One of the virtues of Harvey's foray into imperialism theory lies in his re-iteration of the dialectical relationship between the two logics of power that reside in the heart of imperialism. The dynamics of this symbiotic relationship often are overlooked by Marxists and mainstream writers alike, favouring either the capitalist or territorial logics (economics or the political) leading to one-sided analysis. His exposition is a timely reminder of the interconnectedness of the political and economic layers. Other notable contributions have been the insights into the geographical and temporal nature of the accumulation process, the increasingly predatory nature of the latter leading to a new type of primitive accumulation: accumulation by dispossession. In a refinement of the two logics of power relationship, Harvey adds to the arsenal of analytical tools the further dialectic of the internal and external relations of the state and uses them to posit two new forms of imperialism.

Some criticism has been made of Harvey's lack of a 'proper theory of the state' and fault is found in his not having really defined imperialism (Castree 2006: 43–4). The latter claim arguably is wrong, and even though the former claim may be true it is beside the point, anyhow. Harvey acknowledges the importance of state theory, believing that imperialism cannot be understood without it (Harvey 2005: 183). It was not his intention to develop a fully rounded theory of imperialism, nor for that matter present a comprehensive theoretical view of the state. Both Harvey and Wood have done valuable work in theoretical underlabouring. They have helped raise the bar for Marxist imperialism theory in their clarification and explication of not only old imperial forms but also new strands. This represents real qualitative achievements in the field. The next two writers, Leo Panitch and Sam Gindin, have identified a gaping hole – state theory – in classical Marxist theories that apparently render them obsolete.

Sins of omission: state theory, the gaping hole in imperialism theory

Panitch, a professor of Political Science, and his academic colleague at York University, Sam Gindin, assert that there is a glaring omission in the corpus of Marxist imperialism theory. The lack of a proper theorisation of the state and the international system of states has proven to be problematic for classical Marxist thought and writing on imperialism. Instrumentalist readings of the state cannot cope with the current configuration of the US informal empire. In their critique, they not only point out problems but also advocate the inclusion of state theory to arrive at a sophisticated contemporary theory of imperialism. Their contribution also is indicative of the high level of analysis evident in contemporary Marxist writing.

Panitch and Gindin decry the lack of 'any serious political economy or pattern of historical determination that would explain the emergence and reproduction of today's American empire and the dimensions of structural oppression and exploitation pertaining to it' (Panitch and Gindin 2004: 2). Imperialism, for much of the twentieth century the lodestar for the left, had lost its lustre by the 1970s amidst debates about where the real source of resistance to imperialism was centred – the Third World or in the working classes of the West.

The result of such disputation was a tower of Babel where, according to Arrighi, not even Marxists knew how to find their way (Arrighi cited in Panitch and Gindin 2004: 3). Consequently, there was a rejection of the use of imperialism as an analytical device. This trend continued through the 1990s, from the first Gulf War to the humanitarian interventions of the Clinton presidency, and culminated with the election of George W. Bush. The term imperialism barely rated a mention in critical analysis connected with the foregoing events (Panitch and Gindin 2004: 3). According to the two authors:

> The popularity of Hardt and Negri's tome, *Empire*, had caught the new conjuncture even before the second war on Iraq. But their insistence (reflecting the widespread notion that the power of all nation states had withered in the era of globalization) that *'the United States does not, and indeed no nation state can today, form the center of an imperialist project'* was itself bizarrely out of sync with the times (Hardt and Negri cited in Panitch and Gindin 2004; 3–4 emphasis in original).

The term imperialism was back, but the use made of it by the left was not sufficiently sophisticated to account for the informal US empire. Nor could the stages of capitalism approach be trotted out again. One of the lynchpins of Lenin's version of imperialism – inter-imperialist rivalry – had gradually become an article of faith, yet Panitch and Gindin argue that there were and are no real challengers to US hegemony. Inter-imperialist rivalry currently is a dead letter.

Classical theories: too much economics and not enough politics; where was the state?

The ebbing of globalisation (capitalist expansiveness or globalism) and the inter-imperialist rivalry of the years just prior to, during and immediately after World War I were taken as exemplary by classical theorists of imperialism. This is a fundamental error, which has acted to distort a proper understanding of imperialism through the decades (Panitch and Gindin 2004: 5). In taking the peculiarities of this historical conjuncture (inter-imperialist rivalry, export of capital, the monopoly or finance-capital stage of capitalism) as evidence of the moribundity of capitalist development, Hobson and classical Marxists such as Lenin apparently erred:

> Moreover, the theory of crisis derived from the classical understanding of this period was mistakenly used to explain capitalism's expansionist tendencies. If capitalists looked to the export of capital as well as trade in foreign markets, it was not so much because centralization and concentration of capital had ushered in a new stage marked by the falling rate of profit, overaccumulation and/or underconsumption. Rather, akin to the process that had earlier led individual units of capital to move out of their original location in a given village or town, it was the accelerated competitive pressures and opportunities, and the attendant strategies and emerging capacities of a developing capitalism, that pushed and facilitated the international expansionism of the late nineteenth and early twentieth centuries (Panitch and Gindin 2004: 6).

The upshot of such a catalogue of errors is that the capitalism of this era was not the highest stage; rather it was an early phase that had been misdiagnosed, where there was only rudimentary control over the internationalisation of capitalist social relations.

The problems with classical theorising of imperialism go deeper. There was a tendency in the classical group of writers to reduce imperialism to the playing out of economic forces. The privileging of the economic as explanatory device meant that the two distinct concepts of capitalism and imperialism became blurred or merged (Panitch and Gindin 2004: 6). For writers such as Kautsky and Lenin, mid-nineteenth-century Britain with its free trade and burgeoning industrialisation became a benchmark for 'pure' capitalism. The imperialism of the latter part of that century, for Lenin at least, marked a transition. Such a view was too crude a reading; not enough attention was paid by Kautsky and Lenin to the 'separation of the economic from the political under capitalism' (Panitch and Gindin 2004: 7). To understand the nature of imperialism thus requires not only political theory, but, moreover, a solid theory of the capitalist state. Such a theory needs to cover not only antagonisms between states but also now must cover the 'conjunctural predominance of one imperial state' that has structurally penetrated its former rivals and in the main gets them to accept its hegemony through consent (Panitch and Gindin 2004: 7). Classical Marxist theories cannot provide a basis for understanding this conjuncture because of the instrumental and reductionist reading of the state found within them (Panitch and Gindin 2004: 6).

The neo-liberal era and the end of inter-imperialist rivalry

The reconstruction of capitalism in the aftermath of World War II was a transitional phase. With the recovery of the European and the Japanese economies in the mid- to late-1950s, there was the potential for a challenge or challenges to US economic supremacy. That this did not happen was due to the material and ideological penetration of Europe and Japan, by American capital and by American notions of state-building and global order. Such material and ideological penetration meant states were no longer just responsible for furthering or promoting the interests of their own national bourgeoisie; they had to promote the interests of foreign capital as well. This was due to the interpenetration of US capital throughout Western Europe in the post-World War II era, through such mechanisms as the European Recovery Program (better known as the Marshall Plan). The internationalisation of the state, with the 'state's acceptance of responsibility for managing its domestic capitalist order in [a] way that contributes to managing the international capitalist order', was the bedrock of the informal US empire (Panitch and Gindin 2004: 17).

The hegemony established on the basis of this material and ideological penetration of potential rivals and their integration into the world capitalist economy does not preclude a degree of economic instability. Such instability, however, cannot lead to full blown inter-imperialist rivalry. The classical Marxist use of the latter term may have been insightful 'when economic competition among European states was indeed imbricated with comparable military capacities and [thus] Lenin could assert' that imperialist wars were inevitable (Panitch and Gindin 2004: 24). This did not hold after World War II and especially after the ending of the Cold War. With US military dominance and the material and ideological penetration of potential rival states and even the military integration of leading capitalist powers into US-backed treaties and alliances, economic competition cannot lead to armed conflict.

Nonetheless, the economic instability discussed above can be and is exacerbated by neo-liberalism, which has engendered recessions, deflationary pressures and world dependence on US markets. Correspondingly, the US now is reliant on inflows of capital to manage its expanding trade deficits. Neo-liberalism has helped to increase the complexity within the global capitalist system. Crises still are endemic to capitalism, but Panitch and Gindin argue that capitalist states have more instruments and experience by which to manage such crises. The hegemon leads the way in crisis management: 'The American imperial state has, to date, demonstrated a remarkable ability to limit the duration, depth, and contagion of crises' (Panitch and Gindin 2004: 26).

The unconcealed nature of US empire now in evidence has sprung from the limitations found in the very nature of informal empire. Neo-liberal reforms that started in the US and Britain, such as privatisation, financial deregulation and so on, and which were deemed to be necessary to address the low growth, low profitability problems that plagued capitalism after the Long Boom had ended, did not roll out uniformly through the capitalist states. The widespread adoption of neo-liberalism, promoted by ideologues and state managers in the Anglophone countries, required the co-operation of the member states of the informal empire. The resistance to these reforms in various states has in part caused the less-than-uniform acceptance of neo-liberalism. Take, for instance, the German state's difficulties in introducing labour market flexibility and the lack of progress in the restructuring of the Japanese banking system. The argument that Panitch and Gindin are making here is that the frustrations associated with informal empire have caused a shift in US rhetoric. Famous for long eschewing any imperialist ambitions for itself, the American state no longer baulks at unconcealed empire-building (Panitch and Gindin 2004: 27). A consequence is the crisis of imperialism where 'an American imperialism that is so blatantly imperialistic risks losing the very appearance of not being imperialist – that appearance which historically made it plausible and attractive' (Panitch and Gindin 2004: 31).

State theory *is* required: the merit of Panitch and Gindin

The essay 'Global Capitalism and American Empire' (Panitch and Gindin 2004) serves a most useful purpose by highlighting a real problem in much of imperialism theory. The role of the state and the international system of states have been overlooked or improperly analysed in much of the theoretical work associated with imperial matters (not all analysis has missed the bus; Harvey, too, has given prominence to state theory). The importance given by the two authors to the issue of the state in the era of the informal US empire – or globalisation era – is a direct response to the concept of stateless sovereignty as found in Hardt's and Negri's work. Moreover, their insistence on state theory stems from a unique set of circumstances under conditions of capitalism: the unrivalled power of one state. They also have challenged cherished concepts such as inter-imperialist rivalry, capitalist stages and thus, by extension, the dictum of imperialism being the highest stage of capitalism. These concepts were either wrong from the outset or no longer had currency. Dogmatic faith in certain texts by Lenin, Hilferding and Kautsky, for example, were a hindrance in trying to theorise imperialism in post-Cold War conditions. This is a shot across the bows for many on the left and at the least shows a willingness to confront accepted wisdom. At best, Panitch and Gindin have alerted those analysts working in the Marxist tradition to the pitfalls associated with some constituent parts of classical Marxist writing on imperialism. Not only that but, in their efforts to re-cast imperialism to take account of major changes to global capitalism and geopolitics (the unique American informal empire), they open up debate on imperialism. Their contribution adds to the sophistication, depth and complexity that features in much of the writing on Marxist imperialism theory reviewed above.

Conclusion

Analysis of seven 'globalisation-era' Marxists' engagements with three key problem areas – globalisation, empire and imperialism theory and the state and the system of states – shows that not only has there been an enthusiastic return to the field but the potential for richer more insightful theory is high. This in no small part is due to the contributions of Hardt and Negri, McQueen, Petras and Veltmeyer,

Wood, Harvey, Panitch and Gindin. We have seen the responses to the knotty issue of globalisation and the problems it poses for analysis of capitalism and imperialism theory. The three poles around which our representative writers gravitated indicate the broad parameters of the discourse on the globalisation-capitalism-imperialism nexus. Whilst there are two clear opinions (one certain that globalisation is a junior partner in the relationship and the other sure that globalisation is not a fully-fledged member of the capitalism-imperialism 'family'), McQueen is unclear about the connections. This is put down to a concern that there may be something fundamental about globalisation and thus more empirical research is required. The next two writers engaged in theoretical underlabouring, a process of clarification and explanation. Wood responded to Hardt's and Negri's 'Empire' concept and brought to light the essential differences of the historical forms of empire. Harvey brought to the fore the dialectic of the capitalist and territorial logics, the dynamo of new imperialism and added insights about changes to the capitalist accumulation process. He also proposes that there are two new forms of imperialism. Both are valuable contributions, even if they are not fully developed theories of imperialism. Panitch and Gindin, by pointing out the omission of state theory and the obsolescence of some classical Marxist works, have ensured that there cannot be a return to a re-hashing of the old theories. An invigorated, insightful body of work on Marxist imperialism theory – with its focus on contemporary geopolitics and the global capitalist economy – already is evident, with the prospect of more to come. The high quality of the theorising evident in the work of these writers – the 'globalisation-era' Marxists – is proof that a new phase of Marxist imperialism theory has dawned.

Continuing the engagement: some current writing

The focus in the foregoing has been on the work of 'globalisation-era' Marxists whose work took us up to 2006. In the ten years since, the claim about an invigorated, insightful body of work on Marxist imperialism theory has been further borne out with some of the latest contributions to the theorising of imperialism. Two of the most interesting and challenging books on imperialism written from a Marxist perspective have just been published.[6] It is also fair to situate these contributions under the 'globalisation-era' Marxist rubric for globalisation, imperialism theory and the state system are concerns of them both, to varying extents.

Tobias ten Brink's capitalist geopolitics/imperialism

A very significant contribution to the literature is Tobias ten Brink's *Global Political Economy and the Modern State System* (ten Brink 2015), which strives to develop, an 'analytical framework for the study of geopolitics' building 'on some of the fundamental assumptions of past research' (ten Brink 2015: 1). He prefers to use the word geopolitics instead of imperialism because the 'latter term too often connotes the open use of violence or more specifically war between nation states' (ten Brink 2015: 3). What can be lost sight of when employing the term imperialism suggests ten Brink are the 'multilayered forms of conflict' that underpin the open use of violence mentioned above. Despite the term becoming both over-determined and a political shibboleth especially during the Cold War according to ten Brink, he continues to use imperialism as a synonym for his preferred term of geopolitics. This is evident in his definition of geopolitics where 'we can conceive of the phenomenon of capitalist geopolitics (or imperialism) as an open or latent praxis of individual states to defend, reinforce or extend their power against the backdrop of international economic dependencies and political fragmentation' (ten Brink 2015: 2).

So despite a reluctance to use the term, imperialism (or geopolitics) is the central focus of the book. Moreover, how geopolitics has evolved in relation to and with the 'fundamental structural characteristics of capitalism' is an integral part of ten Brink's analysis (ten Brink 2015: 3). There are four particular structures that he links with geopolitics, namely:

> (1) the internal and external class relations of modern society; (2) capitalist relations of competition and crisis; (3) money relations, and (4) . . . the existence of multiple competing states – or nowadays, increasingly of macro-regional, integrated formations (ten Brink, 2015: 3).

Attention must also be paid to the 'individual dynamics of "economic" and "geopolitical" forms of competition' in order to clarify the 'distinctions between the various forms of partially violent (geo-) politics' (ten Brink 2015: 3). Two forms of the latter that he identifies are 'hard' and 'soft' geopolitics, of which more below. Furthermore, geopolitics/imperialism has to be analysed in its historically specific context and for ten Brink this means that the conflicts – which in the current era tend not to be interstate wars – between the most powerful states feature in his analysis (ten Brink 2015: 3).

It is clear from the above that imperialism/geopolitics comprises both economic and political aspects and ten Brink does provide an overview of the capitalist accumulation system and its structural features in part of a chapter (ten Brink 2015: 39–56). However, his examination of how the global capitalist system works (the logic of the capitalist accumulation process) is less well developed compared with his sophisticated unravelling of the complexities inherent in international politics. The great merit of ten Brink's work for Marxist imperialism theory then is his theorising of the modern state system and its pivotal role in contemporary imperialism.

In the first of the three parts in his book, ten Brink examines the 'past research' mentioned above. The work on twentieth-century global rivalries by critical Liberal, Marxist and neo-Weberian thinkers is given a succinct but critical summary (ten Brink 2015: 13–23). The differences of opinions about inter-state rivalries and causes of conflict suggests ten Brink can be traced back to how thinkers conceptualise capitalism, modern societies in general and the state in particular. In addition, how one categorises 'the implications of globalisation processes of both the world economy and social classes…' can also lead to different views on contemporary geopolitics (ten Brink 2015: 12).

The period from 1875 to 1945 is characterised by ten Brink as the first stage of critical analysis of imperialism and the output of Hobson, Hilferding, Lenin, Bukharin, Luxemburg and Kautsky is outlined sufficiently and need not detain us. The period after 1945 forms a second phase of theorising of imperialism/geopolitics which ten Brink states saw the taking up of North-South relations and in the late 1960s the question of US hegemony and its possible decline (ten Brink 2015: 17). The end of the colonial era heralded the advent of neo-colonial dependencies based on socio-economic constraints rather than formal political control. Dependency theories emerged in response to these changes. It is worth noting ten Brink's astute summation of an important element of dependency theories: 'In (various versions of) dependency theories, direct political control plays only a subordinate role. Instead, the "structural" violence of economic conditions is considered the decisive element in constructing an "imperialist" relationship' (ten Brink 2015: 17). This last sentence is especially noteworthy because the next book on imperialism, John Smith's *Imperialism in the Twenty-First Century* (Smith 2016), reviewed below, adopts such a viewpoint. Such a view of imperialism emphasising the capitalist logic of power whilst ignoring or downplaying the geopolitical (or territorial logic of power) gives rise to narrow and less sophisticated analyses.

A third stage of explanatory models of imperialism begins in 1989 suggests ten Brink, the principal concern of which is 'how to theorise the contradictory conditions in the tendency towards regional and global integration, "US hegemony", and new international rivalries' (ten Brink 2015: 19). The claim made by Hardt and Negri in their *Empire* regarding the supersession of imperialism by an amorphous entity, which is to say a 'world encompassing "Empire" that is, of a single undisputed claim to power' ten Brink concludes is unlikely (ten Brink 2015: 3). Also, contrary to Panitch and Gindin and their arguments about an 'American Empire', ten Brink contends that geopolitical rivalries, international economic instability and inter- and intra-societal conflict renders moot such a formulation (ten Brink 2015: 3).

Writing about the 'New Imperialism' during this third stage received a further boost from the so-called 'War on Terror' proclaimed by George W. Bush after the September 11 attacks. According to ten Brink, the idea that a form of US super-imperialism was now evident gained a foothold amongst some thinkers, in particular Panitch and Gindin. However, he also cites the work of Harvey, Arrighi and Michael Mann (categorised as a neo-Weberian by ten Brink) all three of whom acknowledge qualitative changes to imperialism in the last decades of the twentieth century hence 'New Imperialism' yet they diverge from Panitch's and Gindin's super-imperialism thesis (ten Brink 2015: 21–3).

Displayed in this first part of ten Brink's book is a solid grasp of the essential contributions to imperialism theory made by many of the key contributors over the past century and up to the present. One of the main theoretical approaches in the discipline of International Relations, neo-realism, is also subjected to ten Brink's scrutiny. Passing over his concerns about the limitations of neo-realism, ten Brink identifies a number of ambiguities, ambivalences and problems that he argues beset Marxist theories of imperialism taken as a whole. These are:

> (1) The emphasis on capital export and the related (colonial-) imperialist aspirations can be criticised as an overvaluation of the role of trade with the colonies. . . . In fact, it is not possible to prove a direct correlation between imperial expansion and an increase of capital export . . . (2) The explanation of an historical shift from an era of 'competitive capitalism' to one of 'monopoly capitalism' . . . cannot sufficiently explain the fundamental dynamics of social formation around 1914 . . . (3) Marxist theories of imperialism often described the economic tendencies towards crises too one-sidedly . . . (4) (The classifying of capital) particularly the continued influence of the category 'finance capital' represents an additional theoretical ambiguity . . . (such that) More than a few authors have drawn the incorrect conclusion that 'finance capital' transforms itself into a driving force of geopolitics (which ten Brink argues) does not apply to any moment before 1945 . . . (5) A final problem with Marxist argumentation . . . is its instrumentalist approach to state theory (ten Brink 2015: 32–3).

On the basis of his critical engagement with this 'past research' ten Brink is able to situate his own insights and contentions about contemporary imperialism, this despite a reluctance to use the term. In Part Two of the book, ten Brink constructs the criteria for an analytical framework robust and sophisticated enough to unravel and explain current geopolitics (imperialism) and then in Part Three goes on to test his theoretical framework by analysing what he calls the 'the new world disorder' which appeared after 1989. This is an ambitious project and in the main ten Brink accomplishes what he sets out to do. There is much that warrants close attention and reflection in these two parts, however, there is not the scope here to cover all points of interest. Instead, some points that are worth highlighting due to their relevance for contemporary Marxist imperialism theory will be briefly outlined.

The author makes the claim that the political form of global capitalism is an international system of states. In itself this is not new;

Wood for example always asserted that at the political apex of global capitalism stood sovereign nation-states (see above). What is perhaps more novel is ten Brink's finessing of this claim. To fully comprehend international relations requires moving beyond the received wisdom of the economic and political 'and instead conceive of inter-societal relations' (ten Brink 2015: 64). Inter-societal relations are the gamut of 'social, political, socio-cultural and normative dimensions beyond the state and economy' (ten Brink 2015: 64). By widening the analytical parameters, the pitfalls of 'state-centric' approaches such as neo-realism can be avoided (ten Brink 2015: 65).

Recognising the import of Harvey's and Callinicos' engagement with the capitalist and territorial logics of power and also for the latter, the 'changing forms of *economic* and *geopolitical* competition' (ten Brink 2015: 104 emphasis in original), ten Brink nevertheless observes a deficiency in their analyses. The territorial logic of power and geopolitical competition aspects are not as well handled as their examination and elaboration of the capitalist logic of power. Consequently some additional factors are offered up by ten Brink to augment the theorising of capitalist geopolitics (imperialism) and attendant global rivalries.

The first of the additional factors is the economic dimension of capitalist geopolitics. The economic backbone of a nation is of vital importance in the creation of political-military competitiveness and increasing the strength of that 'backbone' is in the interest of the capitalist state. The second is the role of ideological and normative power in geopolitics. Included here are the normative resources that state leaders rely on to sustain the threat or actual implementation of violence. Unifying measures such as the fear of a strong external threat and nationalism amongst others are pressed into service and continue to have a deep influence in geopolitics. Factor number three is the military dimension. A strong army is not only an indicator of a significantly productive economy it is also an important vehicle for exerting influence geopolitically. Political organisation and formation of alliances are the fourth of the factors. Strong political organisation helped states such as North Vietnam overcome South Vietnam and the US. In addition, the major conflicts of the twentieth century were fought between groups of allies. Political organisation and alliances matter in geopolitics. The fifth factor is leadership and in particular decision-making (ten Brink 2015: 106–7).

It should also be borne in mind that capitalist geopolitics, or contemporary imperialism, does not require direct authority: 'Political threats and military competition function precisely to support the "peaceful" management of international public spaces and to regulate the "anarchy" of international space and inter-societal relations' (ten Brink 2015: 108). What is more, military potential serves as the 'discrete' background information in the international political realm (ten Brink 2015: 108). Such background information enables those states with the capabilities to employ 'hard' and/or 'soft' geopolitics depending on the circumstances. The former is the deployment of military assets, actual armed conflict and/or organised violence. 'Soft' geopolitics being the influence that strong states bring to bear on international institutions for example, using co-option and persuasion, rather than the brute force of 'hard' geopolitics (ten Brink 2015: 108–9).

The final point of interest for contemporary theorising of imperialism that this brief review will discuss concerns the hierarchy of states in the international state system. The hierarchy is based on the capacities of states. At the top of the pecking order are:

> globally pre-dominant or even hegemonic states; second, states in leading positions at the macro-regional level that have a global impact as well; third, leading states at the macro-regional level with less impact internationally; and fourth, strong states with a limited influence. Insofar as these latter states pursue imperialist policies, they can be designated as sub-imperialist powers. By *sub-imperialism* [ten Brink] mean[s] countries that strive for political dominance on a regional scale in ways similar to the most developed capitalist states at a macro-regional or even global scale (ten Brink 2015: 109).

Over the last two hundred years the capitalist world system has witnessed a number of conflicts, conflicts which 'have shifted power relations between states' and have often been brought about what ten Brink, borrowing the term from Kees Van der Pijl, calls 'contender states' (ten Brink 2015: 109). The caveat is added that 'geopolitics itself was transformed in the transition to capitalist imperatives' and has continued to change throughout its historical development. Theorising of geopolitics/imperialism should always historicise geopolitical conflicts (ten Brink 2015: 109).

Such insights help enrich Marxist imperialism theory and the examples given above are only indicative of what is available in the text. There is much more that could be highlighted not least the detailed and insightful exploration of the rise of China and the tension that this engenders with the US in part three of the book. Suffice it to say that whilst some of what ten Brink has elucidated above may not be novel, his critical engagement with Marxist imperialism theory challenges aspects of those theories astutely and is thus deserving of close reading. His analyses of the state, the state system and geopolitics in general are of particular importance, because they address a lacuna in Marxist theorising flagged by Panitch and Gindin. As mentioned above, the sections of the book where he deals with the capitalist accumulation process are not as developed as his rendering of capitalist geopolitics/imperialism but it can be argued, the representation of that process is sufficient for his purposes here. Apart from this quibble, ten Brink's is a theoretically rich book with many insights that can be used to deepen understanding of the current incarnation of capitalist imperialism. As Bob Jessop says in the Foreword: 'Overall the book makes a major contribution to the critical historical re-interpretation of the phenomenon of imperialism as well as to contemporary developments and new forms of state intervention in the current period' (Jessop 2008: xvi–xvii).

John Smith and twenty-first-century imperialism

Passing from a text that is primarily concerned with the geopolitical to one whose focus is on the economic aspects of imperialism, John Smith's *Imperialism in the Twenty-First Century* situates imperialism firmly in the unequal relationships between nations engendered by global capitalism. Like ten Brink's offering, Smith's too is ambitious. Amongst other things, Smith seeks to revive dependency theory, albeit a modified variant, which, he strongly insists, 'remains a crucial reference point for contemporary study of imperialism' (Smith 2016: 206).

Smith starts his book in an attention grabbing way with the collapse of the Rana Plaza, a building in Dhaka, Bangladesh that housed a textile factory, a bank and some shops. The collapse, which happened in April

2013, killed 1,133 garment workers and wounded 2,500 others (Smith 2016: 9). From this shocking disaster a fundamental fact about global capitalism is revealed, namely 'its good health rests on extreme rates of exploitation of workers in the low-wage countries where production of consumer goods and intermediate inputs has been relocated' (Smith 2016: 10). The extreme rates of exploitation of workers in places like Bangladesh, one of many countries in what Smith calls the Global South, are 'the source of surplus value sustaining profits and [the] unsustainable overconsumption in imperialist countries', the latter designated the Global North by the author (Smith 2016: 10).

The bifurcation of the world into the Global North and the Global South is one of the key dichotomies in Smith's analysis of present-day imperialism. This simple classification of nations raises some issues though. What constitutes membership of either group? For example where do countries such as China and India fit in this classificatory system? India is a developing capitalist nation, a former colony, with the presence of multinational companies in its economy, yet also with a number of large domestic corporations, some with a global presence. Is it a member of the Global South, due to numbers of its workers being super-exploited by companies based offshore? Or is it part of the Global North because Indian corporations such as Tata Steel exploit workers in other countries, including those working in the Global North? The reliance on such simple geographical terms when it comes to the complexities associated with global capitalism and the system of states obscures as much as it clarifies. In addition, as we shall see when Smith defines imperialism, simple dichotomies lie at the heart of his understanding of the subject. Here too problems lurk.

Returning to Smith's book, in an approach that mirrors Marx's opening in *Capital Volume 1* Smith zeroes in on three iconic commodities (in Marx's case, of course, he started with the commodity as the elementary building block of the wealth of capitalist society). These are the T-Shirt, the iPhone and the cup of coffee. Smith looks at each in turn, drawing out the exploitative relationships in the production of each of the three commodities. The T-Shirt made in a Bangladeshi factory is

> sold in Germany for €4.95 by a Swedish retail firm called Hennes & Mauritz (H&M). The latter firm pays the Bangladeshi manufacturer €1.35 for each shirt, 28 per cent of the final sale

> price, 40¢ of which covers the cost of 400g of cotton raw material imported from the United States; shipping to Hamburg adds another 6¢ per shirt. Thus €0.95 of the final sale price remains in Bangladesh, to be shared between the factory owner, the workers, the suppliers of inputs and services and the Bangladeshi government, expanding Bangladesh's GDP by this amount. The remaining €3.54 counts towards the GDP of Germany, the country where the T-Shirt is consumed . . . (Norfield 2011, cited in Smith 2016: 13).

A breakdown of the €3.54 that remains in Germany is provided, which shows that German transporters, wholesalers, retailers, advertisers and others take out €2.05, with H&M making 60¢ profit on each shirt; 79¢ going to the German state via VAT and 16¢ going to sundry items (Norfield 2011, cited in Smith 2016: 13). Aside from the difficulty that these last four figures do not add up to €3.54 (they total €3.60), the point that is being made here is that the low wages paid to manufacturing workers in the Global South benefit economically the mass of people in the Global North. Low wages not only make high mark-ups possible, they also enable states in the Global North to collect substantial tax revenues. There is more; according to Smith, contemporary imperialism is predicated upon the 'exploitation of labor by capital and the exploitation of poor nations by rich nations' (Smith 2016: 199). In fact, imperialism is defined by these relationships, as we shall see below.

The transfer of manufacturing and service provision to the low wage countries of the South, especially since the 1980s, has not only disproportionately benefited transnational corporations (TNCs) who have re-located their production to places like China, Vietnam, Thailand and other countries of the South, it has enabled new business practices to emerge which have increased the flow of surplus value (the basis of profits) from South to North. One of those business practices (or strategies) being outsourcing. It is not an entirely new practice, but it has really come to the fore 'during the past three decades' and is the 'continuation . . . of capital's eternal quest for new sources of cheaper, readily exploitable labor-power' (Smith 2016: 39–40).

The increased drive to transfer production to the Global South since the 1980s has its roots in neo-liberal globalisation. One of the fundamental processes Smith associates with neo-liberal globalisation is the globalisation of production, with global commodities such as the T-Shirt, iPhone and the cup of coffee as emblematic products (Smith 2016: 35). However, it is difficult to pin down exactly what Smith means by neo-liberal globalisation. References to a neo-liberal era, neo-liberal globalisation and globalised production are interspersed throughout the text without a clear definition of neo-liberalism or globalisation being furnished. For example, it is neo-liberal globalisation that has extended 'the links in the chain of production and value-creation across national borders ...' (Smith 2016:46). Compare this with the previous page where '[n]eoliberal globalization has transformed the production of all commodities ...' and then in the next sentence we read: 'the globalization of production processes impacts workers in imperialist nations in two ways ...' (Smith 2016: 44–5). It would appear that neo-liberal globalisation and the globalisation of production are interchangeable terms for the author. This is not a matter of pedantry; there is an issue with how Smith defines or does not define certain key terms throughout the book making it difficult for the reader to sometimes comprehend what is meant.

As a consequence of neo-liberal globalisation/globalisation of production, the peripheral countries of the Global South and their industrial workers are now much more integrated in the global economy (Smith 2016: 102). The countries of the Global North, also known as the imperialist countries, (another pair of interchangeable terms) maintain their ascendancy in large measure through the super-exploitation of workers in the South. Such super-exploitation gives rise to super-profits, which, via mechanisms such as outsourcing, ensures that the super-profits created in the South largely end up in the North. Super-exploitation of workers in the South is a central element of Smith's understanding of contemporary imperialism.

Super-exploitation occurs when the wages of the workers making the commodity or providing the service are reduced to below the minimum required to sustain a worker. The super-exploitation contention is based on Marx's analysis of wages and the production of surplus value. Smith devotes considerable attention to the three ways of increasing surplus value that Marx identified, in particular the third of these methods. The first way, absolute surplus value is brought about by such means as increasing the length of the working day. Making workers work longer hours, thus producing more value (in the form of commodities) above and beyond the value (in the form of wages) advanced to them. The second way, relative surplus value, is effected through the introduction of technology for example, which enhances the productivity of labour. Workers may not work long hours but their efficiencies are increased due to technological advancements. Again, more value is produced, beyond the value of wages advanced to them. The third way of increasing surplus value is achieved by depressing the value of labour power, which manifests as the decline of the purchasing power of wages (Smith 2016: 236–7). This third way is pivotal for Smith's argument about super-exploitation of workers in the Global South.

Smith relies on three quotes from Marx taken from *Capital Volume 1* to support his proposition about super-exploitation (Smith 2016: 237–8). Marx did acknowledge that the value of labour power could be driven below its value. But Marx did not go further than mentioning this as a factor in increasing surplus value, instead focussing on the production of absolute and relative surplus value. On the basis of these selected quotes from Marx, Smith claims that combined with rising unemployment, harsh labour regimes and political repression in the low-wage countries, the value of labour power is forced below its value. Such prima-facie evidence allows the conclusion to be drawn that 'the value of labor-power has been forced down much more cruelly in Southern than in Northern nations, *so much so as to force a permanently lower value of labor power upon these workers*' (Smith 2016: 237 emphasis in original).

The claim that workers in the Global South are super-exploited because they are consistently, even permanently, remunerated below the value of labour power is a proposition that Smith shares with Andy Higginbottom. Higginbottom also argues that super-exploitation should be incorporated in the theory of imperialism: 'Super-exploitation is a specific condition within the capitalist mode of production . . . the hidden common essence defining imperialism' (Higginbottom 2012: 284, cited in Smith 2016: 239). Smith concurs with Higginbottom's statement about super-exploitation as hidden essence defining imperialism, suggesting that 'this is a new fact not contained in Marx's theory of value' and only by acknowledging this 'new fact' can a 'value theory of imperialism' be formed (Smith 2016: 239–40).

The claims made about and for super-exploitation have generated discussion about such things as wage differentials between advanced capitalist countries and the less developed countries, and the differing social, cultural, and political conditions that influence wage levels in each country amongst other things.[7] The assertion about the *permanent* reduction of labour power below its value in the Global South is an overstretch. Are the workers in the Global South completely quiescent and do not strive to resist the pressure to drive down their wages? Is the class struggle forever over in the South? These are challenging claims that will spark debate and have done so already. Even if we grant that they are reasonable what is perhaps most questionable is how super-exploitation has been made into an essential defining element of imperialism.

The connection between imperialism and the law of value is drawn out in Chapter Eight. Smith states that Lenin's understanding of imperialism continues to have relevance, and Smith unearths another essential element of imperialism. It is that '[t]he division of nations into oppressor and oppressed [is] the essence of imperialism' (Lenin 1964 cited in Smith 2016: 225). Coupling this splitting of the nations of the world into oppressor and oppressed, with a refurbished law of value (which takes into account super-exploitation) the foundations of a 'value theory of imperialism' are discernible for Smith. Such a formulation is not only simplistic it is deeply problematic. As ten Brink incisively pointed out in reference to dependency theories above, for these theories, the 'structural' violence of economic conditions is the determining feature of imperialist relations. The geopolitical aspects of imperialism (or the territorial logic of power) are passed over in many dependency theories and also in Smith's account, culminating in one-sided analyses. It raises the question about what constitutes imperialism; if it is mainly about economic factors such as super-exploitation, super-profits and the law of value, why not just call it global capitalism? Smith has given too narrow a version of the subject, one that cannot and does not account for the geopolitical complexities that have always been a part of capitalist imperialism.

One of the positive aspects of Smith's contribution to recent work is the wealth of data that he has collected. Such data is an invaluable resource that can be drawn on by others in their involvement with Marxist imperialism theory. Another important aspect of Smith's contribution is that he correctly highlights the overlooking of, or lack of engagement with, the re-location of global production and service provision to the low wage countries, by Marxist theorists. This is a problem that needs to be addressed in any subsequent writing on imperialism by Marxists. In this ambitious book, Smith argues strongly about what constitutes twenty-first-century imperialism, and supports his argument with a mass of empirical data. This is not to say that his position is correct of course. Some of his arguments are questionable and deserve to be challenged and will be challenged. However, in being so challenging Smith's work will open up debate on topics such as dependency theory again, which will act to deepen and sharpen contemporary theorising of imperialism. For these positive attributes alone his passionate, detailed book is worthy of serious and critical attention.

CONCLUSION

This book has traced the evolution of Marxist theories of imperialism over the course of the twentieth century and into the new millennium. In doing so it makes a substantial contribution to the critical literature on these theories. The book not only updates the existing literature on the subject, it has identified a new third phase of Marxist imperialism theory. The third phase of theorising – the 'globalisation-era' Marxist phase – started in 2000, a decade or so after the last critical surveys of the literature were published (Brewer 1990; Polychroniou 1991). 'Globalisation-era' Marxist imperialism theory has not only challenged and critiqued previous theories of imperialism (particularly the classical Marxist's work) but some of the 'globalisation-era' Marxists have made telling contributions to the corpus. The writing on Marxist imperialism theory by Harvey, Wood, Panitch and Gindin adds qualitatively to imperialism theory and deserves the close scrutiny undertaken above. Another key contribution to knowledge made by this book is that, by critically engaging with the theorising of the 'pioneers', the neo-Marxists and the 'globalisation-era' Marxists, a clearer picture emerges of the strengths and weaknesses of the theorising in the three phases.

The strengths of the theories of the first phase writers – the 'pioneers' – are the setting of the parameters for subsequent theorising and the benchmark status some of the theories achieved, most notably Hobson's, Bukharin's and Lenin's. The weaknesses are the problematic notion of inter-imperialist rivalry, the paucity of the political analysis in classical Marxist writings and the overemphasis on economic considerations. The strengths of the neo-Marxists are found in their shifting of the focus of imperialism away from the capitalist heartlands and to its impact on the Third World. In countering the perceived 'Eurocentrism' of the 'pioneers' and others, the neo-Marxists Gunder Frank, Wallerstein and Amin provide a longer term, more global perspective on capitalist development, under-development and imperialism. The principal weakness of neo-Marxist imperialism theories is that over the course of their many contributions these theorists tended to lose interest in imperialism as an analytical tool. Under their stewardship imperialism theory atrophied. Third phase Marxist theorising has a number of strengths. Amongst these are the clear and concise understanding of the constitutive elements of imperialism and their dialectical relationship courtesy of Harvey. Also, the issue of the historical specificity of capitalist imperialism has been clarified by Wood. Another strongpoint of 'globalisation-era' analysis is the identification of a problem in the theorising of classical Marxists and neo-Marxists, namely their poor handling of state theory. Where the 'globalisation-era' offerings are weak is in their high level of abstraction. That is, when compared to the 'pioneers' and especially the contributions of Hobson, Bukharin and Lenin which are empirically rich, there is a dearth of data used to support the arguments made about globalisation for instance. Notwithstanding this deficiency, (a deficiency not found in Smith's work though) it is fair to claim that due to the 'renaissance' in Marxist engagement with the subject matter, there has not only been an updating and a revival of interest in imperialism theory, but also the theorising itself is more robust and more clearly defined. This is seen, for example, in the very recent work of ten Brink summarised above.

Such a picture of the strengths and weaknesses of the three phases of Marxist imperialism theory was arrived at by tracing the continuities and discontinuities in the theories both within and across the phases. Each phase of theories of imperialism was or is a response to contemporary social, political and economic conditions.

Suggestions for improving twenty-first-century Marxist imperialism theory

A key attribute of Marxist writing on imperialism is its capacity for the disentangling of complexities at both the geopolitical and the global economic levels. Bob Sutcliffe suggests that the Marxist approach to imperialism is best thought of as an analytical process which 'tries to integrate coherently two separate aspects of the world' (Sutcliffe 2006: 60). The two separate aspects are the 'hierarchies, conflicts and alliances – political, military and economic – between countries ... [as the first aspect, with the other being the] working of the productive system and the hierarchy of classes which it generates' (Sutcliffe 2006: 60). For Sutcliffe, conventional approaches have tended to view one of these aspects at a time, such as Realism, for example, which focuses almost solely on the geopolitical. On the other hand, as Sam Ashman and Callinicos point out in their essay on Harvey's *The New Imperialism* (2005) the opposite error often is made by Marxists, where the political is bypassed or subsumed in a desire 'to find economic causes for all state policies and actions' (Ashman and Callinicos 2006: 114). Harvey's emphasis on the dialectical relationship between the territorial and capitalist logics of power is a significant corrective to this sort of one-sidedness. A sophisticated theory of imperialism should be able to account for how 'capitalists and state managers [play active roles ...] as the initiators of strategies and tactics designed to promote their own distinct interests' and in the process sometimes bringing them into partnerships with each other (Ashman and Callinicos 2006: 114). Such sophisticated theorising should also provide insights into the unfolding of 'late capitalism' and the US penchant for empire. The provision of such insights is in turn, one part of a dialectical relationship that exists between theory and practice, where imperialism theory furnishes the analysis or understanding that enables political strategising and practice.

Some of the writing analysed in this book emphasises one side of the dialectical relationship that lies at the heart of capitalist imperialism. Most often that has been the focusing on economic development to the detriment of the analysis of the political factors, which are an integral part of imperialism. We have seen this especially in the writing of the classical Marxists and Panitch and Gindin were right to point out this problem. Panitch and Gindin, however, are overzealous in their attempt to redress the omission in the classical Marxist theories. They argue that for contemporary imperialism to be understood then state theory has to be prioritised:

> *Capitalist imperialism, then, needs to be understood through an extension of the theory of the capitalist state, rather than derived directly from the theory of economic stages or crises* (Panitch and Gindin 2004: 7 emphasis in original).

The heavy emphasis these two thinkers place on state theory as the indispensible component of contemporary Marxist analysis of imperialism bends the stick too far. To overemphasise one of the 'logics' (in this instance the 'territorial logic of power') as Panitch and Gindin do is problematic. Nevertheless, Panitch and Gindin have a point and the examination of the role of states in the generation and maintenance of imperialism is necessary. As Callinicos points out, this would not be a simple task due to the unresolved nature of much of the debates over state theory within Marxist circles alone (Callinicos 2009: 73). Difficult yes, but imperialism theory would be richer for the endeavour.

As states do not exist in isolation, it also is important that analysis of the international system of states as a factor in the 'territorial logics of power' be improved. Until recently, Marxist theoreticians working within the discipline of International Relations tended to avoid imperialism as a theoretical resource. Lately there is some interest in overcoming this oversight with Callinicos and Rosenberg arguing for the necessity of more sophisticated study of the international system of states by Marxists (Callinicos 2007; Rosenberg 2009; Callinicos 2009: 73–93). Furthermore, in his considered and sophisticated offering, ten Brink has made inroads into bringing capitalist geopolitics, the system of states and elements of state theory into imperialism theory, which is a very welcome and very recent development. Still, there is a long way to go before the politics of the international system is completely incorporated into Marxist imperialism theory. This is not just an issue of theoretical niceties. The current global political situation sees a dominant power – the US – seemingly unchallenged. Looming on the horizon, however, is the growing presence of China. Issues such as the increasing prominence of countries like China and how the US manages its position as global hegemon and imperialist nation-state *par excellence* need to be part of sophisticated twenty-first-century Marxist writing on imperialism. For too long the pivotal place of the political – both domestic and the international – in the dialectical relationship that defines capitalist imperialism has been neglected. It is only now that it is starting to be addressed.

One of the positive attributes of the writing of Hobson and the classical Marxists Bukharin and Lenin is their use of statistics to support their propositions. Empirical research has not been a feature of third phase 'globalisation-era' Marxist interventions as noted. In part that is due to this group's pre-occupation with pointing out omissions, 'theoretical underlabouring' and the analysis of globalisation and its relationship with capitalism and imperialism. Developments in the capitalist world economy brought on by the ending of the Long Boom have been addressed by some of the 'globalisation-era' Marxists such as Harvey, Petras and Veltmeyer for example. But in the main, issues such as the heightened influence of finance capital or 'financialisation' and the neo-liberal drive to privatisation have not received the empirical study they deserve. As Sutcliffe notes, in their valuable additions to the literature Harvey and Wood are nevertheless 'empirically timid almost to the point of phobia'. Not only would 'a more serious look at the concrete' benefit the work of Harvey and Wood, it would also benefit future research into capitalist imperialism (Sutcliffe 2006: 69). The almost lone figure whose work is empirically rich is the newest member of the 'globalisation-era' cohort, John Smith. His work whilst problematic has a dazzling amount of the 'concrete', which will benefit both current and future research.

The last suggestion offered in this book is not concerned with improving Marxist imperialism theory *per se*. Rather it concerns the relationship that this theorising has with political practice. Apart from the 'pioneers' many of the thinkers whose work has been examined here have been or are intellectuals with little or no affiliation with avowed Marxist political parties. This can sometimes lead to a concentration on theorising with little thought given to the implications for political strategising of that theorising. Whilst there has been a fragmentation of the left, especially since the ebbing of the revolutionary upsurges of the 1960s and 1970s and the 1980s turn to neo-liberalism, there still is an obligation on Marxists to promote informed political practice. For Marxists, theoretical work is not undertaken just to understand or better explain the world as it is, rather the point of theory is to inform the practice of changing the world. This last point means helping to rid the world of the incubus of capitalist imperialism, which has been a blight for the majority of the world's people for over a century. It is imperative, therefore, for those who are going to get involved in Marxist imperialism theory not to lose sight of the dialectical relationship between theory and practice. By highlighting this issue, making some suggestions about how future theorising can be improved and critically analysing the work of the three cohorts of theoreticians, this book makes a contribution to the project of freeing the world from capitalist imperialism.

NOTES

Chapter 2 Imperialism as Unavoidable Consequence of Capitalist Development: The Revolutionaries: Luxemburg, Bukharin and Lenin

1. Howard and King, too, refer to the disagreements between Bukharin and Lenin over the role of the state in monopoly capitalism, as well as national self-determination and the desirability of an alliance between the proletariat and the peasantry, amongst other things. These disagreements strained relations between Bukharin and Lenin in the war years of 1916 to 1917. Howard and King, however, claim that Lenin became reconciled to Bukharin's views about the state after *Imperialism* was published (Howard and King 1989: 249–50). For a more in-depth analysis of the matter see H. Ray Buchanan's article (Buchanan 1976).
2. See also Brewer's concern about the export of capital, where he drew out the vagaries of Lenin's reasons for the heightened importance of capital export, namely the 'over-ripeness' of capitalism in the advanced capitalist countries. Brewer conceded that Lenin had a point when he asserted that the profits from capital exports to less developed countries were high, which, coupled with the use of capital export to secure access and control of sources of raw materials did amount to strong motives for the export of capital. Brewer, however, argued that these reasons were not an adequate explanation or 'a complete theory' (Brewer 1990: 119).

Chapter 8 The Big Three: Globalisation, Empire, State and the Third Phase of Marxist Imperialism Theory

1. See, for example, William Robinson's essay on globalisation and the transnationalisation of the state where globalisation is the fourth epochal shift

in the history of capitalism. This fourth epoch started in the 1970s and is countenanced by Robinson as a fundamental restructuring of the capitalist system (Robinson 2002). His essay has not been critically reviewed in this chapter as he does not examine the globalisation-capitalism-imperialism nexus.

2. For a critique of Petras' and Veltmeyer's view of globalisation as mask for imperialism see (Callinicos 2007). One of the problems that Callinicos sees in Petras' and Veltmeyer's argument about globalisation is that in positing globalisation as an imperial project they run the risk of making it over as a consciously pursued strategy of powerful actors. Overemphasising the role of actors lends itself to conspiracy theories.
3. Wood argues that, despite their disagreements, Lenin and Luxemburg shared the assumption that 'imperialism had to do with the location of capitalism in a world that was not – and probably never would be – fully, or even predominantly, capitalist' (Wood 2003: 126). Subsequent capitalist development has proven otherwise.
4. Callinicos, in supporting Harvey's dialectic, charges Realism in the discipline of International Relations with only dealing with the political side. Marxists often make the opposite error; ignoring the geopolitical in their search for economic causes (see Ashman and Callinicos 2006a).
5. Robert Brenner has called into question Harvey's 'grab bag' approach adopted in his exposition of the processes involved in accumulation by dispossession. Brenner states that many of the processes that Harvey appropriates under the banner of accumulation by dispossession can be classified as normal capitalist exploitation. Brenner acknowledges accumulation by dispossession as an 'impressive job' in the adaptation for the present day of primitive accumulation (Brenner 2006).
6. There have been a number of books and journal articles published on imperialism in the last few years. Books such as *Extractive Imperialism in the Americas: Capitalism's New Frontier* (Petras and Veltmeyer 2015) and *European Bloc Imperialism* (Canterbury 2012) for example. Journal articles such as Tom Bramble's on Australia as a mid-level imperialist in the Asia Pacific (Bramble 2015) and Claude Serfati's on French imperialism (Serfati 2015) amongst others, attest to the continued interest in imperialism theory by Marxist writers. Two books have been chosen which are very interesting, quite challenging and indicative of the current high level of engagement with the topic. Space considerations militated against analysing others such as the abovementioned.
7. For a review and follow up post on Smith's book see Michael Robert's blog (Roberts 2016a) where he reviews the book (discussion about the debate that ensued is found here: Roberts 2016b). In the latter post he canvasses a number of problems with super-exploitation amongst other things.

BIBLIOGRAPHY

Amin, Samir. 1974. *Accumulation on a World Scale: A Critique of the Theory of Underdevelopment*. New York: Monthly Review Press.

——. 1976. *Unequal Development: An Essay on the Social Formations of Peripheral Capitalism*. New York: Monthly Review Press.

——. 1977. *Imperialism and Unequal Development*. New York: Monthly Review Press.

——. 1989. *Eurocentrism*. London: Zed Books.

——. 1997. *Capitalism in the Age of Globalization*. London: Zed Books.

——. 1998. *Spectres of Capitalism: A Critique of Current Intellectual Fashions*. New York: Monthly Review Press.

——. 2001. 'Imperialism and Globalization'. *Monthly Review* 53(2).

——. 2005. 'Empire and Multitude'. *Monthly Review* 57(6).

——. 2006. *Beyond US Hegemony? Assessing the Prospects for a Multipolar World*. London: Zed Books.

Andersson, Jan Otto. 2001 second version. '"Imperialismus" Text written for Historisch-kritisches Worterbuch des Marxismus', accessible online at <http://www.marxseura.fi/archive/imperialism.html>.

Arendt, Hannah. 1968. *Imperialism: Part Two of the Origins of Totalitarianism*. New York: Harcourt Brace Jovanovich.

Arrighi, Giovanni. 1978. *The Geometry of Imperialism The Limits of Hobson's Paradigm*. London: NLB.

——. 2002. 'Lineages of Empire'. *Historical Materialism* 10(3): 3–16.

Ashman, Sam, and Alex Callinicos. 2006. 'Capital Accumulation and the State System: Assessing David Harvey's The New Imperialism'. *Historical Materialism* 14(4): 107–31.

Bagchi, Amiya Kumar. 1983. 'Towards a Correct Reading of Lenin's Theory of Imperialism'. *Economic and Political Weekly* 18(31): PE2–PE12.

Baran, Paul. 1976. *The Political Economy of Growth*. Harmondsworth: Penguin Books.

Baran, Paul, and Paul Sweezy. 1968. *Monopoly Capital: An Essay on the American Economic and Social Order*. Harmondsworth: Penguin Books.

Barkawi, Tarak, and Mark Laffey. 2002. 'Retrieving the Imperial: *Empire* and International Relations'. *Millennium* 31(1): 109–27.

Barone, Charles A. 1982. 'Samir Amin and the Theory of Imperialism: A Critical Analysis'. *Review of Radical Political Economics* 14(1): 10–22.

Bhaskar, Roy. 1989. *Reclaiming Reality: A Critical Introduction to Contemporary Philosophy*. London: Verso.

Bottomore, Tom. 1981. 'Introduction'. In *Finance Capital: A Study of the Latest Phase of Capitalist Development*. London: Routledge and Kegan Paul.

Bottomore, Tom, and Patrick Goode (eds). 1978. *Austro-Marxism Texts*. Oxford: Clarendon Press.

Bramble, Tom. 2015. 'Australia: A Mid-level Imperialist in the Asia-Pacific'. *Historical Materialism* 23(3): 65–100.

Brenner, Robert. 1977. 'The Origins of Capitalist Development: A Critique of Neo-Smithian Marxism'. *New Left Review* 104: 25–92.

——. 2006. 'What is, and What is Not, Imperialism?' *Historical Materialism* 14(4): 79–105.

Brewer, Anthony. 1990. *Marxist Theories of Imperialism: A Critical Survey*. Second Edition. London: Routledge.

Bromley, Simon. 2003. 'Reflections on *Empire*, Imperialism and United States Hegemony'. *Historical Materialism* 11(3):17–68.

Broué, Pierre. 2006. *The German Revolution 1917–1923*. Chicago: Haymarket Books.

Buchanan, H. Ray. 1976. 'Lenin and Bukharin on the Transition from Capitalism to Socialism: The Meshchersky Controversy, 1918'. *Soviet Studies* 28(1): 66–82.

Bukharin, Nikolai. 1973. *Imperialism and World Economy*. New York: Monthly Review Press.

Burchill, Scott. 1996a. 'Introduction'. In *Theories of International Relations*, Scott Burchill and Andrew Linklater (eds). Houndmills: Macmillan Press Ltd.

——. 1996b. 'Liberal Internationalism'. In *Theories of International Relations*, Scott Burchill and Andrew Linklater (eds). Houndmills: Macmillan Press.

——. 1996c. 'Realism and Neo-realism'. In *Theories of International Relations*, Scott Burchill and Andrew Linklater (eds). Houndmills: Macmillan Press.

Cain, Peter. 2002. *Hobson and Imperialism: Radicalism, New Liberalism, and Finance 1887–1938*. Oxford: Oxford University Press.

Callinicos, Alex. 2002. 'The Actuality of Imperialism'. *Millennium* 31(2): 319–26.

——. 2007. 'Globalization, Imperialism and the Capitalist World System'. In *Globalization Theory Approaches and Controversies*, D. Held and A. McGrew (eds). Cambridge: Polity Press.

——. 2009. *Imperialism and Global Political Economy*. Cambridge: Polity Press.

Canterbury, Dennis C. 2012. *European Bloc Imperialism*. Chicago: Haymarket Books.

Castree, Noel. 2006. 'David Harvey's Symptomatic Silence'. *Historical Materialism* 14(4): 35–57.

Chibber, Vivek. 2004. 'The Return of Imperialism to Social Science'. *Archives de Europeenes de Sociologie* 45(3): 427–41.

Chilcote, Ronald (ed.) 1982. *Dependency and Marxism Towards a Resolution of the Debate*. Boulder: Westview Press.

Churchward, L.G. 1959. 'Towards the Understanding of Lenin's *Imperialism*'. *Australian Journal of Politics and History* 5(1): 76–83.

Cohen, Stephen F. 1970. 'Bukharin, Lenin and the Theoretical Foundations of Bolshevism'. *Soviet Studies* 21(4): 436–57.

Day, Richard B. 1976. 'The Theory of the Long Cycle: Kondratiev, Trotsky, Mandel'. *New Left Review* (99): 67–82.

Donald, Moira. 1993. *Marxism and Revolution: Karl Kautsky and the Russian Marxists 1900–1924*. New Haven: Yale University Press.

Eisenstadt, Shmuel N. 1968. '"Empires"'. In *International Encyclopedia of the Social Sciences*. New York: Macmillan and Free Press.

Engels, Frederick. 1976. *Anti-Duhring Herr Eugen Duhring's Revolution in Science*. Peking: Foreign Languages Press.

Etherington, Norman. 1982. 'Reconsidering Theories of Imperialism'. *History and Theory* 21(1): 1–36.

——. 1983. 'The Capitalist Theory of Capitalist Imperialism'. *History of Political Economy* 15(1): 38–62.

——. 1984. *Theories of Imperialism: War, Conquest and Capital*. Beckenham: Croom Helm.

Foster, John B. 1992. 'Paul Alexander Baran (1910–1964)'. In *A Biographical Dictionary of Dissenting Economists*, Philip Arestis and Malcolm Sawyer (eds). Aldershot: Edward Elgar.

Frank, Andre Gunder. 1969. *Latin America: Underdevelopment or Revolution Essays on the Development of Underdevelopment and the Immediate Enemy*. New York: Monthly Review Press.

——. 1971. *Capitalism and Underdevelopment in Latin America Historical Studies of Chile and Brazil*. Harmondsworth: Pelican Books.

——. 1975. *On Capitalist Underdevelopment*. Oxford: Oxford University Press.

——. 1993a. 'Transitional ideological modes Feudalism Capitalism Socialism'. In *The World System: Five Hundred Years or Five Thousand?*, Andre Gunder Frank and Barry K. Gills (eds), London: Routledge.

——. 1998. *ReORIENT: Global Economy in the Asian Age*. Berkeley and Los Angeles: University of California Press.

——. 2000a. 'Andre Gunder Frank'. In *A Biographical Dictionary of Dissenting Economists*, Philip Arestis and Malcolm Sawyer (eds). Cheltenham: Edward Elgar.

——. 2000b. 'Immanuel and Me With-out Hyphen'. *Journal of World-Systems Research* 1(2 Special Issue: Festschrift for Immanuel Wallerstein Part 1): 216–31.

Frank, Andre Gunder, and Barry K. Gills (eds). 1993a. *The World System Five Hundred Years or Five Thousand?* London: Routledge.

——. 1993b. 'Rejoinder and Conclusions'. In *The World System Five Hundred Years or Five Thousand?*, Andre Gunder Frank, Barry Gills (eds). London: Routledge.

Freeman, Alan. 1996. 'Ernest Mandel's Contribution to Economic Dynamics'. In *Ernest Mandel Internet Archive*, accessible online at <http://www.ernestmandel.org/en/aboutlife/txt/freeman.htm>.

Friedman, Harriet. 1996. 'Prometheus Rebounds'. *Contemporary Sociology* 25(3): 319–22.

Fuchs, Christian. 2010. 'Critical Globalization Studies: An Empirical and Theoretical Analysis of the New Imperialism'. *Science & Society* 74(2): 215–47.

Giddens, Anthony. 1990. *The Consequences of Modernity*. Cambridge: Polity Press.

Gills, Barry K., and Andre Gunder Frank. 1993. 'The Cumulation of Accumulation'. In *The World System: Five Hundred Years or Five Thousand?*, Andre Gunder Frank, Barry K. Gills (eds). London: Routledge.

Gilpin, Robert. 2002. *The Challenge of Global Capitalism*. Princeton: Princeton University Press.

Gowan, Peter. 1999. *The Global Gamble: Washington's Faustian Bid for World Dominance*. London: Verso.

Griffin, K., and J. Gurley. 1985. 'Radical Analyses of Imperialism, The Third World, and the Transition to Socialism: A Survey Article'. *Journal of Economic Literature* XXIII: 1089–143.

Hardt, Michael, and Antonio Negri. 2000. *Empire*. Cambridge: Harvard University Press.

Harvey, David. 2005. *The New Imperialism*. Oxford: Oxford University Press.

Hay, Colin. 2004. 'Globalization and the State'. In *Global Political Economy*, J. Ravenhill (ed.). Oxford: Oxford University Press.

Held, David *et al.* 1999. *Global Transformations*. Cambridge: Polity Press.

Held, David, and Anthony McGrew (eds). 2007. *Globalization Theory Approaches and Controversies*. Cambridge: Polity Press.

Henfrey, Colin. 1982. 'Dependency, Modes of Production, and the Class Analysis of Latin America'. In *Dependency and Marxism Toward a Resolution of the Debate*, Ronald Chilcote (ed.). Boulder: Westview Press.

Henwood, Doug. 2003. *After the New Economy*. New York: The New Press.

Hettne, Bjorn. 1995. *Development Theory and the three worlds: Towards an international political economy of development*. Second Edition. Burnt Mill, Harlow: Longman Scientific & Technical.

Higginbottom, Andy. 2012. 'Structure and Essence in *Capital I*: Extra Surplus-Value and the Stages of Capitalism'. *Journal of Australian Political Economy* 70: 251–70.

Hilferding, Rudolf. 1981. *Finance Capital: A Study of the Latest Phase of Capitalist Development*. London: Routledge and Kegan Paul.

Hirst, Paul, and Grahame Thompson. 1999. *Globalization in Question*. Cambridge: Polity Press.

Historical Materialism. 2006. 'Symposium: On David Harvey's "The New Imperialism"'. *Historical Materialism* 14(4): 3–166.

Hobsbawm, Eric. 1977. *The Age of Revolution Europe 1789–1848*. London: Abacus.

——. 1998. *Age of Extremes: The Short Twentieth Century, 1914–1991*. London: Abacus.

Hobson, John A. 1988. *Imperialism: A Study*. Third Edition. London: Unwin Hyman.

Holton, Robert, J. 2005. *Making Globalization*. Houndmills: Palgrave Macmillan.

Howard, Michael, and John King. 1989. *A History of Marxian Economics Volume 1, 1883–1929*. Houndmills: Macmillan.

——. 1992. *A History of Marxian Economics Volume 2, 1929–1990*. Houndmills: Macmillan.

——. 2004. 'The Economic Contributions of Paul Sweezy'. *Review of Political Economy* 16(4): 411–56.

Jessop, Bob. 2008. 'Foreword'. In *Global Political Economy and the Modern State System*. ten Brink, Tobias. 2015. Chicago: Haymarket Books.

Kant, Immanuel. 1972. *Perpetual Peace: A philosophical essay*. New York: Garland.

Kautsky, Karl. 1914. 'Ultra-imperialism'. Marxist Internet Archive, accessible online at <http://www.marxists.org/archive/kautsky/1914/09/ultra-imp.htm>.

Kiely, Ray. 2005. *Empire in the Age of Globalisation: US Hegemony and Neoliberal Disorder*. London: Pluto Press.

Laclau, Ernesto. 1979. *Politics and Ideology in Marxist Theory: Capitalism – Fascism – Populism*. London: Verso.

Leaver, Richard. 1983. 'Samir Amin on Underdevelopment'. In *Neo-Marxist Theories of Development*, Peter Limqueco and Bruce McFarlane (eds). London: Croom Helm.

Lee, George. 1971. 'Rosa Luxemburg and the Impact of Imperialism'. *The Economic Journal* 81(324): 847–62.

Lenin, V.I. 1964. 'The Right of Nations to Self-Determination'. *Collected Works Volume 21*. Moscow: Progress Publishers

——. 1973. *Imperialism, The Highest Stage of Capitalism*. Peking: Foreign Languages Press.

Liebknecht, Karl. 1972. *Militarism and Anti-militarism*. New York: Dover.

Luard, Evan. 1979. *The United Nations: How it Works and What it Does*. London: The MacMillan Press.

Luxemburg, Rosa. 1971. *The Accumulation of Capital*. London: Routledge and Kegan Paul.

Luxemburg, Rosa, and Nikolai Bukharin. 1972. *Imperialism and the Accumulation of Capital*. London: Allen Lane The Penguin Press.

Magdoff, Harry. 1969. *The Age of Imperialism*. New York: Modern Reader Paperbacks.

Mahoney, James. 2007. 'Qualitative Methodology and Comparative Politics'. In *Comparative Political Studies*. (40)2: 122–44.

Mandel, Ernest. 1976a. 'Introduction'. In *Capital A Critique of Political Economy Volume 1*. Harmondsworth: Penguin in association with New Left Review.

——. 1976b. *Late Capitalism*. London: NLB.

Mandel, Ernest, and Alan Freeman eds. 1984. *Ricardo, Marx, Sraffa*. The Langston Memorial Volume. London: Verso.

Martin, William G. 2000. 'Still Partners and Still Dissident After All These Years? Wallerstein, World Revolutions and the World-Systems Perspective'. *Journal of World-Systems Research* XI(2): 234–262.

Marx, Karl. 1973. *Karl Marx: The Revolutions of 1848 Political Writings Volume 1*. Harmondsworth: Penguin Books in association with New Left Review.

——. 1976. *Capital: A Critique of Political Economy Volume 1*. Harmondsworth: Penguin Books in association with New Left Review.

——. 1978. *Capital: A Critique of Political Economy Volume 2*. Harmondsworth: Penguin Books in association with New Left Review.

——. 1981. *Capital: A Critique of Political Economy Volume 3*. Harmondsworth: Penguin Books in association with New Left Review.

Mattick, Paul. 1978. *Anti-Bolshevik Communism*. London: Merlin Press.

McQueen, Humphrey. 2001. *The Essence of Capitalism: The Origins of Our Future*. Sydney: Sceptre.

——. 2003. 'What Happened in Globalization?' *Journal of Australian Political Economy*(51): 103–31.

Meldolesi, L. 1984a. 'The Debate on Imperialism Just before Lenin'. *Economic and Political Weekly* 19(42/43): 1833–1839.

——. 1984b. 'The Debate on Imperialism Just before Lenin'. *Economic and Political Weekly* 19(44): 1873–1879.

Mommsen, Wolfgang. 1981. *Theories of Imperialism*. London: Weidenfeld and Nicolson.

Mooers, Colin. 2006. 'Nostalgia for Empire: Revising Imperial History for American Power'. In *The New Imperialists: Ideologies of Empire*, ed. Colin Mooers. Oxford: Oneworld Publications.

Nettl, Peter. 1965. 'The German Social Democratic Party 1890–1914 as a Political Model'. *Past & Present* (30): 65–95.

——. 1966a. *Rosa Luxemburg Volume One*. London: Oxford University Press.

——. 1966b. *Rosa Luxemburg Volume Two*. London: Oxford University Press.

Norfield, Tony. 2011. 'What the "China Price" really means', accessible online at <http://economicsofimperialism.blogspot.com/2011/06/what-china-price-really-means.html>.

Ohmae, Kenichi. 1996. *The End of the Nation State: The Rise of the Regional Economies*. London: Harper Collins.

Panitch, Leo, and Sam Gindin. 2002. 'Gems and Baubles in *Empire*'. *Historical Materialism* 10(2): 17–43.

. 2004. 'Global Capitalism and American Empire'. In *The New Imperial Challenge Socialist Register 2004*, L. Panitch and C. Leys (eds). London: The Merlin Press.

——. 2005. 'Superintending Global Capital'. *New Left Review*(35): 101–123.

Petras, James, and Henry Veltmeyer. 2001. *Globalization Unmasked Imperialism in the 21st Century*. London: Zed Books.

Petras, James, and Henry Veltmeyer (eds). 2015. *Extractive Imperialism in the Americas: Capitalism's New Frontier*. Chicago: Haymarket Books.

Pieterse, Jan Nederveen. 1988. 'A Critique of World System Theory'. *International Sociology* 3(3): 251–66.

Polychroniou, Chronis. 1991. *Marxist Perspectives on Imperialism: A Theoretical Analysis*. New York: Praeger Publishers.

Reynolds, David. 2001. *One World Divisible: A Global History Since 1945*. London: Penguin.

Roberts, Michael. 2016a. 'Imperialism and super exploitation', accessible online at <https://thenextrecession.wordpress.com/2016/03/07/imperialism-and-super-exploitation/>.

——. 2016b. 'Thoughts on the debate about imperialism', accessible online at <https://thenextrecessio.wordpress.com/2016/03/13/>.

Robinson, William. 2002. 'Capitalist Globalization and the Trasnationalization of the State'. In *Historical Materialism and Globalization*, Mark Rupert and Hazel Smith (eds). London: Routledge.

Rosenberg, Justin. 1994. *The Empire of Civil Society: A Critique of the Realist Theory of International Relations*. London: Verso.

——. 2000. *The Follies of Globalisation Theory*. London: Verso.

Rustin, Michael. 2002. '*Empire:* A Postmodern Theory of Revolution'. *New Political Economy* 7(3): 451–62.

Salvadori, Massimo. 1990. *Karl Kautsky and the Socialist Revolution 1880–1938*. London: Verso.

Serfati, Claude. 2015. 'Imperialism in Context'. *Historical Materialism* 23(2): 52–93.

Shaw, Martin. 2002. 'Post-Imperial and Quasi-Imperial: State and Empire in the Global Era'. *Millennium* 31(2): 327–36.

Sivanandan, A., and Ellen Meiksins Wood. 1997. 'Capitalism, Globalization and Epochal Shifts: An Exchange'. *Monthly Review* 48(9): 19(14).

Smaldone, William. 1988. 'Rudolf Hilferding and the Theoretical Foundations of German Social Democracy, 1902–33'. *Central European History* 21(3): 267–99.

——. 1994. 'Rudolf Hilferding and the Total State'. *Historian* 57(1): 97.

Smith, John. 2016. *Imperialism in the Twenty-First Century: Globalization, Super-Exploitation, and Capitalism's Final Crisis*. New York: Monthly Review Press.

Stokes, Eric. 1969. 'Late Nineteenth-Century Colonial Expansion and the Attack on the Theory of Economic Imperialism: A Case of Mistaken Identity?'. *Historical Journal* 12(2): 285–301.

Sutcliffe, Bob. 1976. 'Introduction'. In *The Political Economy of Growth*. Baran, Paul (ed.). Harmondsworth: Penguin Books.

——. 2002. 'How Many Capitalisms? Historical Materialism in the Debates about Imperialism and Globalization'. In *Historical Materialism and Globalization*, Mark Rupert and Hazel Smith (eds). London: Routledge.

——. 2006. 'Imperialism Old and New: A Comment on David Harvey's *The New Imperialism* and Ellen Meiksins Wood's *Empire of Capital*'. *Historical Materialism* 14(4): 59–78.

Sweezy, Paul M. 1970. *The Theory of Capitalist Development: Principles of Marxian Political Economy*. New York: Modern Reader Paperbacks.

ten Brink, Tobias. 2015. *Global Political Economy and the Modern State System*. Chicago: Haymarket Books.

Townshend, J. 1988. 'Introduction'. In *Imperialism A Study*. Third Edition. London: Unwin Hyman.

Wallerstein, Immanuel. 1974. *The Modern World-System I: Capitalist Agriculture and the Origins of the European World-Economy in the Sixteenth Century*. New York: Academic Press.

——. 1980a. *The Capitalist World-Economy: Essays by Immanuel Wallerstein*. Cambridge: Cambridge University Press.

——. 2000. *The Essential Wallerstein*. New York: The New Press.

——. 2003. *The Decline of American Power The U.S. in a Chaotic World*. New York: The New Press.

Willoughby, John. 1995. 'Evaluating the Leninist Theory of Imperialism'. *Science and Society* No. 3.

Wood, Ellen Meiksins. 2003. *Empire of Capital*. London: Verso.

Worsley, Peter. 1980. 'One World or Three? A Critique of the World-System Theory of Immanuel Wallerstein'. In *Socialist Register* 1980, eds. R. Miliband and J. Saville. London: Merlin Press.

Zhou Enlai. 1973. 'Report to the Tenth National Congress of the Communist Party of China', accessible online at <http://www.marxists.org/subject/china/documents/cpc/10th_congress_report.htm>.

INDEX